Hidden Victims

Critical Issues in Crime and Society
Edited by Raymond J. Michalowski Jr.

Rayond J. Michalowski Jr., Series Editor

Critical Issues in Crime and Society is oriented toward critical analysis of contemporary problems in crime and justice. The series is open to a broad range of topics including specific types of crime, wrongful behavior by economically or politically powerful actors, controversies over justice system practices, and issues related to the intersection of identity, crime, and justice. It is committed to offering thoughtful works that will be accessible to scholars and professional criminologists, general readers, and students.

Hidden Victims

THE EFFECTS OF THE DEATH PENALTY ON FAMILIES OF THE ACCUSED

SUSAN F. SHARP

RUTGERS UNIVERSITY PRESS
New Brunswick, New Jersey, and London

LIBRARY OF CONGRESS CATALOGING-IN-PUBLICATION DATA

Sharp, Susan F., 1951–
    Hidden victims : the effects of the death penalty on families of the accused /
Susan F. Sharp
        p.   cm. — (Critical issues in crime and society)
    Includes bibliographical references and index.
    ISBN 0-8135-3583-2 (hardcover : alk. paper) — ISBN 0-8135-3584-0 (pbk. :
alk. paper)
    1. Capital punishment—United States.   2. Death row inmates—United
States—Family relationships.   3. Prisoners' families—United States.
I. Title.   II. Series.
    HV8699.U5S45   2005
    362.82'9—dc22   2004020835

A British Cataloging-in-Publication record for this book is available
from the British Library

Manufactured in the United States of America

Contents

FOREWORD

"This is the picture of our son that Richard had in his room before he died," said the ninety-year-old woman in her thick German accent. The year was 1986. We were in San Francisco, on the top floor of the Fairmont Hotel, there to do a TV show about the fiftieth anniversary of her husband's execution. As the city lights glistened below, she hugged the picture and sobbed, both her hands clutching my upper arm. After a moment of silence, she slowly muttered, "It still hurts like it was yesterday."

Yesterday. Fifty years. Yesterday.

So said Anna, the widow of Bruno Richard Hauptmann, who was executed in 1936 for the murder of the baby of aviator Charles Lindbergh. To this day, many believe that Hauptmann was innocent. That issue aside, Richard Hauptmann's suffering ended in 1936. Once his death sentence was carried out, he could no longer be punished, and he could not live with the stigma and the memories. His family could; his wife still did, every day for nearly six decades, until her own death in 1994.

In this important book, Professor Susan Sharp focuses our attention on the wives, parents, children, and siblings of death row inmates. Because this is a group that is rarely in the limelight, they can unquestionably be seen as "Hidden Victims" of the death penalty. Over the past twenty-five years I have had the experience of going through last visits with over fifty condemned inmates, sharing those last hours with the prisoner, his or her family, attorneys, and spiritual advisors, and getting to know scores of other families who dread the day when the life of their loved one on death row will be taken. No one has ever done a better job than Professor Sharp of shedding light on these families and allowing their stories to be told.

Supporters of capital punishment argue their position very differently than they did a generation ago. Then, the pro-execution forces saw the death penalty as a deterrent, or as a way to save taxpayers' money, or as a penalty justified by biblical scriptures. Today, few if any criminologists would argue that executing prisoners is a better deterrent than life imprisonment without parole (which is now the alternative to the death penalty in thirty-six of the thirty-eight death penalty states), all would agree that the costs of the death penalty far surpass the costs of life in prison, and there are few issues on which more religious leaders agree than on the basic immorality of capital punishment. Instead, in recent decades the prime (or even sole) justification has become *retribution*: they deserve it, and executing offenders helps families of homicide victims in ways that prison never can.

As Professor Sharp shows us, however, the retributive aspects of the death penalty are applied with shotgun accuracy, with effects that are often invisible to those who are not in the line of fire. Executions tend to create an ever-widening circle of tragedy, often affecting three generations. As we learn about these effects in the pages that follow, we learn that the death penalty punishes the innocent—that is, the families of the condemned—far more than alternative sentence of long imprisonment.

This is possible only because the family members of those under death sentences are among the most powerless in our communities. To be sure, some of the mothers and fathers of these prisoners were terrible parents. Among them are former prostitutes, alcoholics, and drug addicts; some who were abusive and negligent and unbelievably selfish. At first glance, one might feel they deserve punishment as much as or instead of their children. But we learn from Professor Sharp that such traits describe only a small minority of the parents of America's thirty-five hundred death row inmates. Instead, we find that most of the parents of death row inmates are in many ways not all that different from the mothers of police officers, nurses, or college professors. As a group they are people who have usually done their best with what they had. To be sure, many did not have much—poverty is one characteristic that most families of those on death row share—but they did what they could with what they had.

And many are like the mother in William Styron's *Sophie's Choice*, who is forced by a Nazi physician at Auschwitz to decide which of her two children will die. There is no question that Sophie herself would rather die than sit helplessly as the life of either child is taken. Most of us would similarly trade our own lives for the life of our child. Anna Hauptmann, Sophie, we, and the families of death row inmates have much in common. A family's love is often unconditional.

Families of death row inmates are a diverse group; often their differences are as striking as their similarities. The same is true of their condemned loved ones. Some of them got to death row by committing heinous and premeditated murders; others got there by committing impulsive or accidental murders or murders resulting from mental illness. Others are on death row, rather than serving prison terms, only because their attorneys were incompetent. The heterogeneity of death row inmates is paralleled by the heterogeneity of their families.

And some of what these families of condemned inmates have in common is also shared with other groups of troubled families. Some traits are shared with the families of prisoners not on death row. Parallels can also be drawn to families who are in the process of losing a loved one to a chronic illness, especially to a stigmatizing disease such as AIDS. By drawing these parallels, more can be learned about their common situations and experiences.

Families of death row inmates also have much in common with families of homicide victims. While the two groups invite comparison, the bottom line is that pain is pain, and the question "Who suffers more?" quickly becomes irrelevant. Although supporters of capital punishment often cry that the offender needs to be executed as a way of assisting the family of the murder victim, only about 1 percent of American homicides is avenged by the death penalty. While some murder victims' families do indeed support the death penalty, Professor Sharp's work invites us to wonder if executing 1 percent of murderers is the best way to help the families of sixteen thousand murder victims each year in the United States. What other ways can the millions of dollars spent on the death penalty assist families of victims? What ways can we assist these families other than doubling the number of innocent families who mourn the loss of a loved one?

Sometimes the effects do not emerge for years after the execution. Just last week I received a phone call from a twenty-eight-year-old man in Texas whose father was executed in Florida a dozen years ago. He never knew his dad and only recently had learned that he had been executed, and called me after reading that his dad had spent his final hours with me. He had no idea who his dad was, what his life was like ("Oh— he was in the army?"), how he understood his crimes, or even what he looked like ("Please send me a picture"). "At least one good thing came from your dad's life," I tried to reassure him. "You."

Since the death penalty will remain in America for the foreseeable future, the stories of these families—the good, the bad, and the banal— need to be told. It may be that after learning their stories and their sobering struggles for dignity the public will still demand the death penalty, but if so, at least we will have a better idea of what our executioners are doing, and the nature and consequences of our public policies. Without denying the horror of the crimes that most death row inmates have committed or the need for the confinement of those inmates, Professor Sharp raises the question of whether Americans would still support the death penalty if they understood the full range of its consequences. It is a sobering question that readers of this book will be forced to ponder.

—Michael L. Radelet
Professor and Chair
Department of Sociology
University of Colorado at Boulder

Preface

AMERICANS ARE OBSESSED with murder, as evidenced by headlines such as a recent one proclaiming, "Killings Increase in Many Big Cities." As one journalist stated, "Crime reports are cathartic; we feel relief that the victim and offender are not like us."[1] For quite obvious reasons, we do not want to be like the victim, who has suffered or has even died. However, we also do not want to be like the offender, who is seen as possessing some degree of "otherness," to be somehow less than fully human, particularly with murder. When we see the offender as "other," it becomes far easier to sentence that offender to death. Prosecutors and legislators who refer to certain offenders as animals or subhuman further this sense of separation.[2]

But those facing a death sentence do not exist in a vacuum. They are someone's brother or sister, mother or father, daughter or son, relative or friend. Our system of capital punishment often creates stress, hardship, and pain for persons in addition to those accused of a capital crime. Furthermore, the hardships occur whether or not the offender is executed. America's focus on murder and the related response of capital punishment affect the families of those accused as well as those convicted and sentenced to death. Therefore, the problems faced by these family members as well as their responses to the crisis should be explored.

Why study the families of persons facing a death sentence? Some may feel that this topic merits little attention. They are admittedly a small group. Murder itself is an infrequent crime, and prosecutors seek the death penalty in only a small fraction of all murders. Second, the families of those facing potential execution are often seen as culpable themselves. Violent offenders frequently come from appalling backgrounds, fraught with abuse and neglect.[3] Thus, the families of those accused of a capital crime are not only guilty by association, but they may be viewed as guilty in their own right. Why, then, should a book be written about these family members?

In the spring of 2000, two areas of my academic life coalesced into the foundation of this book. My research partner and I had explored the effects of incarceration on families of prisoners, especially women prisoners. That project was coming to an end. I was, therefore, pondering what direction I would be taking with subsequent research. At the same time, I began teaching a senior capstone course for criminology students, focusing on examination of inequities in the criminal justice system. The course had a unit on capital punishment, and as I gathered materials for the class, I became increasingly disturbed by what I viewed as fundamental flaws in our system of capital punishment. I found myself pondering how the families of those facing a death sentence might feel. With some awareness of the social costs of incarceration on families, extending my research to the effects of capital punishment on families was a natural step. The project quickly took on a life of its own.

Locating a population not easily identified was one difficulty that I faced. I thought that the proposed subjects might not want to talk about the problems they faced. Ultimately, I discovered that many family members wanted to be heard, wanted their stories to be told.

The subjects' own words led to the title of the book. Repeatedly, family members stressed to me that they were victims, too. From their perspective, they were being punished for a crime that they did not commit. As their stories unfolded, certain recurring themes emerged that are the focus of this book.

As long as America maintains a system of capital punishment, the costs of that system—both economic and social—should be assessed. The effect of the death penalty on family members of those facing execution is an often ignored cost of the system. The existing literature about families of persons facing executions has stressed the effects that capital punishment has had on their lives. However, to date little is known about how early in the process these effects begin. In the current study, I examine the effects of capital punishment on family members at various stages of the process.

This book focuses on the families of those charged with or facing charges for a capital crime as well as those sentenced to death. I believe that whether or not the person receives a death sentence or is executed, the family undergoes certain types of stress. Furthermore, the study of these families is intrinsically linked with both other prisoners' families and family members of murder victims. Families of those facing a death sentence have many similarities to both. However, the experiences of the families of persons charged with a capital offense differ from the other two groups in some important and fundamental ways that are presented in the following chapters. Each family member's story could and should be a book in itself. But as unique as each story is, the stories are also undeniably similar. I am humbled by the willingness and courage of those who were willing to share their pain in order to help this book come to fruition. I sincerely hope that in weaving their stories together, I have been able to demonstrate what almost every person wanted conveyed. In their words, "We are victims, too."

Acknowledgments

THIS PROJECT COULD NEVER have been completed without the help and encouragement of many people. In particular, I would like to take this opportunity to thank all the men and women who were willing to share their stories with me. This is their book, their project. I am in awe of their courage and their willingness to share their experiences with a complete stranger. While their names have been changed to ensure confidentiality, I hope they will recognize themselves in the following pages and be pleased with the way I have presented their stories.

I would also like to thank Michael Radelet, professor of sociology at the University of Colorado at Boulder. Without his encouragement, I might never have been able to write this book. Likewise, Saundra Westervelt and Kim Cook provided much needed encouragement. Finally, my heartfelt thanks go to the members of the Oklahoma Coalition to Abolish the Death Penalty for their friendship and support.

Hidden Victims

CHAPTER 1

Introduction

THE DEATH PENALTY, VICTIMS'
FAMILIES, AND FAMILIES OF PRISONERS

MEDIA AND OUR
UNDERSTANDING OF CRIME

THE AMERICAN PUBLIC'S understanding of crime is shaped and influenced by the media. Indeed, no other topic garners as much local media attention as crime.[1] This understanding of crime, however, is not based on an unbiased presentation of the facts. Instead, it is often shaped by the concerns and the goals of those Altheide refers to as "the formal agents of social control" (representatives of various aspects of the criminal justice system).[2] Furthermore, representations of crime are "considered good ways to sell papers and sustain viewers." The result is that the American public has developed an intense fear of being victimized. This fear of victimization translates into support for the death penalty.[3]

News media frequently focus on the most appalling offenses, regardless of the state's stand on capital punishment. In Wisconsin, a non–death penalty state, the discovery of multiple victims of Jeffrey Dahmer led to intensive media coverage. The press not only reported the terrible evidence but also covered aspects of Jeffrey Dahmer's personal life in great detail. The general public was regaled with stories of the seventeen murders to which he had confessed and the grisly evidence found in his home. However, media coverage was not limited to the crime. News stories also included information about the type of beer he drank, his cigarette preference, the types of potato chips he ate, and the brand of baking soda he used in his refrigerator.[4] The focus on Dahmer's preference for certain brands served to underscore the gulf between the mundane aspects of his life and the nature of his offenses.

News is not the only type of media that shapes Americans' perceptions about crime. Indeed, according to one criminologist, movies "are a significant source—perhaps the most significant source—of ideas about crime and criminals. Indeed, the author points out a way in which crime films shape our understanding of crime in America, stating, "Seemingly innocuous suburbs are overrun with psychopaths, and because normality never presides in these unpredictable realms, justice and escape are always just beyond reach."[5]

Arguably, this focus on senseless and random murder has helped shape America's attitude toward capital punishment. Faced with the violence and depravity of Hannibal Lecter of *Silence of the Lambs* fame or the Knox couple of *Natural Born Killers*, the average American may find it easy to believe that we are surrounded by senseless violence that must be stopped. To many, the death penalty is the only appropriate punishment for such depravity as they have witnessed in films. Again, media representations have provided support for the system of capital punishment in the United States.

Not all media depictions support capital punishment, of course. In the last decade, there has been a steady increase in books, movies, and news stories that show a different side of the death penalty. These recent releases have often focused on the inherent humanity of those condemned to death as well as on the public's growing awareness of the potential of executing the wrong person. In *The Chamber*, the reader meets Sam Cayhall, a former Klansman, and his grandson, Adam Hall. As the story begins, Sam is facing execution for the murders of two young children decades earlier. Adam, a young attorney who has grown up not knowing his grandfather, represents Sam during his last month. Sam Cayhall is not a lovable character. He is an angry and irascible racist who spent his younger years persecuting minorities. However, Grisham manages to demonstrate that Cayhall, like most of us, has many dimensions to his personality and that his execution serves little purpose. The man the state is executing is not the same man who committed the crime many years before.[6] This argument is frequently put forth by those opposed to capital punishment. The book also develops the theme of the impact on family members. In the movie *The Last Dance*, the audience is introduced to Cindy Liggit, a young woman sentenced to die for murders she committed during a burglary. Cindy does not deny her responsibility, having had years to reflect on why she acted with such violence. Again, this is a character that is complex and evolving. In *The Green Mile*, two anti–death penalty themes emerge: the barbarity of executions, particularly botched ones, and the potential for wrongful execution of an innocent person. No discussion of media and the death penalty would be complete without acknowledgment of the book *Dead Man Walking* and the later movie of the same name. The story surrounds the experiences of Sister Helen Prejean, who finds herself befriending death row prisoners and helping them to find peace and self-forgiveness. The message of this book is far more complex than most of the others. Prejean deals with numerous issues, including the effects of capital punishment on families, the pain of victims' family members, and the humanity found in even the worst members of society.[7] Finally, *The Life of David Gale* suggests not only the potential for wrongful execution but also the level of commitment held by some activists to work toward abolition.[8]

In the news media, stories about wrongfully condemned persons have been on the rise. Increasing coverage of exonerations has probably swayed public opinion, with declining support for capital punishment being reflected in polls as well as growing concerns that we have executed one or more innocent persons.[9]

Although media stories that focus on problems in the system of capital punishment are growing, they are far less representative of the media's focus on crime than those that emphasize the randomness of murder and the inhumanity of murderers. Lead stories on evening news reports are still designed to instill fear. Prime-time television remains filled with "crime shows" focusing on solving brutal murders. And one has only to peruse the new releases on the rack at a local bookstore to see our obsession with senseless and brutal murder.

America's fascination with murder is somewhat difficult to understand given the reality that murders accounted for only 0.1 percent of the Index Crimes and only 1.1 percent of reported violent crimes in the year 2001.[10] Nonetheless, we are obsessed. We love to be afraid, and we love to hate offenders. Indeed, the average citizen wants to distance her- or himself from offenders, particularly those who face a death sentence. Those sentenced to death, the public assumes, are inherently different from the rest of us. Not only are their acts more depraved than those of other murderers, but the offenders themselves are also assumed to be more depraved. This assumption is grounded in America's history with capital punishment.

A BRIEF HISTORY OF CAPITAL PUNISHMENT IN THE UNITED STATES

Capital punishment has been a fixture in the American landscape since colonial times. In 1608, Captain George Kendall was executed as a spy. Since his death, over twenty thousand individuals—primarily adult males—have been executed. High numbers of executions during the early nineteenth century and abolitionists' responses led to a number of reforms, including movement away from mandatory death sentencing, transferring of jurisdiction in capital cases from local to state authorities, and reduction in the numbers of offenses punishable by death. By the late nineteenth century, capital punishment, while still a mainstay of punishment, was used less often.[11]

However, use of the death penalty began to rise again in the first part of the twentieth century. Executions in the United States reached a peak during the 1930s, with over 1,600 executions occurring during the decade. In the ensuing decades, executions began declining, with only 191 executions occurring between 1960 and 1976.[12] High-profile cases such as those of the Rosenbergs and Caryl Chessman, as well as abolition of capital punishment by European and African nations, elevated the debate about capital punishment in the United States. This debate culminated in a series of court cases challenging the death penalty either in principle or in practice.[13]

In 1972, death penalty statutes in forty jurisdictions were overturned and existing death sentences commuted in the *Furman* decision.[14] At the heart of the *Furman* decision was the issue of arbitrary and capricious application of the death penalty. The Supreme Court ruled that existing statutes, but not the death penalty itself, were unconstitutional. Unfettered jury discretion was cited as a violation of due process and equal treatment under the law. This left those states desiring capital punishment with the task of redrafting their death penalty statutes to overcome the legal objections.

Response to the *Furman* decision was immediate. A number of states attempted to rectify the arbitrariness in the imposition of capital punishment by creating mandatory death sentences for certain crimes. The Supreme Court in turn struck down these statutes.[15] However, at the same time, the Supreme Court accepted new death penalty statutes with guided discretion provisions in *Gregg v. Georgia*.[16] This case also led to the acceptance of other important reforms: two-phase trials, proportionality reviews, and an automatic appeal process. Guided discretion meant that juries could impose a death sentence only in cases where certain criteria were met—criteria that would set that case apart from other murders. Trials were bifurcated. That is, the first part of the trial determined guilt or acquittal. If the defendant was found guilty, a second trial would be conducted to determine the appropriate sentence. In the sentencing trial, the jury would decide whether or not the offender should be sentenced to death. Although not mandatory, the Supreme Court also recommended that states engage in proportionality reviews. This meant that similar cases should be examined to ensure death sentences were not given arbitrarily.

Currently, thirty-eight states, the military, and the federal government have death penalty statutes in place. Of those states, six states and the military have not executed anyone in the modern era of the death penalty, post-*Furman*. Only sixteen states have executed 10 or more offenders since 1976. At the time of this writing, these sixteen states accounted for 815 of the executions. Most of those have occurred in five southern states: Texas, Virginia, Oklahoma, Missouri, and Florida.[17]

Since the reinstatement of the death penalty in 1976, Americans have operated under the assumption that capital offenses qualitatively differ from other crimes. The *Furman* decision articulated a "death is different" principle that has shaped our understanding of capital crimes. The requirements of *Gregg v. Georgia* were designed to ensure that those cases resulting in a death sentence could be distinguished from other crimes. We were to sentence to death only "the worst of the worst." The *Gregg* decision required states to set forth guidelines that made a case eligible for the death sentence. The Supreme Court aimed to eliminate arbitrary and capricious sentencing.[18] The American people could now breathe a sigh of relief, assuming that capital punishment would be administered in a fair manner. "By forcing states to articulate their theories of the 'worst offenders,' the narrowing doctrine purportedly guards against 'overinclusion'—that is, the application of the death penalty in circumstances in which, notwithstanding the sentencer's decision, the sentence is not deserved according to wider community standards."[19]

However, intentions and reality do not always coincide, as noted by Governor George Ryan in his speech commuting the sentences of the entire death row of Illinois[20] Governor Ryan has not been the first voice to speak out about the continuing problems with capital punishment. In a dissenting opinion in 1984, Justices Brennan and Marshall wrote about the forms of "irrationality that infect the administration of the death penalty." They further stated, "Rather, for any individual defendant the process is filled with so much unpredictability that 'it smacks of little more than a lottery system.'"[21] Concerns about the inability to ensure that the death penalty was applied fairly led Supreme Court Justice Blackmun to state:

> From this day forward, I no longer shall tinker with the machinery of death. For more than 20 years I have endeavored—indeed, I have struggled, along with a majority of this Court—to develop rules that would lend more than the mere appearance of fairness to the death penalty endeavor. . . . Rather than continue to coddle the court's delusion that the desired level of fairness has been achieved and the need for regulation eviscerated, I feel morally and intellectually obligated simply to concede that the death penalty experiment has failed. It is virtually self-evident to me now that no combination of procedural rules or substantive regulations ever can save the death penalty from its inherent constitutional deficiencies.[22]

Hugh Adam Bedau argues that the changes to imposition of the death penalty in the post-*Furman* years are "largely cosmetic." The changes brought about by the *Gregg* decision have not eliminated discrimination and randomness. Instead, it is administered in a way that is fundamentally unfair, applied primarily to the poor and to nonwhites. Another aspect of unfairness is that capital punishment is largely reserved for those who kill white victims. He also points out that discretion of the prosecutor is a key element. Even if juries can be trusted to navigate their way through the often confusing death penalty statutes in deciding whether an offender lives or dies, those decisions are relevant only when the prosecutor seeks a death sentence.[23]

Some states reserve aggravators that may be conveniently applied to almost any murder for cases in which the prosecutor seeks a death sentence. These aggravators can be applied whether or not the case is qualitatively different from cases in which the death penalty was not sought. Two aggravators used in Oklahoma help illustrate this point: Heinous, Atrocious, and Cruel (HAC) and Continuing Threat to Society.[24] These conditions are vague and broad enough to be applied whether or not a murder case is different from others receiving lesser sentences. Critics of the system suggest that political aspirations of the prosecutors may be more of a determining factor than characteristics of a particular crime.[25]

According to some critics, some aggravating circumstances have a less visible aspect. These aggravators honor certain types of victims, including innocent victims in drive-by shootings or carjackings as well as law enforcement officers. This approach serves to delineate a gulf between "people like us" and those qualitatively different that "threaten us."[26] This type of case frequently attracts significant publicity. The general public thus assumes that the murder is far worse than other murders, the offender far worse than other offenders. These offenders are "other"— inherently different from the rest of the populace.

The offenders in death penalty cases are not the only ones seen as different. Their families become tainted with a degree of "otherness" by association. Borg described a vicarious victimization process where those close to the victim become co-victims. The family members of someone accused of a capital crime become "vicarious offenders,"[27] and they may find themselves publicly shunned. Or when they walk into a room they may find people staring at them. Even when not deliberately ostracized, they may begin avoiding social situations, fearing the reactions of others and feeling guilt or shame. The relatives of those facing death may become obsessed with concerns about how others view their family member and, by extension, themselves. Many also feel responsible in some way for the offender's actions and may obsess about how they could have prevented the murder. Like the families of victims, the families of those sentenced to death must live with the loss of a relative. However, "They must also live with the humiliation and stigma of being related to a person deemed so vile that he had to be exterminated."[28]

At certain stages in the capital punishment process, a relative's case may become the focus of media attention. Journalists and television reporters bombard the public with details about the murder, the murderer, and at times the family of the murderer. In the most publicized cases, the offender becomes a celebrity of sorts, with television specials, books, and movies about his or her life.[29] Often, these stories revile the family of the offender. As execution approaches, the media circus escalates, reporting on the final hours of the offender's life, including the last meal and final visits from family members. Private grief of the family becomes public entertainment.

The family members of convicted Oklahoma City bomber Timothy McVeigh provide one example. McVeigh's two sisters, fearful of consequences from their brother's act, kept their whereabouts unknown. Shy and private, his father nonetheless granted a few interviews. Even the most mundane features of his daily life were fodder for the hungry media. "He bowls regularly with other U.A.W. retirees and plays golf. He helps out at the fire station. In addition to the bingo at the American Legion, he runs games at Good Shepherd Catholic Church. He goes to Mass every Sunday."[30]

According to recent statistics, 6,754 men and women have been placed under a sentence of death since reinstatement of capital punishment in 1976. In "the modern age of execution" (post-*Furman*), almost 900 men and women had been executed in the United States by late 2003. In 2000, 85 executions occurred, in 2001 another 66 persons were executed, and an additional 71 executions took place in 2002. At the time of writing, 3,517 prisoners remained on death row throughout the country. These numbers exclude those who were charged with a capital offense but through plea bargain, acquittal, or lesser sentence avoided death row.[31]

Most of these offenders have families, many of whom have been affected by the death sentences. While some of those convicted of capital offenses have little or no contact with their families, that does not mean the family has not been affected. Indeed, some family members avoid contact with the offender due to shame or concern that their neighbors, friends and coworkers might find out about their relationship to someone who has committed a heinous crime. This issue will be addressed in detail in subsequent chapters.

Families of those facing a death sentence, of course, are not the only ones affected by crime. Families of victims are certainly traumatized.

Suddenly faced with the shock and pain of their loss, they know that a murderer deprived them of a chance to say good-bye, and they may agonize over their family member's suffering. But the criminal justice process and the media circus that surrounds the death penalty often make their pain worse, especially in death penalty cases that receive excessive attention. In these cases, they may find it difficult to turn on a television or pick up a newspaper without being reminded of the terrible details of their relative's murder.[32]

Furthermore, the justification of prosecutors asking for the death penalty has shifted to the survivors of the victims in the post-*Gregg* years. This has emerged in response to the *Lockett v. Ohio* ruling that allowed the presentation of mitigating evidence. The decision of whether or not to impose a death sentence has become a process of weighing mercy for the offender against the claims for vindication by the families of the victims, often in flagrant disregard of those families' desires.[33] Notably absent in this process is any mention of the feelings, rights, or desires of the family of the offender.

FAMILIES OF MURDER VICTIMS COMPARED TO FAMILIES OF THE ACCUSED

Like the families of those sentenced to death, families of murder victims experience trauma and grief. However, they also differ from the families of those facing execution in several significant ways. Both families face financial loss, grief, and trauma. When a family member is murdered, the survivors may lose the income of the victim as well as income from their own jobs as they take off work to deal with detectives and prosecutors or attend a trial. In this sense, they are similar to the families of those charged with a capital offense. But family members of a person charged with a capital crime do not have resources that may be available to relatives of murder victims.[34]

Almost fifteen thousand people are murdered each year in the United States.[35] Most victims leave behind several family members who must cope with the aftermath. These families face immediate financial costs, including funeral costs, lost wages of the deceased, medical bills, and their own lost wages. Additionally, the trauma resulting from sudden loss and the violence frequently associated with murder may result in high levels of fear and rage. They may feel disoriented, overwhelmed by efforts to make sense of the tragedy. Many family members seek counseling to deal with the grief and anger surrounding the death. Finally, these family members often feel repeatedly traumatized. Murder victims' family members (or co-victims, as they are sometimes called) may react to the combined stress of their loss and of dealing with the criminal justice system with increased anger or depression.[36]

The family of the person facing execution experiences many of the same negative consequences. If the arrested relative was employed, they suffer an immediate loss of income. Even if the person facing execution was not the primary wage earner, they usually face expenses. At a minimum, the family members lose wages as they attempt to seek help. Those who hire private defense attorneys often mortgage their homes or use their life savings. Furthermore, although their family member is still alive, the family deals with a lingering expectation of death. This can lead to what Vandiver refers to as "anticipatory grief." Loss is a universal human experience. However, when a family member is condemned, the loss is not easily resolved. The lack of certainty and the often futile hope of a reprieve place the family members in long-term tenuous situations, preventing them from resolving their grief.[37]

Families of the individual who faces execution are more fortunate than the family members of murder victims in one important way. Their family member is still alive, and they can have contact, although limited. The family members of the victim had no time to prepare themselves for loss. On the other hand, the protracted death process or "anticipated death" faced by families of those sentenced to death can take a toll, resulting in anger, depression, and frustration. Social isolation is also common.[38]

Furthermore, some resources are available to the families of murder victims. Crisis counseling and emergency financial assistance are sometimes made available to them, although these are usually inadequate. The family of the person facing execution has no government-funded resources and very few support groups. Instead, these relatives may face public hostility and an outcry for the family member's death. The lack of support, in conjunction with shame, often leads to isolation.[39]

The criminal justice system itself sometimes offers resources to victims' families. The National Organization for Victim Assistance (NOVA) developed in response to concern for victims. This organization has fought for victim representation at several stages of the process, asking for the ability to influence the penalties for crimes. Two important elements exist in the victim's rights movement. The first promotes assistance to victims and their survivors, while the second focuses on the legal rights of victims. Families of victims have been co-opted as part of the prosecution team in many jurisdictions. At first, the Supreme Court ruled that victim impact statements (VIS) would divert attention away from the crime itself as well as the criminal, focusing instead on factors about which the offender would have had no knowledge. Victims with better verbal skills would be more likely to obtain retribution in the form of a death sentence. However, subsequent decisions have resulted in increased use of victim impact statements in determining sentences.[40]

A Victim/Witness Assistance Program is housed in the prosecutor's office in Oklahoma County, Oklahoma. The program description emphasizes the importance of victims: "One of the most important services offered by the District Attorney's office is the Victim/Witness Center. This program provides valuable assistance to the *most important people in the criminal* justice system—the victims of crimes"[41] [emphasis added].

Family members of homicide victims who participate in this program receive support throughout the trial, often from other victims' family members. In Oklahoma County, the grandmother of a young murder victim founded a homicide survivors group. The group is pro–death penalty, providing moral support to families throughout the homicide trial, often accompanying the family not only to legal proceedings but also to the execution.[42] This group focuses on advocating for the legal rights of the victims, with assistance being secondary.

Not all victims' relatives support capital punishment. Murder Victims' Families for Reconciliation (MVFR) is a national organization for those who oppose it. In some areas of the country, these families may be harshly criticized and receive little support from officials. They may even be treated as if they themselves have committed some type of crime. In Nebraska, the state supreme court ruled that victims' families who opposed the death penalty could be denied the right to address the board of pardons. Thus, state-supported advocacy for victims' families is at times limited to those family members who support the prosecutor's desire to seek the death penalty.[43]

Support is not readily available to the families of defendants. According to King and Norgard, state governments, sentencing courts, prisons, and victim's programs do not provide needed support to these individuals. The small number of death row prisoners, confined to a single prison in most states, decreases the odds of connecting with others in the same situation. Thus, the family members of the accused or convicted frequently find themselves in a social vacuum, with few if any people with whom to share their feelings and fears.[44]

Relatives of accused murderers feel alienated as well as isolated.[45] They experience severe stigmatization and may lose their individual identities, becoming subsumed under the category of "relatives of murderers."[46] Few sources of support are open to them, usually small and localized groups of prisoners' families. These families may experience a sense of helplessness, often accompanied by feelings of guilt and shame.[47] Indeed, some relatives, particularly parents of the accused, find themselves vilified in the media when the offender's life is examined for mitigating factors. Furthermore, they may find themselves needing to embrace and support the accusations, rightfully viewing them as a potential source of leniency or clemency. They are placed in a situation with no positive choices. They may allow themselves to be portrayed as abusive and dysfunctional, in hopes that the accused person's childhood will be seen as a mitigating factor. While this could potentially save the life of the offender, there is no guarantee that it will. Public portrayal in a negative light often results in alienating them from others in the community.

The physical structure of the trial further alienates these families. In many trials, law enforcement officers are present to "protect" the family of the victim, thus implying that the family of the accused may attack them. Furthermore, in the penalty phase of a capital trial, the victim's family members but not members of the offender's family are allowed to testify about the impact of the murder on their families. The only information they may offer during the penalty phase is related to childhood traumas, again placing them in the position of testifying about their own failures. Thus, efforts to save the family member can further isolate the family.[48]

However, critics of the criminal justice system point out that participation in the trial is not always helpful to the family members of victims. One difficulty with the use of victim impact statements in trials is that the process is based on vengeance and anger. Indeed, many family members report that they do not feel better after testifying about their loss. Critics of the victim's movement as it currently exists point out that an unspoken goal is to give legitimacy to a punitive approach to crime.[49]

In cases where the victim's family does not support the death penalty, the family may lose their status as victims. In a recent court decision, the state of Nebraska ruled that the victim's family members did not have a right to be present at a hearing to state their desire that the offender not be executed. Other family members have found themselves excluded from the decision-making process and treated as outsiders.[50]

Recently, restorative justice for family members of victims has provided some healing. Two states, Texas and Ohio, have victim-offender mediation programs for violent crimes, and programs are being attempted in a few other states. The programs bring together willing offenders and survivors in a controlled environment to allow the family members to ask the offenders questions about themselves or about the crimes. While these programs are rare and research on them is limited, the findings to date are promising. Over 90 percent of the victims reported high degrees of satisfaction with the programs. In Texas, victim-offender mediation is available in capital cases as well. This type of mediation appears to have the opposite effect of testifying for the prosecution. Instead of increasing the anger and rage experienced by the victim's survivors, they report feelings of relief and peace.[51] This type of support is certainly not available to families of those executed. The "perpetrator" of their relative's death is not an individual but instead the criminal justice system. Imagine the prosecutor, judge, and jury sitting down with the family for mediation!

Finally, some victim's survivors end up befriending the offender as a result of the healing process. Although this uncommon, it does occur through letter writing between the survivors and the offenders. In some cases, the victim's survivor has served as a witness for the offender at the time of execution.[52]

Although the type of support available to victim's survivors varies, organized support does exist. In many jurisdictions, survivors may receive financial assistance, counseling, and emotional support. Families of offenders do not have these options. Instead, they must face the anticipated death of their relative with little support and at times in social isolation.

The families of other prisoners also experience trauma, even when the death penalty is not sought. A brief comparison of families of the accused with families of victims and families of other offenders may illuminate some of the similarities and differences.

Families of Non–Death Penalty Prisoners Compared to Families of Death Penalty Prisoners

The families of other prisoners can also be compared to the families of those charged with a capital crime. Again, similarities as well as differences exist. Families who have a member sent to prison usually can expect that person to eventually be released, although the current trend toward giving life without parole does constrain that possibility.

An extensive literature documents the effects of incarceration on families. Currently, more than 1.5 million minor children have an incarcerated parent, and more than 7 percent of African American children have a parent in prison. Prisoners' families frequently experience severe financial difficulties, often losing their residence or having trouble meeting other basic necessities. Additionally, children may become difficult to discipline in the absence of a father. Problems with depression are also commonplace, in addition to school problems and aggressive behavior. Some researchers have even suggested that current incarceration trends are causing community breakdown, as large numbers of young adult males are imprisoned. We could expect to see some or possibly all of these negative effects when the family member is facing the possibility of execution, often to a far greater degree.[53]

Family members of both types of prisoners may be able to visit, although prisoners are often housed at considerable distances from their families. In some cases, the relocation of prisons to remote areas makes visitation difficult if not impossible. For some families, contact with the offender occurs only via Internet connections. Of course, this type of "visitation" is less than optimal. Connections frequently fail, and there is no physical contact.[54]

Many families do reunite upon release of the inmate. This, however, is not as likely when the offender is sentenced to death. Thus, the family with a member facing execution must cope with the potential of permanent loss, punctuated by periods of hope during the appeals process.

Having a family member in prison has become "normal" in some communities, even at times a mark of honor and "coolness" for some youth.[55] According to Clear, the high incarceration rate since the 1980s may have reduced the negative view of prison.[56] Many children have a parent in prison in the United States, and many more children will have a parent incarcerated during their lives. In communities with high incarceration rates, little stigma may be attached to incarceration. Incarceration is such a pervasive feature of neighborhood life in some of our cities that it can increase status within the subculture. This has severe consequences for families of the imprisoned, with children of prisoners far more likely to be incarcerated themselves.[57] Children of an individual facing execution, however, may not be as likely to see the parent's offense as something in which they can take pride. Under the *Gregg* ruling, death penalty cases are theoretically set apart from all other murders. To be facing execution, the person is believed to have done something truly horrendous, something that demonstrated their "otherness." By association, family members are seen in a negative light.

Realistically, the guided-discretion guidelines derived by most states under the dictates of the *Gregg* decision frequently do not truly distinguish between those cases that receive a death sentence and those that do not.[58] However, the general public views capital offenders as somehow intrinsically different, and it is doubtful that the children of someone charged with a capital offense will feel pride in their parents' sentence, nor will it seem "normal."

Finally, in most cases, non–capital offenders are allowed contact visitation at some point during their incarceration. However, in most jurisdictions, no physical contact is allowed with death row prisoners. Only five jurisdictions with the death penalty allow contact visits in all cases, and fourteen more allow contact visits in only some situations. Appendix A provides a detailed description of the contact visit policies for the jurisdictions with the death penalty.

The remainder of this book is devoted to the stories of men and women who have been affected by our system of capital punishment. Chapter 2 provides a description of the subjects of this book as well as a discussion of the methodology. In chapter 3, the focus is on the coping mechanisms employed by the families of the accused. The protracted grief process they undergo is described in chapter 4. Chapter 5 describes the experiences of several families with the execution itself, using their own words whenever possible, while chapter 6 is devoted to the aftermath. Some families have faced unique circumstances, and entire chapters are devoted to them. Chapter 7 focuses on the families of those who may have been wrongfully accused or convicted. Whether the offender is exonerated, has a sentence commuted, or is executed, these families will never be the same. Families who are relatives of both murder victims and offenders are the subject matter of chapter 8. "Fictive kin" and death row marriages are addressed in chapter 9. Chapter 10 revisits the comparison of death penalty families with those of victims and those of other prisoners. Finally, chapter 11 deals with the author's reactions and perceptions as well as the difficulty of maintaining both empathy and academic rigor.

Chapter 2

Dealing with the Horror:
"We're Sentenced, Too"

Families of Individuals Facing a Death Sentence

The chapter title includes a quote from one of the individuals interviewed for this book. The stories and words of sixty-eight subjects are the focus of this book. Unlike most prior studies, this study is not limited to families of death row prisoners. Instead, it takes the approach that the effects of the death penalty start *before* conviction, when the first discussion of whether or not to seek a death sentence begins. To truly understand the effects of the system of capital punishment on families, we must examine these families' experiences at all stages of the process. A recent study of families of individuals involved in capital trials illustrates that the effects begin prior to sentencing.[1]

A proposed death sentence separates the family members from others in their social milieu, subjecting them to many of the traumas faced by those with family on death row. The *projected loss* and the sense of *alienation* and *social isolation* are related to having a family member who may be guilty of a crime that is theoretically different from other crimes. Bedau argues that we must look at the cost of capital punishment as a system, citing the research on costs of pretrial investigation through execution.[2] The effects on the family are also part of a system, not just a product of the ultimate execution. Thus, we must look at the costs of our system of capital punishment to these families by examining the effects of the entire system of capital punishment. From the horror and shock experienced by the young wife whose husband's face is in the news as a brutal killer to the artificial atmosphere of visitation and ultimately to the anguish experienced by the mother watching her son's execution, the process takes a toll on families.[3]

Amnesty International (AI) refers to the system of capital punishment in the United States as "state cruelty against families." AI points out that families, like the condemned, experience alternating hope and despair. The report gives the example of Jay Scott, who received a reprieve minutes away from death, only to be executed a few weeks later. Despair can take a terrible toll. Gerald Bivins's mother was in intensive care when he was executed, having attempted suicide after her last visit with her son.[4]

The limited research in this area has illustrated some important issues. First, the families frequently suffer severe financial hardships, at times using their scarce resources to assist in the accused's defense or appeals. Furthermore, "The families of executed inmates are also violently bereaved."[5] This bereavement is not sudden, however, but drawn out over a period of years. The protracted deathwatch is marked by a cycle of hope and despair as the offender and family members proceed through the criminal justice process. The family members may enact a sort of dress rehearsal of the grief process, preparing for the final loss. This *anticipatory grief* may lead to distress and delayed recovery. Indeed, the offender's family may experience "frozen sadness" as a result of the repetitive cycle of hope and hopelessness. This type of "ambiguous loss" also occurs in situations such as when a family member suffers from terminal illness or a soldier is missing in action. However, unlike the families of the terminally ill or missing soldiers, the families of offenders often have little social support and may even be the object of scorn.[6]

Research on the families of the condemned is often a difficult and complex task. Vandiver and Berardo point out methodological flaws with most research on families of condemned inmates. Research is rarely done with random samples, and large samples are rare, thus limiting the generalizability of the research. Furthermore, the samples are usually limited to family members in contact with the condemned.[7] The research described in this book did not eliminate those flaws, although the sample drawn is from a slightly different group, families of those facing a potential death sentence as well as families of those condemned to death.

One limitation of the current study is that the sample is not representative of all families of those accused of capital crimes. Some death row prisoners have had no contact with family years prior to the crime. These families may not even know of the charges. If they know, they may not be affected. There is no way to know what their experiences are like. However, many family members are in contact with those accused of capital crimes. Again, the subjects of this book may not even be representative of this latter group. Participation in the study was voluntary, and those who chose to participate may differ from those who did not. The degree to which the experiences and feelings of the subjects of this book compare to all families of the accused, unfortunately, cannot be determined.

Vandiver and Berardo also point out that extant studies have not used comparison groups (i.e., families of prisoners with life sentences).[8] This is a valid criticism. However, there is an inherent problem with comparing these two groups. Many prisoners with life sentences originally faced capital charges. The reversal rate of death sentences is extremely high; almost two-thirds of death penalty cases are reversed, and many former death row prisoners have had their sentences commuted to life. The overlap between death row prisoners and those serving life sentences could make comparisons difficult. Moreover, most studies are based on a one-time interview, prohibiting the researcher from assessing the effects over time.[9] In the current study, I reinterviewed fourteen subjects, five of them both before and after execution of their relatives.

THE SUBJECTS OF THE STUDY

The study was conducted using in-depth interviewing with sixty-eight subjects. (A detailed description of the interview subjects is provided in appendix C.) The sample covered a range of relationships. Fifty-three interviews were with family members. Originally, I planned to conduct only face-to-face interviews with family members, thus limiting the research primarily to Oklahoma. The Oklahoma Indigent Defense System and the Oklahoma chapter of CURE referred family members to me that were willing to be interviewed.[10] From these initial interviews, I obtained other subjects. The community surrounding death row prisoners is sadly united by their common experience. Many family members meet while visiting their relatives and develop friendships based around their common problems. Some of my earlier interview subjects referred additional family members to me. Twenty-five interviews were conducted face-to-face.[11] I used a short interview schedule of questions to elicit their stories (see appendix B).[12]

I quickly learned that many of these families desperately wanted to be heard. Subjects began calling me regularly, asking about the research and then bringing me up-to-date on their situation. Currently, I still hear regularly from a number of the family members that I interviewed.

The additional twenty-eight interviews with family members resulted when one individual, noting my request for interview subjects in the CURE newsletter, put a notice of my research on a national listserv. As a result, I began receiving e-mails from around the country. Most of the e-mails came from family members asking to be included in the project. At that point, I returned to the Human Subjects Institutional Review Board at my university to modify the protocol. Permission was granted to conduct the research using postal mail, electronic mail, and telephone interviews. I received e-mail responses and telephone calls from over fifty individuals about the research. After receiving more information about the project, a few decided not to participate. However, twenty-eight family members and fifteen "fictive kin" returned electronically signed consent forms and typed their responses to the questions on the open-ended questionnaire. One woman sent me about sixty pages she had written about her son's life. These long-distance interviews had both advantages and disadvantages. On the one hand, the individuals were able to take their time answering questions, resulting in thoughtful responses. In some cases, we corresponded back and forth several times. On the other hand, the responses were sometimes less candid, and I was unable to observe body language and affect. In two cases, I interviewed the family members by telephone, taking handwritten notes.

Family members in this study had relatives who were ultimately not charged with a capital offense, relatives who were charged with a capital offense but ultimately not sentenced to death, relatives currently under a death sentence, relatives whose death sentences had been overturned or commuted, and relatives who had been executed. My contention is that the *entire process*, rather than only the death row and execution experiences, affects the families. Because "death is different," the effects begin at the time that a prosecutor announces that he or she plans to seek the death penalty. From the beginning, their relative is separated from others accused of murder. By relationship, the family members are thus separated from "ordinary people," too. Therefore, throughout the book I use the global term "accused" for those to whom my subjects are related.

I conducted face-to-face interviews with a variety of relatives, including parents, stepparents, siblings, adult children (some of whom had been minors at the time of the arrest), uncles, aunts, cousins, nieces, grandparents, and spouses. The interviews were audiotaped with the subjects' permission and later transcribed, with the exception of one interview where the tape recorder malfunctioned for the first thirty minutes. In addition to taping the interviews, I took extensive notes throughout all interviews, including body language and subjects' responses. Thus, I was able to reconstruct much of the conversation from the missing portion of tape in the interview where the recorder malfunctioned. Additionally, I reinterviewed this subject one additional time, allowing me to regain the lost details.

All interviews were confidential, and the names of the subjects and their relatives have been changed to preserve their anonymity, with one exception. One couple has been the subject of national as well as international media attention. Because the details of their experiences are somewhat unique, I was concerned about my ability to preserve their anonymity if I used much of their story. They wanted their story told, and they assured me that they had no desire to be anonymous. Thus, Jim and Ann Fowler are the only family members whose identities are disclosed in this book. I have described the situations and experiences of other family members in general enough terms to protect the privacy of my subjects.

I interviewed twenty-one mothers, two fathers, one stepmother, two wives, seventeen siblings, two nieces, two cousins, two daughters, one aunt, one uncle, and two grandmothers of prisoners. Additional informal conversations were held with a father and a sister. The majority of the subjects were white, although in many cases I did not know the race or ethnicity of the electronic subjects. The ethnicity of subjects is noteworthy, as nearly half of the individuals on death row are African American. I believe I had difficulty accessing African American subjects for two reasons. First, the majority of the subjects for face-to-face interviews were accessed through defense attorneys and an advocacy group. African Americans, especially those in the lower classes, are less likely to become actively involved in organizations due to more immediate concerns such as providing food and shelter. They also are less likely to remain in close contact with prisoners on death row due to transportation difficulties. Second, twenty-eight of the subjects contacted me electronically. African

American households are less likely to have computers and Internet access. The sample, therefore, is not truly representative of families of those facing death sentences or those executed.

Fifteen other subjects were interviewed. Their stories are presented in the chapter on fictive kin. Most of these responded to the listserv postings. The fictive kin include pen pals of death row prisoners as well as persons who subsequently married them. While these subjects could not respond to questions about the initial stages of their relatives' cases, their stories are nonetheless important. Four fictive kin were eliminated from the final book because they provided insufficient information to describe their experiences. The remaining four subjects of the chapter include an attorney, a spiritual advisor, and two family members of victims. With their permission, I have identified three of these subjects. The individuals represented by the attorney are well-known, and it would have been impossible to keep his identity confidential. The two women who are victims' family members are also well-known, and the details of the related cases would make it easy to identify them, as well. As the research progressed, I became increasingly networked into the death penalty community, meeting a wide range of people affected by the system. Notably, ministers, defense attorneys, and their investigators often seemed to experience symptoms similar to those experienced by families. The formal interviews of fictive kin were supplemented with materials from conversations and written correspondence with other individuals, all of whom gave written consent to have their stories included. Finally, materials from Web sites, magazine stories, newspaper articles, and books about this group of hidden victims supplement the interview material. I would be remiss if I ignored this source of information.

METHODOLOGICAL NOTE: USE
OF A NONREPRESENTATIVE SAMPLE

The findings cannot be generalized to all family members of persons charged with capital offenses. This is a limitation of this study. My sample is limited to those family members who chose to be identified as such and to participate in the interviews.

This is an unfortunate reality when researching a hidden population. It reflects the tension between quantitative methods, which stress the importance of generalizability to a larger population, and qualitative methods, which focus on the depth of the material but often are not generalizable to the larger population.[13] Ideally, the methodology used should be based on the nature of the questions asked. Qualitative methods and intensive interviewing are particularly well suited for obtaining information about sensitive or emotional matters. My goal was to have a clearer understanding of the experiences of family members, arguably both sensitive and emotional. A brief survey of family members with fixed-choice answers could easily fail to tap into their feelings and realities. "Many social situations (experiencing grief over the loss of someone or something one cares deeply about, for example) may be masked in everyday interaction and thus be directly apprehensible through intensive interviewing."[14]

Ferrell and Hamm argue that field research allows us to examine crime and deviance from a perspective other than that of the institution of criminal justice. Grounded research allows the perspectives of those whose lives are under examination to shape the findings.[15] When I began this undertaking, I felt it was essential that the stories of the family members take precedence over any preconceived ideas that I might have about how they experienced the capital punishment process. If I had approached this research from a more positivistic and quantitative position, I might have been able to give summary statistics about emotional states and perhaps actions taken by family members. In a sense, the findings would ultimately be "people-free."[16] The effects of capital punishment do not occur to statistics, however. Real humans are affected.

A more focused qualitative study is more appropriate than a larger quantitative study for another reason. Identifying the entire population of family members would be impossible. Some of the accused have not been in contact with their families for years before the offense. In other situations, family members may break contact after the arrest due to their own concerns about being identified. It is not methodologically sound to use a nonrepresentative sample to make inferences about a larger population. Indeed, the potential for bias in the analysis increases as the sample gets larger.[17] Therefore, I used qualitative methods to do this research, and my sample is not representative of all families. However, the people I did interview reported many similar experiences, leading me to believe that there are certain patterns that do occur. Furthermore, a few subjects had broken off contact with the accused, yet they reported similar experiences.

CHAPTER 3

Trying to Cope

Withdrawal, Anger, and Joining

When an individual is implicated in a violent crime, family members are faced with a variety of emotional dilemmas. How should they react? Should they distance themselves from their relative? Or should they rally to his or her defense? Should they be angry with their relative for engaging in a criminal act or angry at the system that is targeting him or her? Should they reach out to others for support, including those with similar experiences, or should they try to resolve their feelings alone?

The individuals' responses to these dilemmas are based on many factors. Personality type, attachment to the accused, and the situation all play a role.[1] In many ways, the families in this book resembled those of persons dying from AIDS. Essentially, the family may be "disenfranchised." Social stigma is an inherent aspect of having a relative accused of an appalling crime, similar to AIDS. Families may experience internal conflict; some members feel anger toward the accused, while other members want to rush to his or her aid. The result is that some family members end up isolated, due to both rejection by others and their own efforts to maintain secrecy or avoid being shunned. Depending on the circumstances, they may feel anger toward the accused for engaging in actions that could have been avoided. Additionally, they may be angry at a system they see as unfair. The convergence of the trauma of the accusal with disapproval of the relative's behavior can produce "bereavement overload." In this situation, there are simply too many problems and issues to deal with.[2]

Coping Responses Used by Families of
Those Facing a Death Penalty

In the families that I interviewed, some basic patterns emerged. Family members tended to respond to their experiences with withdrawal, with anger, or by joining supportive groups. Their responses were not static, however. Individuals moved between the categories, depending on the situation and their resources at any given time. Some family members responded in one way the majority of the time, but others moved back and forth between response categories.

Some of the subjects reported that they dealt with the initial situation by withdrawing from other people. Family members using this response to the strain of having a relative facing a capital sentence eliminated social interaction with anyone but close family members. Depending on other relatives' attitudes toward the prisoner, these family members sometimes withdrew from extended family as well as from friends and neighbors.

Others responded initially as fighters. Fighters responded to the situation of having a relative facing a death sentence by attacking the system itself. These individuals were often angry and felt as if they were fighting some overwhelming enemy alone. Fighting, however, is draining, and many who were initially fighters ended up either withdrawing or joining as they became exhausted from their efforts.

Becoming joiners was a third response. In some cases, family members dealt with the strain of having a relative facing a capital sentence by joining organizations or groups for support. They became active in churches, in abolitionist groups, or in support groups for families of inmates. Joining was a cathartic experience for some of these subjects. They reported that being surrounded by people who were willing to listen to their pain helped them cope. Frequently, joining also took away their sense of helplessness, particularly when they became involved in abolitionist groups.

The following individual cases illustrate the family members' responses. Examples of withdrawal, anger, and joining are described, with attention paid to the movement in and out of the different coping responses. Most of the subjects used different coping responses at different stages of their experiences.

The first subjects, a retired couple, were parents of a young man who was executed in January of 2001. This couple, Jim and Ann Fowler, have been the subject of numerous articles, television specials, and stories, making their anonymity almost impossible to preserve. They have given me permission to use their real names throughout this book. In Ann's words, "I don't see that we've been anonymous at all throughout this process."

In 1985, their youngest son, Mark, was arrested for three murders committed during the course of a grocery store robbery in an affluent suburb of Oklahoma City. They were informed of his arrest by an early morning telephone call from a family friend. Ann took the call. "And on the Fourth of July, bright and early the phone rang. And it was one of our very dear friends. And she said to me—I answered the phone—she said, 'What's Mark's middle name?' And I said, 'Andrew. Why?' and she said, 'I just heard on the radio—or maybe she said TV—that a Mark Andrew Fowler had been arrested for murder, in Edmond.' And I don't remember anything else, except I asked her, 'Can you come?'"

Early in the process, the Fowlers became "joiners." They turned to friends and to their church for support, stating that they were able to survive the ordeal through "the three *F*'s, as we call it: family, friends, and faith." Friends, in particular, were important at this stage, offering both emotional and tangible support.

One friend offered the use of a vacation condominium to the Fowlers for times when they needed to get away from the crisis. The family also turned to their church for support. Jim's brother-in-law from his first marriage was a Catholic priest, and he provided strong support to the family. Because of this connection as well as their faith, the church provided solace to the couple. However, "there was not . . . just an endless stream of priests coming in and out of the house . . . other than my brother-in-law."

During the months leading up to the trial as well as during the trial itself, Jim and Ann began feeling overwhelmed by the system. They began trying to get their son assistance, unsuccessfully. The trials of Mark and his codefendant were not severed. Additionally, the defense attorney appointed to Mark's case was handling his first capital trial. The two defense attorneys, Mark's and the attorney of the other defendant, agreed to avoid blaming the codefendant. The results were disastrous for both boys, each receiving a sentence of death. The Fowlers were devastated. Jim summed up his feelings succinctly, stating, "It makes you realize you're not near as smart as you thought you were. . . . You just realize that you're not—that you just really don't have any control. And that's pretty terrifying when you stop to think about it."

However, after the trial, the couple was unable to sustain their high level of involvement. In part, this was due to another tragedy that struck the family shortly after their son's trial and death sentence. Jim's elderly mother was brutally raped and murdered just three months after his son was sentenced to death. A man was charged with that crime, convicted, and sentenced to death, creating a rift in his family. Jim's siblings wanted a death sentence, while Jim did not. According to Jim, his family supported capital punishment, "just not for Mark." While this did not destroy family support, it did weaken it. After the trial, Jim walked up to the defendant's father, put his hand on his shoulder, and said, "I know exactly how you feel." The other members of Jim's family, however, did not understand the pain a parent faces when his or her child is condemned to death. "We had the biggest division in my family over the . . . death of my mother. And uh . . . they're for the death penalty big time. So there's separation so far as the thinking in that respect. . . . We don't talk much about the death penalty."

Eventually, the stress of dealing with the two trials and the reactions of those around them became overwhelming for the Fowlers. Additionally, both parents were angry with Mark for his participation in the crime, so they did not visit him or have much contact. "The first year that he was down there, we didn't go down at all . . . we were just so upset with him—and angry. It took us awhile to get over that."

They had friends and family in other states, and the couple moved to Washington and then to Florida to get away from the stress associated with having a family member on death row. At this point, they became withdrawers, wanting no association with anyone or anything related to capital punishment.

During this time, Jim and Ann had minimal contact with their condemned son and avoided any discussion of the death penalty or his conviction. Then in 1994, Jim's other son, Jimbo, was killed in a motorcycle accident, and the couple returned to Oklahoma. The loss of Jimbo led them to focus on the remaining members of their family, Ann's children from her first marriage and Mark, the son on death row. They began rebuilding a relationship with him, visiting him regularly.

Meanwhile, DNA evidence indicated that Robert Miller, the man who was convicted of murdering Jim's mother, was innocent. This ultimately led to his release in 1998. Jim and Ann began reevaluating their feelings about Mark's crime. According to Jim, the realization that an innocent man could have been executed for the murder of his mother forced him to reevaluate his opinions about capital punishment, leading him to conclude that it was a "broken system."[3]

By this time, Mark's case was fairly far along in the appeals process. Eventually, an investigator in the defense attorneys' office suggested that they might find support by attending meetings of an abolitionist group. The Fowlers took her advice and attended a meeting of the Oklahoma Coalition to Abolish the Death Penalty. They became active in that organization as well as in their church, and Jim began speaking out about the death penalty in public forums. During the last two years before Mark was executed, the couple was extremely active in abolition work.

Mark Fowler was executed in 2001. His parents remained active in the abolition movement as well as in abolition efforts in their diocese for approximately two more years. According to Jim, this was his final promise to his son, to help abolish the death penalty. Jim is a charismatic man who passionately presents his views on capital punishment. His efforts have not gone unnoticed. Mark Fuhrman, former Los Angeles police detective, credits Jim Fowler with changing Fuhrman's position on capital punishment. Fuhrman, who recently completed a nonfiction book about Oklahoma's system of capital punishment, was unabashedly pro–death penalty at the beginning of that project. He credits Jim Fowler with showing him that closure comes not from vengeance but instead from forgiveness, "because my investigation brought me into contact with Jim Fowler, who, more than any other person, made me begin to reexamine my opinion concerning the death penalty. . . . Jim Fowler showed me the peace that forgiveness and compassion can offer. If he, who has suffered so much, can forgive, then why can't the rest of us?"[4]

In recent months, Jim and Ann have moved away from their intense involvement in abolitionist groups. According to Jim, they "hit the wall." The high level of emotion and constant efforts to abolish the death penalty had taken a toll on both of them. They also found that the pain of losing Mark had not gone away. As Ann commented, "You'd think it would get better after time, but it doesn't." However, they have not completely withdrawn. Jim actively lobbies state legislators about abolition of the death penalty on a regular basis, and he writes letters to the editors of a wide range of newspapers. Additionally, he remains active in his church and speaks to religious and civic groups at every opportunity. He was recently named an honorary lifetime board member of the Oklahoma Coalition to Abolish the Death Penalty.

The Fowlers were not alone in reaching out for support. Paula is the single mother of three children. Her older son (age sixteen at the time) was charged with a capital murder in Alabama. According to the evidence and the testimony of his codefendants, her son was not present at the murder but was actually passed out a few miles away. However, he was considered to be the mastermind of the crime and was charged with a capital offense. Her initial reaction was, "Shock, horror, disbelief. . . . I knew he was innocent and couldn't believe this was happening to us. I cried for hours. I think I was in shock for days. I felt like I was walking around doing what I had to and the world was going on around me . . . while my life and world was being destroyed."

Paula reached out for support from her mother as well as her church. In her words, both were supportive. Paula reported, "My church family came to the house after the word was out. They were tremendously supportive. I really needed them, I felt like there had been a death in the family."[5]

The church remained supportive, with members accompanying Paula to the preliminary hearing. Then, Paula's ex-husband died suddenly of a heart attack, leaving her feeling abandoned as a parent. She began reaching out to other friends but often was rebuffed. Shortly thereafter, her closest friend died suddenly, increasing her feelings of alienation.

Because the victims were also teenagers, Paula and her family became the targets of severe harassment. Beloved pets were killed, tires were flattened, and harassing telephone calls were received. The family moved to reduce the harassment, but this lessened some of their support because they moved away from their staunchest supporters.

During and after the trial, Paula continued to receive strong support from her church, often resulting in reprisals against the minister and other church members. Paula muses that without their support, she does not know how she and her other children would have made it through the trial.

The accused adolescent received a sentence of life without parole, according to Paula, because the families of the victims felt that was a worse punishment than death. Her response to his sentence has alternated between withdrawal and fighting. She found it difficult to deal with her work life as well as her personal life. "My employer was anything but understanding. My supervisor would say he understood and do what I had to. Then if I ever called in he would have me written up."

Eventually, the stress took its toll on Paula. She was unable to work for several years. She also found that her support was limited. Family members other than Paula, her mother, and her two children have responded to the accusation and conviction of Paula's son with withdrawal. They appear to have erased Paula's son from their lives and memories. "My family . . . they do nothing . . . ask nothing . . . don't write him . . . he is simply forgotten. They won't even ask how he is. It has made us all pull totally away from the rest of the family."

Paula feels the trial was not just and that she has received little support from family or community, other than her church. This has resulted in withdrawal from others in the community, former coworkers and friends, and her extended family members:

> I think most of my family just assumed he was guilty from the beginning. My mother was the only one that stood by him and has continued to stand by him. None of my family would come to the trial because they didn't want to be associated with him. Afraid of the repercussions . . . affecting jobs . . . clients, etc. Made me sick and to be honest, I have not had much use for them since. I have also quit attending any of the family functions. They do not offer to help me find a lawyer or help in any way to secure his freedom. It hurts me to even see them, so I don't.

Although there has been some withdrawal from specific people, Paula's response since her son's conviction and sentencing has been primarily joining and fighting. She reached out actively to her church and found support. More recently, she has linked her battles with other groups, especially those promoting abolition of the death penalty. Paula established a Web site about her son's case, accusing the police and prosecutors of unfairness. Several of the abolitionist groups now have a link on their Web sites to her son's Web site. Paula has also had periods characterized by a fighting response. Feeling she was alone in coping with the charges and the trial, she sent angry letters to politicians and newspapers, accusing the police and the prosecution team of misconduct and political motives.

Paula was not the only family member I interviewed who seemed to benefit from joining. Karen reported that some family members had pulled away from her because she has remained close to her son. Other people have also been distant. Some, she commented, "did not want to listen and wanted the death penalty" for her son. She has dealt with the loss of those relationships by connecting herself with individuals she sees as supportive, "primarily other abolitionists."

Similarly, Alice reported mixed support within her family, adding to the stress. Her situation was made even more difficult by lack of support from friends and within her community.

> Our oldest son, the college graduate, told us he got what he deserved. . . . My mother-in-law told me if we had kept him in he couldn't have gotten in trouble.
>
> Most people seemed [to] avoid us like we had the plague. Up until his arrest, we went out [every] weekend [to] eat with a couple, we did vacations together. Then nothing. About three yrs. later she called and asked me [to] stay with her, she had had surgery. Well, I went. During that time I asked her why we didn't see them any-more. She said, "Your problems were [more] than we could take. . . ." WELL—hello! Wonder what she [thought] they were [for] us.

Alice's lack of support was further complicated by the involvement of a preacher in her son's offense, leading to her alienation from orga-nized religion, which is often a source of support. Although she was a regular church attendee prior to her son's offense, she has withdrawn from involvement in organized religion, stating, "I have been in a church three times in thirteen years. Used [to] be pretty regular."

Alice not only has withdrawn from church involvement but also has quit participating in other activities that she used to enjoy. Her family had always enjoyed camping, but they no longer have time. Now, vaca-tions are limited to visiting her sons. The son who is sentenced to death is incarcerated over four hundred miles from where Alice and her hus-band live. Furthermore, Alice expressed that dealing with her son's situa-tion has made it difficult to deal with other people. I asked her what had been most difficult for her. Alice responded, "Facing people, answering the door, late night phone calls. I used [to] be a positive, strong person. I let this thing steal my self-esteem."

Alice and her husband have both experienced health problems as a result of their experiences. Her husband's blood pressure and blood sugar are, in her words, "out of control." Alice herself has experienced both physical and emotional health problems. "I have gained sixty lbs., take Prozac, see a shrink because I almost took my life. Doubled my smoking until I was hospitalized with lung disease. I stay in a state of depression."

Other family members have moved back and forth through different coping responses. Jim and Sharon are the parents of a man whose death sentence has been overturned and reinstated twice already. Like the Fowlers, they are a middle-class retired couple. Their son was not arrested until more than two years after the murder for which he was sentenced to death, although he was questioned several times. One of the issues in his conviction is that he was originally eliminated as a suspect in the crime based on examination of a hair that the police chemist later testified was his and proved he committed the murder.

Sharon initially reacted to her son's arrest by becoming a fighter. She wrote letters, called attorneys, and tried to get someone to listen to her concerns. She and her husband ended up taking out a second mortgage on their home to help pay for some of the expenses.

Their son's arrest could not have come at a less opportune time, in Sharon's opinion. Their relationship with their son was better than it had been for some time. During his early adolescence, the family had to move away from a small town where there were few options for work, taking him away from his girlfriend. In the urban area to which they moved, he had difficulty fitting into existing peer groups. He began rebelling, using drugs, and getting into trouble. He was arrested several times prior to the murder that landed him on death row. Shortly before the latter arrest, the relationship with his parents took a marked turn for the better. He was living at home, and he was staying away from drugs. To Sharon, it was as if she finally had her son back. However, he became a prime suspect in the case in part due to his past. In his mother's words, "I feel like he was convicted for his lifestyle."

The strain took a toll on her health, and Sharon became ill. She ended up having an organ transplant and spending a large portion of her time in a wheelchair. Due to her health as well as the strain of dealing with her son's death sentence for more than fifteen years, she became a withdrawer, having very little contact with anyone other than her family. Her health continued to decline. Sharon expressed her despair, stating, "Sometimes it was just too hard to get out of bed. The only thing keeping me alive is that I wanted to be there for [her son] 'til the end. But I had no hope, no energy."

Then, information came to light that pointed to her son's possible innocence. She began to seek outside support, networking with other prisoners' families, support groups, and abolitionist groups. She also has made contact with the Innocence Project at Cardozo Law School, seeking assistance.[6] Although her health keeps her from being as active as she would like, she uses her computer as a tool to stay connected. She is currently volunteering for an abolitionist group by sending birthday cards to death row prisoners. "I'm glad the guys are enjoying the cards. I feel helpless to do anything, so that's a small way of saying I care, and I really enjoy sending them."

Her husband, Jim, tends to follow her lead. When she withdrew, he withdrew. As she has become more of a "joiner," so has he. He says little, other than expressing disillusionment with the criminal justice system and appreciation for the work that others have done to help his son. Jim reflected, "I had always believed in the system. I thought it was fair. We were shocked at the way [the DA] lied in court. Now we know it can happen to anybody."

Recently, their son's case has garnered new attention from the courts, with the possibility of either release or yet another trial. Sharon is cautiously optimistic but at the same time concerned that the proper legal actions may not be taken. The strain of the years of having a son living on death row has made her cautious as well as exhausted. She questions whether anyone is paying attention to her son's case. Sharon is reaching out for assistance, but she fears getting too hopeful.

Dan was also a fighter. He was extremely angry about the way his stepson's case had been handled as well as the way that he and his family had been treated by the police and the community. He was connected only tangentially with any supportive groups, and his wife coped with her stress by working extra hours. Dan's anger was palpable during the interview, and I was not surprised to hear a few months later that he had severe health problems related to stress.

One of the most interesting interviews was with a woman whose son had faced a death sentence in the pre-*Furman* years. Lydia was eighty-seven years old at the time of the interview, but she recalled the events surrounding her son's crime as if they had just occurred. As soon as I walked into her apartment, she pointed to a picture of her son on the wall. "Here he is, up here. He was a good-looking guy. He was a good ball player and when he was in remission, he played football."

As she told the story of his life, she pointed out that her son had been disturbed since she could remember and was diagnosed as a schizophrenic in his teens. In the 1950s, her son was in Fort Worth, Texas, and apparently broke into a shop. The owner hit him in the head with a blackjack, and her son shot him. He was kept in jail in Fort Worth, and the district attorney announced he was asking for the death penalty. Lydia and her husband lived in Oklahoma but made frequent trips to see their son in jail. Lydia was a social worker, and she used her knowledge to fight the system. Her sister gave them money for an attorney, and they located a doctor who was a specialist in mental illness. Eventually, she was able to convince the court to hold a competency hearing, and her son was declared insane, suffering from paranoid schizophrenia. Although Lydia and her family dealt with capital charges, they never faced a trial. Her son was committed to the state hospital for the criminally insane, where he eventually responded to treatment and was released after eight years. He died at home of heart failure.

Lydia was both a fighter and a joiner. She has always been extremely active in social causes through her church and her work. During her family's ordeal with capital punishment, she successfully fought the system, in part because of the connections she made to others. She and her husband formed a support group for families of the mentally ill during the period that their son was being held pending trial. She has remained both a joiner and a fighter to this day, and she is an avid opponent of capital punishment. She still writes constantly to elected officials, urging them to abolish the death penalty, often sending me a note about what she has sent.

Some family members have been more likely to use withdrawal as a primary response. Naomi's son was executed in 2001. Her response has most often been withdrawal. Her primary support has been the attorneys involved in the case. She is not active in any faith-based groups, but she did sporadically attend a support group for prisoners' families. However, her attendance was never consistent, and she did not network with others involved in the group. She often came late and left early. Her other support was a pen pal of her son's who is a staunch death penalty abolitionist.

Naomi was a Hispanic woman whose son was executed for a crime he committed while arguably mentally ill. Prior to the crime, he actively sought mental health services but was turned away. This evidence was never introduced at his trial, nor was his history of mental illness presented. If those had been presented, her son would probably not have received a death sentence, as he was not capable of standing trial until stabilized in a hospital. Naomi, who was fatalistic, believed that there was nothing she could do to change the outcome. She suffered from severe depression. Naomi told me, "I don't have money, I don't know nothing about the law. What can someone like me do? I just go home and crawl into bed, hoping this will go away."

In the weeks prior to the execution, Naomi made some effort to be a joiner again. She began showing up at abolitionist functions and family support groups, always coming late and not speaking to others. Since the execution, she has not attended any meetings. She continues to suffer from severe depression. "Since they killed [her son] life has been unbearable. I watched my boy draw his last breath, and it felt like it was my last breath."

Naomi's experiences are not unique, although she was more isolated than most of the family members that I interviewed. Louise is the mother of a man executed in 2001. Early in her son's imprisonment, she was a joiner, attending support group meetings for family members of prisoners. She developed a few close friendships with other parents of death row prisoners that she met through the support group or at the prison during visitation. Louise quit attending the family support group, however, because it was not specific to families of those facing a death sentence.

Louise felt that the concerns she had differed from those voiced by families of non–death sentence prisoners, who were focused on issues such as the cost of telephone calls or how to get a family member moved to a better facility. This is a frequent problem faced by death row prisoners' families. Because most states have only one death row, the family members often live in various areas of the state, making it difficult for death row families to organize as a group. Many try joining prisoners' families support groups but end up dropping out. Support groups of prisoners' families are dealing, overall, with very different issues.

Louise began withdrawing more from interaction with other people, including several family members who supported the death penalty. At the time of the interview, she acknowledged that she maintained relationships with only two people: her own daughter and the mother of another death row prisoner. Her health began failing, leading to more isolation, and she collapsed after the execution. About one year after her son's execution she died of heart failure.

Lynette was also a withdrawer, with only a brief attempt to reach out to others for support. Her two sons had been arrested and charged with capital murder and were awaiting trial when she reached out to a local church for support. The minister of the church introduced her to an abolitionist group. Several group members offered to accompany her to the trial or to assist her in any way they could. Lynette attended the group twice, and then she abruptly broke off contact with the church as well as the abolitionist group. Efforts to find her were fruitless, as she had moved and her telephone number was no longer in service. The minister who introduced me to Lynette told me she had disappeared from the church as well. However, Lynette's sons' trials have not yet occurred, so she may eventually use some other coping response.

Some family members used withdrawal out of their own concerns about being identified with the offender or due to their own anger about their relative's actions. Frequently, family members experience intensive negative publicity. Lisa, sister of a man executed in 1998 for the murder of a woman and her five-year-old child, described this eloquently, stating, "Little did I know that the [victim's family's] pain turned into hatred not only for [her brother] but for my entire family. Everyone in [town where murders occurred] wrote nasty letters to the editor all the time. There were blurbs on the television for the entire ten years. I can't tell you the hell it put my mother through and still is putting her through."

This woman withdrew not only because of the hostility directed toward her family but also because of her own anger about the crime:

At first, I hated [her brother], too. I didn't acknowledge that he was even alive. So did my sister. She harbored bitterness and hate for him the entire time. My sister and he finally made peace about eight hours before he died. After about two years, I finally started writing to [her brother]. Mainly for my mother's sake, so she didn't have to bear the burden alone. As I started writing, I asked questions so that I could understand Michael better. We became close over the years and I understood him. Forgiveness finally came, and I understood all of the why's and how's.

Although she was eventually able to forgive her brother and forge a relationship with him prior to his death, the experience was terrible for her. She had planned to attend the execution but broke down at the prison.

Lisa did not find any support other than from her immediate family even at the time of the execution. She remains cautious, telling few people about her brother. Even people who have appeared initially supportive have later rejected her. She told me, "There was one lady who really disappointed me along the way. She claimed to be a Christian Counselor, and I got to know her months before I told her about [her brother]. She cried with me for awhile after I told her, and then after that, she avoided me like the plague. People look at you funny when they know. They say that they don't but they do. They associate me with being crazy or a murder [*sic*] or something must be wrong somewhere for me to come from that kind of family."

Lisa also reported rejection from childhood friends, from the beginning of her family's ordeal all the way through the execution. This has added to her tendency to withdraw. "I haven't told but a handful of people over the last eleven years. I don't want people to, because they will look at me differently. All my friends from Oklahoma just abandoned me. They didn't support me at all during the years, and when I came down for [her brother's] execution, not one of them showed any support. Not one of them called or came over. NOT ONE!"

However, not everyone rejected Lisa. She did find support from one coworker. Although she still is very cautious about talking to anyone about her family's ordeal with capital punishment, she is more fortunate than some of the family. "One lady at work was very persistent. If it weren't for her, I wouldn't have gotten any kind of counseling. She convinced me that mental health was part of me, not some dirty word. She helped me break through. I tried to share this idea with my sister and nieces, but they didn't welcome the idea. Instead, they turned to drinking."

Lisa also experienced loss of support within her family. Her mother remained close to her brother, and Lisa initially made contact with him in order to relieve the burden her mother was carrying. This angered other family members.

> This tragedy did affect our whole family's relationship, and still is. . . . My sister and I were very close when this happened, but it drove a wedge in our relationship. She didn't agree with me, when I started writing to [her brother]. She thought I was just trying to score brownie points with mom, which at first, I was. We grew apart. It got to the point where we didn't talk, and we still don't talk. . . . Our family relationships now are terrible. We just all live separate lives and when we come together, we just hold our breath until it is over. Everyone avoids the word [her brother's name]. Nobody talks about their feelings. It is like a bunch of strangers sitting around trying to get to know one another. We talk about the weather and current events. We never talk about family history or feelings.

Lisa has experienced health problems since her brother's arrest. She reported problems with high blood pressure, migraine headaches, depression, and sleeplessness. Her doctor told her they were all stress related. She believes that her inability to find support and holding her feelings inside have contributed to her problems.

Withdrawal is frequently the response of family members who feel somehow tainted by their relationship to someone accused of a capital crime. Many family members, like Lisa, talked about their fears of other people finding out about their relationship to someone charged with a capital offense. Jason was concerned about someone possibly intercepting his e-mail to me and finding out that his brother had been executed. Jason chose to send me his answers through the postal service because of bad experiences he had had in the past when people around him found out. In response to the question about what he wanted people to know, he responded, "There are to [sic] sets of victims. The victims' family and the family of the person who is on death row."

Jason belonged to a church and to counseling and twelve-step recovery groups but did not seek support from these groups for the emotional pain related to his brother's conviction. He had an experience with negative reactions from members of one group in which he participated, so he felt that his mother was the only person he could talk with about his brother. Throughout his letter to me, he stressed that he was only able to have friends and hobbies because he did not tell anyone about his brother. Poignantly, he described a major concern. "When your [sic] dating someone, when do you break the news to that person about your brother? I have lost relationships with women right after I told them about David. . . . Can you think how hard this is to tell a new relationship or lover?"

Siblings appeared to be particularly prone to fears of co-identification with the accused. Dana is the younger sister of a man currently on death row. She was a high school student when her brother was arrested and convicted. Her response has consistently been withdrawal. Dana had difficulty talking about her experiences. She had some contact with her brother on death row, visiting him from time to time, but overall she withdrew from most people. One of the difficulties Dana faced was that at the time of the crime, she attended school with a family member of the victim. Her family received threats from the victim's family. Dana had to deal with reactions from others at school and work.

> You have people give you looks, and it was hard to go through the days at school, but I somehow managed. . . . I had my best friend that was very supportive, always been there.
>
> My coworkers were very understanding, and then the only problems I had was when his ex-wife would come in with her family and she would be hateful to me and say that she wanted somebody else. I was assistant customer service manager and there was nobody else there. So, it was just hard on that aspect. And they would come in once or twice a week or something.

Dana not only faced rejection from others but also had to deal with changes in her family. Her mother, fearful for her remaining children, became very strict. Dana's social life was curtailed. Dana told me, "My mom became very protective of both me and [young brother]. She made sure that we were home by 10:00. I don't know, just everybody's attitude changed. Whether it was 'Be home by 10:00' or 'No, you can't go with that friend, I don't know that friend.' She was really picky about how we chose our friends from then on."

Dana left home shortly thereafter. She got pregnant before her brother went to trial and married her high school boyfriend. She has coped with the situation by trying to ignore it. For example, if a show comes on television about the death penalty, she comments, "I will usually just turn the channel off and not listen to it." Dana worries about what to tell her children about their uncle. Currently, he is facing a resentencing trial, so his name is again in the news.

Another sibling also used withdrawal as a primary coping response until his brother had an execution date scheduled. At that time, he became a joiner briefly, seeking support and resources from various sources. Matt's brother is a death row prisoner. He originally withdrew, letting few know of his relationship to someone charged and convicted of a capital offense. Because his brother is in another state, Matt has had limited contact with him.

One subject talked about her sister's inability to cope with their brother's charges and sentence. The sister did not attend the trial even though she lived in the town where it occurred. According to her, "My sister came once, came to one hearing, and told us later that night it emotionally set her back ten years, and so she just would not be able to attend anymore. . . . I don't understand that. To me, you just deal with what you have to deal with, but she can't do that. . . . I kind of resented it for my parents' sake, not for me."

After his brother was convicted, Matt developed severe depression and an anxiety disorder and was eventually declared disabled. For the three years prior to the interview, he had not been able to work. Matt blames his illness largely on the stress of dealing with his brother's death sentence. "It's put a lot of stress on my life from the point of I have panic attacks and all and I get so scared at times. I just could go and hide in the closet and I don't even want to face the world."

Matt's first marriage failed, in large part due to his battle with depression. He has recently remarried and appears to be doing better. According to Matt, he sought support early on from a church and was told that his brother deserved execution, with the pastor reminding him, "An eye for an eye." Matt stated he faced tremendous rejection in his hometown, leading him to withdraw from people and to not seek any support. He stated, "There's people that know I'm [prisoner]'s brother, and you know, I feel like they look down on me for what my brother has done—the crime he has done. . . . I've heard people talking as I pass by and stuff. . . . When it first happened, when I was living in [town name omitted], I was paying the light bill and two ladies was whispering, 'There's the brother of the murderer.' And it did hurt."

At the time of the interview, however, Matt had recently become a "joiner." His brother had converted to Catholicism while in prison, and Matt began investigating that religion. His brother's execution date was set, and he reached out to both the Catholic diocese and an abolitionist group for support. Matt sought and received financial assistance from both groups to drive to the prison where his brother was incarcerated pending execution. The execution was postponed, and Matt again withdrew, ceasing contact with the church and the abolitionist group. Occasional telephone calls to him elicited responses similar to this one: "I just don't want to think about it, ya know? I mean, I just end up crawling in the closet and thinking about killing myself. I planned to kill myself at the same time they killed him. He's my brother, he's all I have, really. When he's gone, why should I stay alive?"

Matt was not the only family member to use withdrawal as his main response, changing only at the time of the execution. When family members have few resources, withdrawal or fighting seems to be the response most often used. Bobby is the younger brother of a woman who has been executed. He was still a teenager when his sister was sentenced to death, and at that time his response was withdrawal. He said that other students ridiculed him for having a "killer-sister," and he ended up dropping out of school. However, this may not be the only factor in his decision to quit. Bobby is low functioning, with difficulty controlling impulses. He has spent time in prison for drug possession.

As his sister's execution approached, Bobby switched from withdrawal to fighting. He became angry and vocal in the last thirty days before his sister's execution. At this point, he was clearly in "fighter" mode. He was caught on television cameras yelling that this was "because we're poor." At his sister's clemency hearing, his fighter response became extremely obvious. Despite the fact that the hearing was held at a prison in a room with prison guards, he jumped up from his chair and began threatening to beat up the brother of the victim, who spoke at the hearing.

Bobby and his family were under constant media attention during this last month, due to the fact that a woman was being executed, and in each news clipping that I saw, he was angry and yelling. After the execution, he threatened to kill his sister's defense attorney and investigator because they were unable to get clemency for his sister. He also threatened a minister who spoke on his sister's behalf at the clemency hearing. From Bobby's perspective, the world was against him and his family. The options he saw available to him were limited, and he responded by either withdrawing from public scrutiny or lashing out.

Not all siblings used withdrawal to cope. Mandy's brother was sentenced to death in Texas. She lived in another state but began looking for support. She became active in Murder Victims' Families for Reconciliation, an anti–death penalty organization of victims' family members. In her words, "I am a victim, too."

Kendra also had a brother on death row, but her response was somewhat different. At the time of the first interview, he was in the final stages of the appeals process. He has since been executed. Kendra was eighteen years old when her family's ordeal began. She had seen the reports of the crime on the news but was shocked when her mother called to tell her that her brother was one of two men arrested for the murder.

Kendra's main support came from her mother, Louise. Other members of her family are strong supporters of capital punishment. They are also, in her words, "dysfunctional." One of her other brothers recently got out of prison and another is still incarcerated. Kendra associates with most of her family only on holidays. She has remained in close contact with her brother on death row and with his attorneys, although the latter group has frequently frustrated her. She also spends considerable time with her mother and with her brother's two children, who were toddlers at the time of his arrest.

At work, she has at times felt ostracized, especially recently since her brother's case has been in the media frequently. One coworker commented that Kendra had the same uncommon last name as a man on death row that was going to be executed soon. Kendra acknowledged that it was her brother, and so the word got around the business. She tries not to let it bother her, commenting, "Generally, when people do act different towards me I just think that's an angry person and just can't see past that. That's not me—that's my brother. A lot of times I think that people don't know the difference."

Kendra does have some outside support, mainly from her church. She has also occasionally reached out to the abolitionist community but is not currently active. She is concerned about her mother's health, stating that although she was only fifty-five, she appeared more like someone in her sixties.

Other family members were not as concerned about being judged by others. Eugene is the uncle of a man on death row. They live in different states, making it difficult for him to see his nephew. Eugene is a "modified joiner." Although he is not active in a church, a family support group, or an abolitionist group (he lives in a non–death penalty state), he maintains contact with other families of death row prisoners via the Internet and e-mail. He also has built his own support network, including coworkers and a tenant. Eugene feels that most people have been very supportive of him, perhaps because he talks to them about the case and about his feelings. When asked who had been supportive of him, he replied, "Just about everyone I talked to." He also claimed that he had not suffered any health problems, nor had his hobbies been affected. Other family members have been less fortunate. Eugene reported, "One of my sisters in NY is embarrassed and has not told her friends and coworkers and is afraid to reenter local politics in fear of his situation being used against her (she left for health reasons and is now recovered)."

Jane's cousin was executed in 2001. Jane has responded primarily as a fighter. She is a well-known activist in her home state and works for a large national organization that often engages in issues related to prisoners' rights. As her cousin's execution approached, Jane was very outspoken in her efforts to save her cousin's life. She sent information to a number of organizations requesting support in her cousin's bid for clemency. She outspokenly criticized the system as well as her cousin's trial. While always respectful of the victim and his family, she was adamant about her feelings.

Another woman's response to her cousin's death sentence was very different. Martha coped with his sentence by withdrawal. She lived in a different state from where the crime had occurred, and she maintained no contact with the offender or with any type of support group. Martha tried to deal with her feelings by herself, and at the time of the interview told me that she had not spoken before about her feelings to anyone. Interestingly, several months after the interview she told me that she had written to the offender and that she was feeling some lessening of her anger toward him.

Wives of death row prisoners face a particularly difficult situation, as they often must become the sole breadwinner for the family following the husband's arrest, find funds to help with legal assistance, and deal with their feelings alone. This may leave little time for involvement in support groups, as in the following case.

Linda is a young mother of two adolescent boys. She is also the wife of a death row prisoner. Her husband was one of three men convicted of a drug-related murder in a small town in the Southwest. Linda has been a joiner since her husband's arrest. She is active in her church and receives strong support there. Linda reflected, "As far as I know, nobody has ever said a negative thing about me or the boys. Everyone has helped. I really don't think I could have gotten through this without my church and my family."

However, Linda says she has no time to participate in any support or abolitionist groups. Linda responded to the crisis in her family by taking on a second job. Eventually, she was able to purchase a small business. The demands of her work and taking care of her two sons take most of her time. Her sons join her at work each day after school. She says she feels no shame about her husband's crime, and she is too tired to worry about what people think or to try to fight the system. Twice a month, she and her sons make the long drive to the prison. They used to go every week, but Linda finds that she is too tired and has too many responsibilities to go that often anymore. For emotional support Linda has networked with a few other prisoners' families that she has met while visiting death row. However, despite the support she receives, she deals with emotional pain that she doesn't think anyone could under-stand. "It's hard, though. Sometimes I think about my husband holding our first son on his chest, and I realize that he will never be able to touch either of his children again. But what else can I do but go on? I have two wonderful sons to live for. They're good boys. They help me after school—they're in football and soccer."

Linda was not typical of most of the people I interviewed, because rather than shifting, she had maintained one response from the time of her husband's arrest until the interview. However, her husband has been on death row for about six years, while some of the other interview subjects had dealt with having a relative on death row for more than fifteen years. It may be that over time she changes her response to the situation. However, her joining is primarily limited to participation in her church activities. The church was a part of her life before the crime occurred. She has not joined any other type of support group or cause, and her responsibilities as sole parent to two young boys leave her with little energy for fighting the system. Thus, she is in less danger of burning out than some of the family members who have been more engaged in fighting or joining new groups.

PATTERNS IN COPING RESPONSES

Three patterns are apparent when looking at the experiences of family members of those charged with a capital crime, sentenced to death, or executed. First, most family members moved back and forth between responses. At some time in the process, a family member may be a joiner, seeking support and assistance from others, especially church and abolitionist groups. At other times, the same person may be a fighter, attacking the system and those who support it. Withdrawal is also a response used, and most family members withdraw at some time during the process. An interesting aspect of withdrawal is that the adjustment of the individual may in part depend on whether or nor he or she withdraws at the beginning of the process or later on. Those whose initial response is to withdraw tended to fare worse than those whose initial and dominant response was fighting or joining. Family members who primarily withdraw often report stress-related health problems, as in Lisa's case. Additionally, those who withdrew from the beginning reported still feeling isolated at the time of the interview.

Fighters did not fare as well as joiners if they maintained a high level of anger for an extended period of time. Fighters tended to report health problems, perhaps due to the stress and lack of support. They appeared to feel impotent in their efforts, alone, and victimized. Fighters frequently developed severe health problems or mental health problems, leading to their becoming withdrawers. Both Dan and Sharon experienced severe health problems. Neither the withdrawal nor the fighter adaptation is as healthy, overall, as joining, if maintained over a long period of time.

Finally, most family members, even those whose primary response was withdrawal, at some point in the process became joiners. Family members often turned to organizations and churches for support in the months preceding the trial and sentencing. These individuals maintained a higher level of activity at those times, attending meetings asking for help. After sentencing, however, many seem depleted emotionally and physically. Most of these then become withdrawers. It may well be that they are simply unable to maintain the continued level of emotional involvement. Some of these family members became joiners again as execution approached.

Some family members are "quasi-joiners," seeking help only in periods of crisis, such as immediately before trial and immediately before execution. As we saw in the cases of Naomi and Jason, these individuals often only minimally connect with groups for support. Quasi-joiners do not benefit as much from their involvement as those who remain active for extended periods of time. However, individuals like Eugene take a modified approach to joining that seems quite beneficial. Eugene created his own support network, and he reports little negative effect on his life.

While joining is the healthiest response in some ways, those who become involved in abolitionist efforts frequently reach the limit of their abilities and have to withdraw for a while. Jim Fowler put it succinctly when he stated, "We just hit the wall." The frustration of being involved in failed efforts to stop an execution or to abolish capital punishment caught up with the Fowlers. Additionally, they needed time to deal with their emotions, and they realized that they wanted and needed to spend a lot of time with their remaining children and their grandchildren.

Most joiners take periods of respite from the high level of involvement. Several subjects acknowledged that they simply had to take a break from focusing their life around the death penalty, that it was too stressful and painful. Likewise, those whose primary response is fighting cannot keep the high emotional response constant. And those who respond by withdrawing often need to reach out for support during the most stressful periods such as the trial or the weeks leading up to the execution.

Not only are the responses to the experience of having a family member facing a death sentence varied, but many families also experience a somewhat predictable cycle. Although considerable variation exists in how the subjects experienced the grief process, there are also striking similarities. In the following chapter, I describe a grief cycle experienced by many, using the family members' stories to illustrate the different stages through which they pass.

CHAPTER 4

The Grief Process

DENIAL AND HORROR, THE BADD CYCLE (BARGAINING, ACTIVITY, DISILLUSIONMENT, AND DESPERATION)

THE GRIEF EXPERIENCE

GRIEF IS ONE of the major experiences of family members of individuals facing execution. A brief examination of how individuals experience grief may help illuminate the experiences of these families.

Some debate exists about whether or not grief is experienced similarly by all individuals—whether the bereaved experience some type of process. Over thirty years ago, Elisabeth Kübler-Ross described the five stages that a dying patient goes through: Denial, Anger, Bargaining with God, Depression, and Acceptance. Numbness and disbelief are characteristic of the Denial stage. Stage 2 is characterized by rage and anger, including anger at oneself. In the Bargaining stage, unrealistic feelings of guilt lead to attempts to somehow fix the situation. Eventually, in the Depression stage the person accepts the reality of the loss but feels helpless and without energy. Acceptance comes when the person deals with the loss and makes some type of new beginning.

Kübler-Ross developed her theory of grief based on in-depth interviews with dying persons. The Kübler-Ross model differs from other models dealing with grief, particularly with bereavement, in some important ways, however. Kübler-Ross developed her model to describe what terminally ill patients experienced *prior* to their death. Thus, she introduces the phase of Bargaining with God, which would not be appropriate for describing what individuals experience after the death of a loved one. However, it is relevant in a discussion of how families deal with a protracted death process. Families of those sentenced to death may experience this stage or something similar.[1]

Kübler-Ross's stages have been applied to other forms of grief, including a loved one's death as well as combat exposure, but with limited success. Other research suggests that the model works fairly well to explain individual responses to job loss in the automotive industry. The idea of the model is that the individual moves through the stages in a somewhat chronological order, eventually reaching the acceptance stage. However, Kübler-Ross acknowledged that not everyone would experience the stages in the order she proposed or even experience all of the stages. Indeed, in her own research no single patient went through all five stages in order.[2]

Kübler-Ross's approach has been criticized as being too simplistic. As one expert commented, "We do not become as much alike when we grieve as that kind of thinking suggests." He goes on to elaborate on his opinion. Grieving, he explains, is a response to loss. The bereaved person must change in all areas of his or her life: emotionally, psychologically, behaviorally, physically, socially, intellectually, and spiritually. Another critic suggests that individuals may experience emotions not mentioned in the Kübler-Ross model. In contrast, yet another author argues that mourning is a natural process with identifiable stages, but the patterns are not usually as simple and straightforward as Kübler-Ross suggests. Another critic acknowledges that while the model is simplistic, it also has strengths. The danger in the simplicity is that an individual's feelings and experiences may be easily dismissed as "part of the process" rather than being recognized as personal and painful. On the other hand, there may be comfort in knowing that others go through similar experiences.[3]

Others have developed their own models of the grief process. In one model, the bereaved individual must first accept the permanent reality of the loss. Next, he or she must experience the pain associated with the loss. Then, the individual must adjust his or her life to exclude the deceased. Finally, a new relationship with the deceased is developed. Another model examines grief through coping theory. This model is based on the perspective that coping is contextual, a process, and multidimensional. This grief theory is referred to as a dual process model of coping because the person is believed to appraise both the negative event and his or her options for dealing with the event. This is a dynamic theory of grief because it emphasizes ongoing changes in coping based on changes in the relationship with the environment.[4]

Freud is considered an early expert on the subject of grief. In his writings, one of the primary tasks faced by the bereaved individual was reclaiming the energy that had been invested in the loved one. We are naturally reluctant to give up a person we love, and the process is slow. Freud considered it important for the individual to refocus energy that had been invested in the relationship with the deceased. Later theorists added to our understanding of grief by reflecting on the role of socialization and the relationship with the deceased in the experience of grief. Bowlby identified four phases through which the grieving person passes: numbing, yearning and searching, disorganization and despair, and reorganization. Still others have suggested that grief responses are predictable, regardless of the individual's personality characteristics and personal coping skills. A recent theory posits five phases or stages through which the individual passes: shock, awareness of the loss, conservation–withdrawal, healing, and renewal. The author goes on to suggest that grief is not only psychological but also biological and represents the individual's movement toward reintegration or balance.[5]

One concern frequently expressed by critics of stage models of grief is a general misunderstanding about how the stages are experienced. The average person and even many mental health practitioners tend to see the stages of grief as linear and as descriptions of how grief should be experienced. This can make grieving individuals feel as if they must "progress" through the stages in a timely manner and that something is wrong if they do not. The authors of the various stage models did not make this assumption, however. Instead, they acknowledged that how grief is expressed, the timing and sequence of stages, how long grief lasts, and the coping responses used were varied. One final criticism of the Kübler-Ross model and other stages of grief models bears examination. These models assume that the outcome of the grief process will be a return to a more "normal" psychological state. Some experts suggest that one does not ever return to the state of mind prior to the loss, and long-term grief may be normal for some people. Instead of "letting go" of the deceased, individuals may redefine their relationships with those they have lost.[6]

The debate about whether or not grief is a process that occurs in identifiable stages is essentially an argument about whether or not each individual's experience of loss is unique or whether common themes and experiences exist that all bereaved individuals experience. The two may not be mutually exclusive, however. While a variety of factors affect the grief experience and make the responses to grief different, that does not mean that no similarities exist in the stages of grief experienced by individuals. Personality type, social support, and the individual's outlook on life could all affect how he or she responds to the death of a loved one. However, each individual must respond to that death and is faced with certain tasks that must be accomplished if the individual is to return to a more functional state.

Complicated grief refers to grief experiences that are extraordinarily severe and painful. Complicated grief may occur when the circumstances surrounding the loss itself are difficult. This can result in fixation on the trauma, replaying it over and over in our minds. It may also occur when the individual lacks sufficient coping skills to deal with the loss. Grief is further complicated when some degree of uncertainty is present about whether or not the loss is real and permanent. Loss can shatter the individual's view of the world and life in general. This is particularly true when the situation is traumatic. This shattered worldview may make it difficult for the individual to find meaning and a sense of purpose and security. Complicated grief frequently is associated with a number of physical and mental health problems, including heart problems, high blood pressure, digestive disorders, cancer, substance abuse, suicidal thinking, and lack of energy.[7]

COMPLICATED GRIEVING

Families facing the execution of a relative may experience a complicated grieving process. Their grief upon facing the potential execution may not be a regular and straightforward progression. Because the process is long and unpredictable, individuals may find themselves bouncing back and forth through stages. Their whole outlook on life is frequently turned upside down. They are not unique in this regard. Other family members who face uncertainty and a prolonged death process have similar experiences.

For example, wives of servicemen missing in action face uncertainty about their loss. When told their husband is missing, they initially hope for his return. As time passes, they begin to think he might be dead but do not dwell upon the idea. Eventually, the up and down emotions become overwhelming, and the wife often just wants a definitive answer, not caring whether or not her husband is still alive as much as she cares about knowing for sure what happened. Predictably, this creates guilt. They then revert back to the idea that maybe their spouse is still alive, and the cycle starts over. There is no resolution, no orderly progression through clearly defined stages of grief. Instead, the cycle feeds on itself.[8] In some ways, their experience is not different from that of death row families. Families with a loved one facing or convicted of a capital charge are on a similar merry-go-round. They have initial hope, then fading hope. Eventually, the roller-coaster ride of appeals takes its toll, and they feel exhausted and drained. They experience guilt as a result, and many renew their efforts to save their relative, putting them back at the beginning of the cycle.

These two types of families are similar in other ways as well. Both experience not only the prolonged grieving process but also considerable anger. Both groups tend to focus their anger on the government. They often feel betrayed and misled. They also are frequently angry with their loved one as well as themselves. Furthermore, both groups have difficulty finding support from others with similar experiences. Wives of missing in action (MIA) servicemen do not feel like they fit in grief support groups where death is certain. Similarly, families of those facing a death sentence do not feel like their issues are the same as those experienced by the families of other prisoners not like families who have already experienced the death of a relative. Additionally, both groups are small in size and spread out geographically, making it difficult to form support networks.[9]

These two types of families experience what Boss has referred to as ambiguous loss. One type of ambiguous loss occurs when someone is physically absent but psychologically present, as in the case of the families of MIA pilots. Another occurs when someone is physically present but psychologically absent, as occurs with Alzheimer's patients. Arguably, having a family member facing a death sentence could create both types of ambiguous loss. The person could be seen as missing but still a part of their lives, much like the MIA pilots. Or, the family may view the condemned prisoner as physically alive but no longer psychologically part of the family. In a culture that does not allow for much ambiguity, the uncertainty of the situation can create a host of problems, including family conflict, depression, and anxiety. Those experiencing ambiguous loss may have difficulty determining how they should react. At one time, they may deny anything has changed; at another time they may act as if their relative is already dead. Eventually, the uncertainty of the situation can create frozen sadness or numbness to all feelings. This frozen sadness is what many families of those facing death sentences experience.[10]

Another group has experiences that are similar to those faced by families of the condemned. Partners and caregivers of AIDS victims deal with prolonged bereavement prior to the death. The eventual death was expected, but much of the distress occurred prior to the death. AIDS caregivers dealt with this stress in part by using "active problem-focused" coping strategies. That is, they dealt with the ongoing stress by focusing on tasks they could carry out in the immediate present. When they were able to successfully complete a task, it created a sense of mastery or being in control. They also used "positive reappraisal," redefining the situation in a more positive light.[11] It is easy to draw parallels between the issues they faced and those faced by family members of those facing a death sentence. In both cases, the death is expected, but a prolonged period of grieving and loss takes place before the death occurs. There may be periods of renewed hope. In the case of caring for AIDS patients, new medical protocols may provide a reprieve and hope for some measure of recovery. For the families of the condemned, strong appeals cases, new technology such as DNA testing, and hearing about other cases being overturned may bring temporary hope. These two groups are also alike in another way. In both cases, their relative is stigmatized, and these family members and friends are also stigmatized because of their relationship. There may be rejection by family and friends, and they tend to seek support from others in a similar situation.

Grief and Families of Those Facing Death

In the current study, identifiable stages in the grief process prior to execution emerged. Of course, all subjects did not go through all stages, and some subjects were trapped in certain stages, repeating those several times. Nonetheless, the following stages are helpful in examining their experiences.

Stage 1: Denial and Horror. Almost all subjects reported that their initial reaction alternated between denial and horror. Most reported that their initial reaction was disbelief, the thought that a mistake had been made.

Stage 2: The BADD Cycle: Bargaining, Activity, Disillusionment, and Desperation. Perhaps the most destructive aspects of capital punishment occur in this cycle. Like the family members of someone with a terminal illness, the family members of someone facing capital punishment experience a cycle of raised and diminished hopes. However, when the prospect of capital punishment is included, the family member also experiences periods of intense activity trying to change the feared outcome as well as disillusionment with the criminal justice system. Eventually, they become desperate, trying to save their family member any way that they can.

Stage 3: Surrender. Family members eventually need to come to terms with what is happening, although they do so in different times and in different ways. For some, surrender means giving into depression and hopelessness. For others, it means accepting the inevitability of execution and reframing it in a more positive way, such as focusing on the fact that their loved one will no longer spend his or her days in a tiny cell.

Stage 4: Picking Up the Pieces. After exoneration, commutation, or execution, the family then moves on. Families vary in how well they do in this stage. Some respond with anger, others withdraw or collapse. Those who seem to fare best are those who have developed strong support networks.

A striking feature of the grief process experienced by these families is that the process is not simply a straightforward progression through well-defined stages of grief. Instead, many get caught up in multiple repetitions of the second stage, the BADD cycle. The very nature of the capital punishment process can lead to periods of renewed hope and efforts to save the family member, followed by disillusionment with the system and desperate attempts to save the relative's life. Some families are caught in this cycle for ten to twenty years. Being stuck in a stage of grief for years can become pathological and create psychological and often physical hardship for the bereaved individual.[12] The current chapter deals with the first two stages of this process. Stage 3, Surrender, will be dealt with chapter 5. Stage 4, Picking Up the Pieces, is the subject matter of chapter 6. The following chapter concerns family members who believe their relative is innocent.

Stage 1: Denial and Horror

Most subjects reported that their initial reaction alternated between denial and horror. Their initial reactions were disbelief, the thought that a mistake had been made. Ann and Jim Fowler recounted the following experience after they received word that Mark had been arrested for the grocery store murders. "You don't have any experience like that. So you don't—I mean it's just like you kind of stand around looking at one another, because there's nothing you can do. The—the reality of it just doesn't sink in on you for a long time, I don't think."

Another family member, Jim Fowler's first wife's brother, talked about his initial reaction during a newspaper interview. Jim Fowler's first wife, Caroline, had died of cancer during Mark's early adolescence. Mark, who was adopted, had felt abandoned. During his mother's illness, he was sent to his uncle's temporarily. He and his uncle, Father Greg Gier, became quite close. He considers his family unusual because they had built closer bonds to their condemned family member, while many families withdraw. A newspaper interview reported, "'It affects your self-concept,' Gier said. 'You are suddenly a criminal by association. You have created this person; this person came out of your home life; this person is your relative.' "[13]

This family was somewhat fortunate in that a close friend broke the news and then arrived to provide support. However, all families were not so lucky. Dan, the stepfather of a young man charged with killing his girlfriend and her children, reported that his family found out when the police arrived at their home. He, his wife Carol, and Carol's other two children were at home when the police came. His stepson was also in the house at the time. There had been a slight indication in the news that their son was a suspect, but the family did not take that seriously until the police arrived. Another former boyfriend of the victim had been arrested for the crime. Then, suddenly, they found the police at their front door. Dan described what happened that night: "They arrested him at our home and violated our house. If you've ever been served a search warrant in your home, let me tell you, it's an experience you'll never forget. They burst into the door and had their guns drawn and I said, 'Hey'—right there in my foyer—'I've got two younger children. You don't need those guns.' He said, 'Step out of the way, sir.'"

The entire family was traumatized. Dan's wife was taken into a separate police car and questioned for hours. She was told she did not need an attorney, but in retrospect she believes that she should have had one present:

> I said, "I don't understand what all these questions are about. . . . And I said, "What are you going to do with these questions? I don't understand why you're asking me all these questions anyway. Are you going to use all these questions against my son? I mean, you've not read me any kind of rights, now you're questioning me. I don't understand why you're questioning us." I don't know what all they were questioning us about.
>
> It was 9:00 at night or something. We were surprised at the timing and what a big deal they made out of it. . . . There was like . . . five or six police cars surrounding our house.

The two younger children were in the home when the police arrived and were frightened by the events occurring. Their daughter was about fourteen; their younger son was thirteen. Dan talked about that as well, commenting, "That's when our hell on earth began. This happened in 1993, so, you know, they were thirteen and fourteen, something like that. They just sat there and cried. I mean, you know, they came in here and ransacked [my] house."

The police went through everything and put things into paper sacks without showing them what they were taking. Some of the things taken by the police were never recovered, including a watch belonging to their younger son that the suspect son had just put on. Carol reported, "They didn't show us anything that was in the sacks. . . . And see, like the watch—it wasn't his, it was [the younger son's]. And, we never did find that watch. It's never showed back up. And that's when our nightmare began. . . . And it was Christmas time, so we had Christmas packages all wrapped and—they just threw them all over the place."

Their younger son suffered the most. He was very close to his brother. His closest friend had moved away a few months before, and so he had gravitated toward his brother. After the arrest, he began getting in trouble himself, and his parents sent him to live with his grandparents in another state. That bothered him even more. He did not want to be there, and he rebelled. Their daughter, Dana, was more fortunate. A few of her friends rallied around her and supported her from the day of the arrest through the trial. I interviewed her at a later date, and she shared her initial reactions with me. "I was in shock. I was in shock. It was kind of like a movie because you see nine million cops. As soon as you open the door, they don't give you time to say anything. They just ran in . . . I was on the floor crying. First, I didn't know what was going on and then I just remember crying and that's about it."

The arrest of her brother and search of their home was particularly traumatic for this young woman, a high school student at the time. Not only was she faced with the intrusiveness of the initial entry, but the search of their home also resulted in damage of sentimental keepsakes. "It seemed like forever. They went through every room in the house. I remember that I had sentimental things that were broken that I couldn't keep. I had some dried roses and stuff that had been wrapped up in a box. I mean, they were nicely wrapped so that they—you know, of course, dried roses are going to fall apart but they were all over the floor, thrown out of the box."

One of the more difficult things experienced by this family was other people assuming their son was guilty and would be eventually executed. They found themselves constantly insisting he had not yet been tried. Carol talked about an incident at work.

The Sunday paper, front page . . . showed [her son's] picture. I don't know if it showed his name at all or exactly what. Gayla [a coworker] said, "Did you read this? Isn't that awful?" I said, "Well, that's my son." And she didn't say anything else. No, she did say something—this was before the trial, too, since he had gotten arrested. . . . And during one of the breaks she said to me, "Oh, I'll bet you are really glad they have lethal injection in Oklahoma." I said, "I don't understand what you mean." And she said, "Well, that's a much easier way to go than other ways." So I think I said, "Well, [her son] hasn't been tried yet."

Dan also found himself denying his stepson's guilt. He was taking his younger stepson to practice, and some men were talking about the police having finally caught the man who had killed the young woman. Another woman, whose son was in prison, called him later that evening to offer her sympathy and understanding. "She called me and she says, 'I'm sorry.' She said you had to sit back and take it. And I said that there were two differences. 'You get to see him [her son].' . . . And I said, 'Has he [his own stepson] been tried yet?' "

Kendra, the sister of a man who was executed shortly after our interview, typified the initial reactions with her response, stating that she got the news from her mother that her brother had been arrested for a highly publicized crime. "And I was shocked, you know, and I said, '[her brother] was arrested for that?' . . . When you've been with somebody from the moment you were born and you've grown up with that person—I don't think anybody wants to think that somebody they love . . . could commit such a crime."

Kendra's family was traumatized when her brother was charged with the murder. Although being arrested and even incarcerated was common in the family, she made a distinction between "normal" crimes and a capital crime.

Similarly, Laura was shocked when her son was arrested. Her son had been using drugs, so their contact was not as frequent as she would have liked. According to her, they spoke on the telephone once or twice a month during the months prior to his arrest. Shortly before the crime occurred, she sent him money to come to the state in which she lived, but his girlfriend convinced him to stay in Oklahoma, where the murder occurred. Prior to his involvement with drugs, he had been a model son. Finding out that he was charged with a capital offense was something she had never anticipated. Laura stated, "My best friend, who lives near Tulsa, called and told me, then [her son] called me and told me what had happened. I was blown away. I would have sworn he was not capable of something like that. . . . I was in shock, as was my husband and my mother. I did not believe it—he was such a lovely child, the perfect child until he became involved with drugs."

Sarah, another mother, described her initial reaction to the news of her son's arrest more succinctly, simply stating, "Shock, disbelief, horror." Her words were echoed by many of the family members that I interviewed. Similarly, the mother of a young woman on death row, Carla, stated, "I always called her on Saturdays to have coffee and chat with her. On [date not given to protect confidentiality], when I called to talk to her I was told to call the police station. The nightmare began at that time."

The damage done when a family member faces death can never be erased, even when the accused is later exonerated. Beverly's son spent a year in jail awaiting trial before he was released. Beverly initially was not sure that her story was "bad enough" for inclusion in this book. In our initial contact, she first noted that she and her family were "lucky" because her son was freed, then she commented that the "ordeal ruined our lives." "I'll be happy to talk to you, but I'm sure you are looking for people that have suffered much more than we did. Although, again, I can't imagine any worse than it was for us. There is nothing, not words or anything else, that can explain the terror of what I felt when I thought the state was going to kill my only child. I had nightmares, asleep or awake, trying to imagine me going into a chamber where my child was strapped down and being injected with poison."

In some cases, members of the family had never been in any trouble, making the charges difficulty to believe. Eugene, the uncle of a death row prisoner, received a telephone call from his sister, the accused man's mother, the night of the arrest. Like most of the subjects, he was caught off-guard. When asked about his reaction, he stated, "Shock, no one in our family had ever been in trouble before—speeding was the highest offense."

Kathy's story is similar. Kathy has a brother on death row who is disabled and has a mental illness. However, despite his problems, she never expected him to commit a murder. She reflected on this. "If someone had told me that one day I would be talking about what it was like to have a family member on death row, I would have said, no way, that no one in my family was capable of killing another human being. I simply wouldn't have believed it was possible. I would have told them that I come from a good family, a normal family, and that everyone in my family is a good, decent caring person. Including my brother."

Linda, the young mother whose husband was sentenced to death for drug-related homicides, first found out about the crime while in the grocery store. A television was on, and the news was covering the murder. Linda's initial reaction was fear that her husband might have been involved. Although they were separated at the time because of his drug use, she knew that he had been shot a week before by one of the victims. So, she called her husband, who reassured her that he did not know anything about the murders. She believed him and let go of her concerns. Then, a few days later, she received a telephone call from her father-in-law letting her know that her husband had been arrested. She described her initial reaction, stating she felt, "Horror! It was like a nightmare." Linda's world was turned upside down by her husband's arrest. She told me that her husband was never a violent person, so it was hard to accept. For the first two years following his arrest, she slept on the couch, unable to face the empty bed. Nothing made sense to her. She sought answers but could not find any explanation for what had gone wrong.

Linda had the additional burden of breaking the news to her two young sons. According to her, they handled it well. She went to the school to talk to their teachers, and there has not been a problem with other children taunting them. But it has been terribly hard for her. "It was hard, knowing his life was over. He will never have another chance. He had never been arrested except for a DUI [driving under the influence], years ago. After the arrest, his mind was not right for a long time afterwards."

Another woman, Lisa, provided a poignant and graphic description of her initial reaction to her brother's arrest in another state, describing both the physical and emotional components:

> I'll never forget that day. . . . My sister called on the phone, and I answered the phone. I didn't even know it was her. She was sobbing, and I actually thought it was a prank call. I said, "Who is this?" She replied, "It's your sister and we have to go to Oklahoma. [Their brother] has killed someone and is in jail." My first reaction was shock. I went completely numb. I didn't know how to think or act. It is almost like time stood still for about five minutes. Everything

seemed to be in slow motion, and I felt like I had just gotten off of a roller coaster. . . . My boyfriend at the time kept asking me what was wrong. He sounded like an echo. I couldn't even form one word in my mouth.

The person faced with the death of a loved one from terminal illness has to deal with the denial of impending loss, the cycle of hope and disappointment, and the grief accompanying the eventual death, while the family member who loses a relative to a sudden catastrophe such as an accident, cardiac arrest, or a violent crime has to deal with denial and the shock of the death. However, these two groups often receive extensive support and sympathy from friends, acquaintances, and the larger community. Those whose loved one is accused of a capital offense deal with the same types of problems—potential long-term loss as well as immediate shock. Unlike the former two groups, however, the family member of the person arrested for a capital crime must also deal with the negative reactions of others. While some family members did report receiving support from friends, others found themselves ostracized immediately.

One family experienced severe harassment at their home immediately following the arrest of the oldest son. According to his stepfather, the media attention increased the family's problems. "They showed right on TV where our house was. That's when the phone calls started. That's when people drove by and started honking their horns and making all kinds of obscene calls and shouts. . . . I have felt violated ever since then."

Sometimes the reaction is less severe, occurring in the community. For young family members, this can be quite difficult. Dana, the sister of a man on death row, was faced with the ordeal of going to school and work, knowing that others looked at her strangely. She was harassed at work by her brother's former wife, despite the fact that Dana had done nothing wrong. Dana did receive support from her boyfriend and a few close friends, making the ordeal bearable. But even years later she found it painful to talk about her experiences surrounding her brother's arrest.

Sometimes not even family is supportive. One woman talked about how other family members reacted to her son's arrest. Margaret's father, who had helped raise her son, never spoke to him again after his arrest and died shortly after her son was sentenced to death. Several other family members have been unsupportive as well. Margaret told me, "Most of my family thinks I should just write him off and forget him. Most of them do not even acknowledge that he is still alive. . . . One of my sisters thinks he should have been executed as soon as he was convicted. And she shares this with me every time his name is mentioned. Also, his sister thinks I should have nothing to do with him. She makes no effort to have anything to do with him."

Although friends and coworkers were supportive to her face, Martha often had their negative comments repeated to her. Even people she did not know often made negative comments. According to Margaret, "Most people just flat out said I had raised the devil himself. This came from friends, family, and complete strangers." Martha withdrew, quitting work and moving to another town. What little support she had was now gone.

Even when the family does not receive direct threats or comments, the damage can be quite severe. Several subjects experienced ostracism. The following comments help illustrate their feelings.

> I was forced to leave my employment by the Doctor I worked for at the time. He harrassed [sic] me until I felt I had to quit. (Carla, mother of woman on death row)

> I was asked to leave my church. My grandchildren, my son's children were ridiculed in school. I took them out and home schooled them. Still do. . . . People all around me acted different about us. (Beverly, mother of a man who was charged with a capital offense but never tried)

> I felt strangers were looking at me and talking behind my back—like at the grocery store, I felt the stockers who might have known him were talking about us. Customers I used to checkout knew I was his mother, and I felt they were staring at me. (Doris, mother of a man on death row in Texas)

Another woman whose brother was sentenced to death but later acquitted talked about the victim's family's hostility. She commented that if the victim's father had still been alive, "He would have thrown the switch himself." The victim's family would not talk to her family, and they still believe her brother committed the murder, even though he has since been acquitted in a retrial. This woman also worried about whether her parents would have support, fearing that their friends would reject them. Fortunately, this did not occur.

On the other hand, a few family members did report receiving significant support. These individuals seemed to deal with the denial and horror better than those who reported ostracism or harassment. Denise, the sister of a man on death row, had that experience. She told me, "At first, people would stare at us and whisper, but that only lasted a couple of days. . . . We have enormous support throughout the community with friends and the church."

Even some who lacked community support did report help from family and close friends. Doris, who commented about the reactions of her former customers, also talked about the support she has received from friends. "My friends have all been very supportive, coming by to check on me and calling. Some brought food, others offered money to send to him. Some send books or magazines and write him a letter."

Linda has a very supportive family who has helped her face this ordeal. She and her husband had been high school sweethearts. In her words, "We were meant to be." He was like a member of her own family, close to her brother and her parents. Her father had died prior to her husband's arrest, but the rest of the family "has always stood by me. They were as devastated as I was." Linda and her sons have also not received negative reactions from others. "Nobody has been negative. They've been good. People will ask things out of curiosity—it's not your normal situation. But, nobody has treated us bad [*sic*]. It's a small town and everyone knows everyone else. People have watched out for the boys and me."

Overall, most people reported receiving little support initially. They were much more likely to report that they were either ostracized or actually harassed. The few that did report receiving initial support seemed to have fared better throughout the process, underscoring the importance of social support in dealing with a family member's potential death sentence.

Family members in this stage of grief tended to respond with either withdrawal or anger. Some, like Lisa and Jason, reported wanting to avoid contact with other people because of their fears of rejection and their own unresolved reaction to their relative's arrest. Others, like Dan, initially responded with anger. The anger was frequently directed toward the police and the criminal justice system.

Another thing worth noting is that regardless of the outcome of the case (i.e., the accused was not convicted, was later freed, is currently incarcerated, or was executed), the family member experienced this stage of grief. Thus, the effects of maintaining a system of capital punishment occur as a result of the existence of the death penalty, not as a result of the application of it.

Stage 2: The BADD Cycle:
Bargaining, Activity, Disillusionment, and Desperation

The most destructive aspects of capital punishment occur in this cycle. Like the family members of someone with a terminal illness, the family members of someone facing capital punishment experience a cycle of raised and diminished hopes. However, when the prospect of capital punishment is included, the family member also experiences periods of intense activity trying to change the feared outcome as well as disillusionment with the criminal justice system. Eventually, as the execution is set, the family may become desperate.

Initially, some family members bargain with God or turn to their religion for help. Donna, the mother of a mentally ill condemned prisoner, shared her experience. "I am one of Jehovah's Witnesses. . . . My ministry help [*sic*] me cope because I'm helping others to know God and that this life is not what He intended for mankind."

Others, however, turn away from their religion because they feel God has in some way failed them by letting the circumstances occur. Martina, a sister of a death row prisoner, shared the following. "I stopped going to church because I felt like I didn't want to serve a God that would let this happen to my brother. He let them take away the only person that I felt close to."

Other family members reported becoming confused about what God wanted. Matt, whose brother is on death row, talked about his confusion. He is considering resolving the dilemma by changing religions. "I'm active in church but we go to a Church of God, and I have been thinking about converting to Catholic myself. . . . It's really my conscience pulling me that a way because I feel like their stand against the capital punishment is a good stand, and I was raised as a Southern Baptist. On that end of it, they believe a woman can't have an abortion, but when they kill someone through the death penalty, they're all glory in the aisles saying, thanks, God, you know, we took another life of a murderer."

Matt went on to say that he does not understand how someone can be both pro-life and pro-death, so he is thinking about conversion to Catholicism. He believes that God will listen to his prayers for his brother then.

Another aspect of the bargaining stage is the belief that the criminal justice process will ultimately exonerate the family member. Doris, the mother of a man on death row, shared her experience with hope and later disillusionment. "The thirteenth juror sent the lawyers a letter stating that he would have voted for resonable [*sic*] doubt and even the judge couldn't believe he was found guilty nor his office staff—what am I to think now? I can only pray somehow this nightmare will end. . . . He is a sweet kid, a gentle soul—who was taken in by a con artist."

Paula, whose son ultimately received a life sentence, originally had faith in the system. However, her experiences soon changed her mind. "I never thought they would find him guilty. I always believed that innocence will prevail . . . how naive can a person be. There is no guilt beyond a shadow of a doubt."

The second part of the BADD cycle consists of frantic activity, either to gain acquittal for the family member or to survive economically. Gloria, the mother of two young brothers awaiting a decision about how her older son would be charged, lost about twenty pounds in the month following her son's arrest due to stress. Additionally, she lost her job as a bartender due to missed work as she frantically attempted to seek assistance. She and her sister sold or mortgaged everything they owned to get the young man a good attorney, only to find that the $20,000 they raised was simply insufficient for retaining private counsel in a capital case. Although the state eventually decided to seek a life sentence, the damage had been done.

Her experience was not that unusual. Many families talked about their efforts to seek assistance for the accused and about their resources being depleted. In another chapter, we will look at the experiences of Sandra and her family in greater depth. Sandra's brother has been exonerated. However, he was initially convicted and sentenced to death. Her parents used up their savings and later mortgaged their home to hire attorneys and post bond for her brother when he was granted a retrial. Her brother's property was sold off to help pay expenses. The family has never really recovered financially, despite the fact that her brother was eventually acquitted.

Similarly, Linda commented, "We've used up all our resources." Additionally, she points out that she and her two young sons are not eligible for the kinds of help often received by other families with an absent parent. "Me and the kids did nothing wrong. In the absence of a parent, you usually get Social Security. This is no different than death."

Many family members reported health and sleep problems during this stage. Carla, the mother of a woman on death row, described her problems with sleeping. "I suffer from insomnia and either have to take a tranquilizer or have a drink of alcohol to enjoy a few hours of sleep but, when I do sleep, I frequently have horrible nightmares."

For Tanya, the effects of the system of capital punishment on her mother bothered her the most. She was quite angry about what her mother had experienced, stating, "My mother has gotten to know other mothers, and I think that has helped a little."

Jim and Sharon have had a terrible ordeal because of the multiple trials. Their son's conviction has been overturned, followed by a new trial and a new conviction. Then, his sentence was overturned, followed by a new death sentence. Currently, the court has again overturned the sentence. They are once again caught up in the frantic activity to save their son's life. Sharon is often frustrated with the efforts of the overworked defense attorneys. A frequent comment that she makes to me is, "I am afraid they are going to get him killed." Sharon's health is poor, and the ongoing stress in her life makes it worse.

Jim and Sharon live in continuous upheaval related to their son's case. They reach the end of hope, only to have a new development in their son's case renew the need for efforts. Their son was convicted in part due to evidence presented by Joyce Gilchrist, a police chemist whose work has since been discredited.[14] In 2001, shortly after my first meeting with them, a major scandal developed surrounding the testimony of Gilchrist in a number of trials. This led to renewed legal efforts in their son's case and renewed efforts by Jim and Sharon.

In the most recent interview, Sharon, the mother of the condemned man, indicated that she was extremely desperate. According to her, she has made many attempts to get in touch with her son's attorney. Then, she began attempting to contact two nationally known attorneys for assistance. The family is currently awaiting results of DNA testing. However, because the evidence in that case is under investigation by the Federal Bureau of Investigation due to allegations against the police chemist, the family is distrustful. Sharon expressed her fears, stating, "They're going to get him killed—those attorneys don't seem to care at all—nobody cares. I just don't know where to turn or what to do."

Jim and Sharon's experiences are not unique. The Fowlers experienced a long cycle before their son was ultimately executed. At the time of the initial interview, the execution had not yet taken place.

> Well (*sighing*), I—I think you get paranoid. You wonder if people are watching you everywhere you go, and stuff like this. And in my business—I don't think I lost any business, you know, but, uh, my capacity to function and to perform as well as I had before was damaged. . . . And you never know what the hell hit you. You don't know what happened. . . . We're all victims. We're all in the same terrible bucket. Our loss is that we lost Mark the day he was arrested for that terrible crime. And we've been going through a—a fifteen-year period of—of hell.

Kendra talked about a recent stay on her brother's execution so that DNA testing could be done. Her hope was that, while there was no doubt that her brother had been involved in the robbery related to the murder, the DNA evidence might help exclude evidence that had been used to convict him. At the time of the interview, she was nervous about the potential outcome of the testing and looking for other alternatives. She focused considerable energy on helping the attorneys any way that she could. However, despite the fact that the DNA tests did not implicate her brother, he was eventually executed.

Linda, the young mother, gave a poignant description of how her life has been affected since her husband's arrest. This woman has two young sons. She and her sons live in a small town. After her husband's arrest, Linda worked two jobs to support the family until she bought a small business recently. Her sons now help her after work. "My life has changed a lot. I had a $468 house payment. I had two children. You know that you can't get weak. I only missed one-half day work other than the trial. There was no slack time, no time to regroup. I just had to go on. I work all the time. I don't know if I'll ever be normal again, really. I wish life could be different. There's no time for counseling. I just go on."

For the first two years after her husband was sentenced to death, Linda and her sons visited him every week at the prison. Eventually, the strain of arranging to drive across the state to see her husband became too difficult for her. They now visit every other week instead. Linda goes through periods of renewed hope. Several months after I interviewed her, she called me to ask me what I knew about a particular type of brain research. She had found some information on it, and she was hopeful that the new information could be used to get her husband's sentence commuted. However, she eventually gave up pursuing that idea. Linda has focused on supporting her family, working long hours and at times working two jobs. Her young sons help her in the business she has recently purchased. She expressed sadness that she has little time in her life for things other than work.

Jeannette's son was on death row at the time of our first interview, although he has since been executed. Jeannette was extremely active in assisting her son's attorneys with his appeals. Her attitude was upbeat and cheerful, and she said that her faith kept her going. Jeannette was a joiner, active in a support group for families of prisoners as well as in an abolitionist group. Although she lived more than an hour away from the city where the two groups met, she tried to attend fairly regularly. She participated in protests against the death penalty frequently and was respected for her energy, upbeat attitude, and enthusiasm.

The third aspect of the BADD stage is disillusionment. Gloria, the mother of a defendant who ultimately was given a life sentence, was shocked and disillusioned that the key state witness was a young woman who had quite likely actually pulled the trigger in the murder. The witness was offered immunity for testifying. Gloria had difficulty believing that someone who was quite possibly guilty and had at the very least been in the room when the murder occurred could be given complete immunity. How, she wondered, could the state justify not charging the young woman with anything and just taking her word about what had transpired?

Gloria was just one of several subjects who had become disillusioned with the criminal justice system. Another father, Jim, was extremely angry and disillusioned. One of the pieces of evidence presented in their son's trial was testimony by some of his friends that he had been in the area near the murder that night. They testified that his car had broken down and that they had pushed him to get it started again. Jim's son was not arrested until over two years later, and recall of the date the car had been pushed would have been questionable in any circumstances. However, in this case, the testimony was definitely false. The car the witnesses described pushing had not been purchased until nine months after the murder. Jim and Sharon provided their son's attorney with the tax and insurance records documenting the purchase. Jim believed that should have resulted in the evidence being dismissed. It was not, however. The testimony about the car was presented as key evidence in the case. He commented, "I always believed in our justice system, you know. And I figured we'd go down there and prove when we bought the car, and it would be all right, you know?"

To Jim's amazement and consternation, the prosecutor suggested to the jury that the family could have faked the records. Jim was livid with anger about the suggestion that he had provided false evidence.

This family has been caught in the cycle for seventeen years. Their son was not charged until more than two years after the crime occurred. The victim had been an acquaintance of his as well as the daughter of a highly respected law enforcement officer. Thus, the trial was somewhat unorthodox. Despite the fact that they were witnesses for the prosecution, the parents of the victim were allowed to hear all other testimony from the judge's chambers, where the door was left open, in the first trial. To date, he has had three trials. The first conviction was overturned due to prosecutorial misconduct. He was retried, and the second death sentence was then overturned, resulting in a third trial. The family hired an attorney for the first trial, getting a second mortgage on their home to pay him. However, the attorney had no criminal experience. Eventually, the attorney got disbarred for five years. A state witness, the police chemist, was reprimanded in the trial for testifying beyond the scope of the evidence. Jim and Sharon both ultimately lost faith in the system, although both had strongly believed in it before their son was arrested. However, they experienced disbelief at a number of things, including a sleeping juror and the behavior of the judge in the preliminary hearing. At the time of the interview, Sharon's health was extremely compromised. Although only fifty-five years old, she was confined to a wheelchair much of the time. She commented to the researcher that she was "just trying to stay alive until this is over—to be there for [her son]."

Other subjects also reported frustration with attorneys. Kendra, whose brother has been executed, was appalled when an attorney put no effort into her brother's case. Her brother was able to get support from an international organization, but the attorney did not follow up on it. He submitted an old appeal that had been denied. Kendra felt that he was going through the motions so that he could be paid, but that he did not care how the case turned out.

> What this attorney did, he took the same appeal, changed the dates on it and sent it back in . . . one that had already been denied. . . . I compared it to the other one and it was exact word for word. And that's when it really started getting frustrating because I knew he didn't know what he was doing. . . . [Her brother] got an agency to agree to fund the DNA testing, 'cause the attorney at the time kept saying he'd applied for the funding. They faxed him [the attorney] several forms, you know, to wire him the money. And that's when I was about to go crazy, you know. The—the court said, you know—we don't have the money to fund DNA. So, [her brother] gets people to say—OK, we will give the money to fund this DNA test—and then his attorney didn't even take advantage of it.

That attorney was not the only one she felt had put minimal effort into his case. At an earlier stage in the process, her brother was appointed an attorney with no capital trial experience and a questionable personal history. "They had put this one attorney on his—on his case. And, uh, again, later on I found out that he had gotten a few DUIs and misdemeanor criminal things. But the main thing was that he did not know about trying a capital case. And it just amazed me, you know, that they put him on [her brother's] case and he didn't know a thing about the death penalty. It—it shocked me."

Marie and her husband had spent all they had to provide a private attorney for their grandson. Unfortunately, unless one can afford a top attorney, this is not always a good solution. In their case, they felt like the trial was unjust. Their grandson now has a public attorney for his appeals, but that frightens him. Marie commented, "He does not have the money to hire an attorney, so the state of Florida is representing him, but he feels as though they also work for the state, so they aren't going to do the best job for him. His trial was so unbelievable, and he immediately filed suit against his attorney, hired by us. We live in Indiana and cannot afford a reliable attorney."

Sandra and her family also were shocked by the lack of concern exhibited by attorneys in her brother's case. The family had hired private attorneys to represent him. Shortly before the trial, they had done nothing, and they hired a new attorney. This turned out to be an even worse mistake. However, it was because the attorney was so ineffective that her brother is alive today, she commented.

> They said that [her brother] could have represented himself better. And it turned out—it took five years—but it turned out to be a blessing because if you have an attorney that even does a halfway decent job, it is real hard—I mean if you lose it is real hard to get a new trial because they are going to say, "Well, you know, somebody had to lose and he did a halfway decent job." But in [her brother's case], you either want to have the very best attorney that money can buy or you want to have the very worst.

Dan and Carol also expressed disillusionment with the system and with their attorneys. They hired private attorneys for their son, using up their entire savings. Unfortunately, Dan and Carol had no experience with criminal cases, and their attorneys were not experienced in capital trials. Furthermore, Carol and Dan believed both had substance abuse problems.

CAROL: It took everything we had, and the attorneys would have taken more and we would have paid more, but our attorneys weren't good. We didn't know that until it was too late. . . . The one was on drugs. We didn't know that until well into the trial. He was overmedicated on Valium, and he was taking codeine for pain, and I don't what all he was taking—he just really had a pharmacy and the other one—
DAN: The lead counselor was drunk all the time. I mean, you could smell whiskey on his breath.

CAROL: And see, we didn't know all those things. And of course, at his point in time, we paid—I don't know if we paid him $15,000 up front at that point in time or what, but it's not like we are going to get any of our money back. But I mean, I didn't have another $15,000 to $20,000 to go like shopping for another attorney.

DAN: They asked for more money in the middle of the trial, which is not really legal from what I understand. So I don't know how much they got out of the community and county, and yet we paid for the transcripts and we paid for the expert witness to fly down.

CAROL: The doctor that never did see him.

DAN: Yeah, the monkey that they told us was going to see him.

CAROL: And you know the state has a bottomless pit to spend, and you know, not very many people—like O. J.—can outspend, but you almost have to outspend them to win. . . . We did the best we could with what resources we had. And now it's just—it's just been a nightmare and we just can't wake up from it.

Not only did they have problems with their attorneys, but they also felt that the deck was stacked against their son in the trial. Because they had little knowledge of the criminal justice system, they did not know what to expect in the courtroom. They quickly learned.

CAROL: They really fix it, if you don't know how it works, and we didn't. So here we show up, there's me and [Dan] and maybe one of our friends, there was three of us. OK, on the victim's side they have everybody that they can pull in from everywhere so that the whole side of the courtroom is loaded. And I kind of think they do that— I think that's a ploy.

Two of the people on that side of the family worked for the police department and the sheriff's department or something, and so they wore their uniforms to court all the time. Like this doesn't have an effect on the jury. And the one on the final day wore his sidepiece into the courtroom and that's not even legal. . . . But that's real intimidating and it's not appropriate and if it's not legal, you know, why do they allow things like that to happen?

In the BADD stage, social support seems to ameliorate some of the negative aspects of getting caught in the cycle of bargaining, activity, and disillusionment. Joiners seemed to fare best during this stage of the cycle, although few were able to maintain a high level of involvement over an extended period of time. Some family members became actively involved in abolitionist groups in an effort to save their loved one's life. They not only found support but also exchanged information with other families at times, as the following mother did. This woman commented, "All of the friends I have now are very supportive. I also belong to a couple of Internet support groups that are parents and loved ones of inmates, going through the same thing as myself."

One of the most striking features of the BADD stage of the cycle is that most family members get caught up in a repetition of the cycle. They move from bargaining to frantic activity to disillusionment, only to have some new hope arise. Then they move through the process again. This may go on for years, creating severe hardship and distress, or what Boss calls frozen sadness.[15]

Doris talked about the effects of the ongoing strain on herself and her parents. In the two years following her son's arrest, the stress started taking a tremendous toll on her health.

> I suffer from headaches every day. I don't sleep much at night. My hair is falling out and turning gray. Some days, I don't get dressed or leave the house. . . . I cry every day. Some days I don't eat and when I do it makes me sick to my stomach.
>
> There are days I get caught up in the what-ifs and what should I have done to prevent this from happening. And I'm angry all the time—it just sits below the surface wanting to explode, and I never know what is going to set it off or who will catch it.

Some subjects also reported considerable family disruption during this phase of the cycle. In some cases, the disruption has been financial; in other cases the family itself has been disrupted, as in the case of Carol's younger son. According to her, "We moved [inmate's brother, who was thirteen at the time of the murder] then up to my parents. He didn't do very well in school, so we sent him up to my folks."

Carol and her husband have had difficulty dealing with the ongoing stress of the appeals process. Since the interview, her husband has experienced a heart attack. The couple divorced last year. The younger son has gotten into legal trouble himself, including involvement in a burglary ring while staying with his grandparents in another state. Carol herself has suffered health problems since the beginning of their ordeal. "I went to the doctor and they put me on antidepressants, and I think they gave me some leave time, too, because I went to a psychiatrist. He said, 'You have no business working during this period or even attempting to work.' Because, I thought, well, I'd be able to work evenings and still go to the trial, because, I mean, we needed the money. We had to have an income. And, he said, 'No, you can't do that.'"

Dan retired because he was unable to work. He said he could not concentrate and was getting violent. "And I'm not a violent person by nature. I mean, I couldn't sleep at night, and I was just—at this point, I had to come to terms. I just couldn't work under those conditions anymore," he said.

The immediate family members were not the only ones affected by Carol's son's arrest, trial, and death sentence. Both Dan and Carol expressed concern about her parents. Carol told me, "My children are my folks' only grandchildren, and they really needed [her son] to help on the farm. And they ended up having to sell the farm because my dad can't keep it up, and that just broke his heart because it was in the family for so many years."

Surprisingly, Carol considers her family to be more fortunate than most families of death row prisoners. In addition to seeking help from a psychiatrist, she has coped by throwing herself into work and school:

> We've been pretty lucky, because I think that most people—you know, I've been able to go on, go to school, and go to my job, and not everybody can. [Her husband] retired, but he kept working until just the last year and a half. But it affects you so bad that most people just can't go on. You know, I don't know what they do. Some of the people go on welfare. I don't know what they all do or if they finally get some sort of Social Security disability. I don't know what they do. But I know that many of the people are not able to hold like real jobs. . . . I think I'm a workaholic and possibly that is my way of coping, is just throwing myself into all of that. . . . It is stressful. But I think I did it as an escape.

Lynne's family also experienced significant disruption. Lynne's father was on death row at the time of the interview. Lynne was the oldest of four children. She was in close contact with her father by mail, and when she had a telephone they talked weekly. Lynne felt that her father's conviction had destroyed the cohesiveness of the family. Her father had always been actively involved in his children's lives although he was divorced from their mother. She related a story about her brother illustrative of the disruption the family was experiencing. Her brother, who was two years younger than her, depended upon their father for guidance. Shortly before the interview, he had attempted suicide. According to Lynne, "It wouldn't have happened if Dad had been there. [Her brother] always depended on Dad. He never was the same after Dad went to prison. He just felt hopeless and lost. He didn't know how to be a man. He had to grow up too soon."

Lynne's father died in prison of natural causes. The family was not able to pay for a funeral and sought help from an abolitionist group. Their older half brother, from her father's first marriage, was not in the state and was not notified of his father's death. I received an e-mail message from him when he discovered that his father's case was inactive.

Yesterday I visited Okla. Dept. of Corrections web page to check the statis of my father . . . the censis sheet shows that he was Discharged on 11 Dec. 2002, & his ODC number is Inactive. I did NOT see a record of his execution in any of my searches. I am wanting to know if the MURDERIOUS BASTARDS let Dad go, because I have been in prayer to Yahweh to help my Dad. . . . The prison put a black list on my mail to my Father, I was unable to write to him, at all, in the past, well, since 1997, that is six years. I could not send him a letter. Let me know. I shall die in peace. . . . I have liver & pancreais cancer, very advanced. (spelling and punctuation in original)

I had the sad task of informing this man that his father had died in prison from an aneurysm. Like his siblings, he was devastated, but unlike them, he did not find out until a few months after his father's death because he was not allowed direct contact with his father.

Doris reported widespread family problems related to her son's conviction and death sentence. Not only did she experience health problems, but other family members were also affected and family relationships were strained. Doris reflected, "My parents have grown old overnight—I blamed my parents for spoiling him and making things easy for him. I have had to learn to forgive my mother and leave the past in the past. Mistakes were made and can't be changed now. My mother has a heart condition, and if I had stayed angry with her it would have added more stress for her, and I was afraid she would have another heart attack."

Finally, whether the accused is convicted or sentenced to death, the family goes through this cycle. A family where the offender received a life sentence talked about their experiences:

> You know, uh, we just kept thinking that if we turned over enough stones, found the right character witnesses, hired the right attorney, then we could save [his brother]. And Mom lost her job because she was taking so much time off, and uh, I flunked out of school. But we thought we had to do it because nobody would. And then, come to find out, the attorney didn't ever even talk to us and hardly to my brother. If the DA hadn't dropped the death sentence, [brother] would be on death row. Mom still isn't the same—she still hardly laughs. (brother of offender who received a life sentence)

In another case, the charges were dropped against the accused because the real perpetrator confessed. Beverly, the mother of the accused, spoke about going through phases of bargaining, activity, and disillusionment despite the fact that her son never went to trial:

> My son was wrongfully arrested for capital murder two yrs. ago although six days before the trial the actual killer admitted the truth. Believe me I am one of the lucky ones but it is hard for me to believe that. The ordeal nearly ruined our lives. I ended up in the hospital twice with what the doctors said it was a heart attack, but it was a broken heart.

This woman became disillusioned, not only with the system but also with people in her community. She was particularly angry with the prosecutors:

> When I tried to convince the DA my son was innocent, her reply was "Lady, I don't care whether he did it or not, he is the one going down for it." That sentence has stayed with me all this time. They just did not care.
>
> I was ask [sic] to leave my church. My grandchildren, my son's

children, were ridiculed in school. I took them out and home-schooled them. Still do. The church did call back after it was on television that my son was wrongfully arrested. I didn't return.

Eventually, the offender approaches execution. Thus, family members become more desperate in their attempts to "save" their relative. Some become more involved in the abolitionist movement, organizing protests or other activities to try to halt their relative's impending death. Others become involved in their church. During this stage, hopes are slowly extinguished. However, even as the family becomes more desperate, they still experience renewed hope followed by disappointment, only to have hope renewed yet again.

Mark Fowler's case was one in which efforts to save his life continued until the execution. At the time that I met the Fowlers they were awaiting word on Mark's last appeal. In October of 2000, the word came down: the appeal was rejected. An execution date would be set. The execution date was set for January 23, 2001.

After years of efforts, there was still one last chance. Their son would have a clemency hearing. Jim Fowler's brother-in-law was a Roman Catholic priest in Tulsa. He had been very close to Mark, his nephew, who had lived with him during the terminal illness of Jim Fowler's first wife. Together with the Fowlers and the defense team, he helped organize the clemency effort. The following is an excerpt from a letter he sent out requesting assistance from Catholics in the state:

Needless to say, I and my family would appreciate your prayers and support. We would also deeply appreciate your presence at the Clemency Hearing. When my nephew was tried in 1986, the District Attorney, Bob Macy, objected to any Catholic as a juror. . . . With Pope John Paul's recent strong stand on this subject, we hope to bring the issue before the Board with a strong representation in McAlester to ask for clemency. This would not require you to speak but to be present. Archbishop Beltran and Bishop Slattery have agreed to speak to the subject as will myself and our lawyers.

To assist us in this endeavor in the Tulsa area, the Benedictine Sisters at St Joseph's Monastery have agreed to help organize buses and transportation to the hearing. We are hoping for an extremely strong show of support. . . .

Thank you for your interest and concern over these many years. Fifteen years is a long time to live with something like this, and many of you have been very supportive and helpful to me during these years.[16]

Mark's uncle's efforts were extremely successful in garnering support, although the outcome of the hearing was denial of clemency. Over two hundred people attended the execution, most of whom had to remain outside in freezing weather. The room in the McAlester penitentiary could hold only sixty people. Almost three times that number waited outside the gates, with icicles hanging off the trees over their heads. The priest sent another message out after the hearing, thanking the supporters. He then commented on how difficult the process had been for him. "I sat with my sister for five nights before she died and I held my father in his dying breath; that was easy compared to yesterday [the day of the clemency hearing for his nephew]."[17]

The Fowlers had clung to hope that the clemency process would result in commutation of their son's death sentence. The family held on to the hope that Mark's good attitude, the problems with the trial, and the plea for clemency from high-ranking clergy would save his life. Jim tried to convince himself that anyone could see the logic.

And our prayer is just, you know, get his conviction turned over to life without parole. And, uh, then something could—with all these people on death row, there's got to be some good in those minds, you know. Rather than our taking on the job of trying to make their lives—their lives miserable—they already made their lives miserable—by putting themselves in prison—OK, contain them and then see if you can't get some good out of those lives that are still there. And there's some pretty smart people in prison. I don't know if I mean to say smart. There's some good down there, there's ideas.

Jim Fowler made the previous statement shortly before his son's clemency hearing. Immediately after the hearing, Jim wrote, "Well, we have just experienced another exercise in futility! As Mark's dad, I was terribly disappointed with the outcome of the hearing, but not surprised. After all, thirty-five years of saying no is a long tradition to break."

The reaction of one of the Pardon and Parole Board members after the hearing was one of the most frustrating things for Jim. The board member apparently did not have a good understanding of the meaning of clemency, instead focusing on the issue of guilt versus innocence. As Jim walked past him, the board member reached out to shake his hand, commenting that if there had been any DNA evidence indicating some degree of innocence, he would have voted for clemency. Jim expressed his anger, frustration, and desperation after this incident. "I was stunned. This was not a trial. We were not there to determine guilt or innocence; we were there to ask for their mercy, their clemency. I state to [the board member] that DNA did not apply. . . . He then told me I should contact the governor. I said to him, 'Man, that is what you do. He won't listen to us. That is why we came to the Pardon and Parole Board.' Obviously, this man and maybe the entire board do not understand their job."

Jeannette, the mother of a man who has been executed, also experienced desperation. On the day of the execution, there was a temporary stay. She contacted numerous people, both in support groups and in the criminal justice system, hoping to avoid the execution. Her efforts and the efforts of her supporters did not achieve the desired result, however, and her son's execution was carried out.

Matt also experienced desperation. When his brother's execution date was set, he began frantic attempts to stop the execution. When he had little success, he then began a desperate attempt to gather money from support groups, agencies, and churches to go to see his brother. He made the trip to another state, and after visiting in person with his brother, he appeared to have some relief. He reported, "We had a very good trip with [his brother]. We all laughed and cried and had a very emotional visit together. Overall, he was in good spirits. The last day was the hardest. We got to see him late because it was very foggy, and thirty minutes before that [his brother] was very emotionally upset. When we saw him, he was crying. But in general it was all great."

As described earlier, Matt's overall response to his brother's situation was withdrawal. However, after his brother received an execution date, Matt became a temporary joiner, seeking support from abolitionist groups and churches. After his visit, his brother reinstated his appeals; thus the scheduled execution date was canceled. Matt again withdrew.

WHEN THE FAMILY MEMBER IS
RESPONSIBLE FOR ARREST

Three of my subjects deserve special consideration because of the special circumstances surrounding their situations. Both of the men turned their family member in to the legal authorities because of their concerns for public safety. In both cases, they felt that by seeking the help of the police, they would be able to save the life of their relative as well as potentially save the lives of future victims. In one case, the family member received a life sentence. In the other case he has been executed. In another family, the mother talked her son into turning himself in to the police.

Although I did not formally interview the first person, I have had the opportunity to meet with him, talk about his experiences, and listen to him speak in public about his experiences. His story is well-known and published in many places. David Kaczynski is the brother of convicted Unabomber Theodore (Ted) Kaczynski.

Unlike most of the interview subjects, David realized his brother was quite possibly responsible for a series of killings long before authorities were aware of his potential guilt. Instead, David and his wife became increasingly concerned that his reclusive brother might be the person responsible for sending bombs to various people because they noticed a similarity in the Unabomber's writings and those of his brother. His wife first suggested the possibility in late 1995. Although the realization came to him gradually, David did experience initial denial.[18] He wrote, "I made a trip to the public library and read everything I could about the Unabomber's seventeen-year bombing spree. It relieved me that none of the victims' names were known to me, for it made it appear less likely that my brother Ted would have targeted them."[19]

David's suspicions continued to grow as he read the Unabomber's manifesto. He was torn between concern about his brother and concern about the victims. He drew a parallel between his experiences and those of the family members of murder victims. "'I never thought it would happen to my family.' I often hear this remark when I speak with family members of murder victims. But it applies equally to me and to other family members of serious offenders. The shock wave from a violent act spreads out in all directions. It isn't possible to be prepared in advance.

You may try to imagine how you would feel, but imagination never comes close to the crushing reality."[20]

Eventually, David and his wife reached a decision to share their experiences with federal authorities. At this point, their experiences began to be more similar to those of other family members of accused capital defendants. They entered into the BADD cycle.

Initially, David believed that by turning his brother in to the authorities, he would be able to bargain for his life on the basis of his brother's mental illness. He also bargained extensively with authorities about keeping his involvement confidential. However, that was followed by disillusionment when authorities failed to keep the agreements.

One of the most painful experiences was that he did not get the chance to break the news to his mother before there was massive media coverage. He stated that he did not want to worry his mother, hoping that his brother would somehow not turn out to be the Unabomber. Thus, he postponed telling her until the day of Ted's arrest. Not only did the government break its promise to not have massive media coverage, but also the Kaczynski family was quickly targeted. As he watched the coverage of his brother being led out of the wilderness, he realized that a media circus was occurring outside his home.

The government also had indicated willingness to not seek the death penalty, but that willingness quickly evaporated. David had hope for a fair evaluation of his brother's mental condition. Ted was a paranoid schizophrenic, and David hoped this would deter the government from seeking the death penalty. However, his hopes were dashed. Prosecutors enlisted the efforts of a psychiatrist whose main job was to portray Ted Kaczynski as a cruel and inhuman monster rather than a mentally ill man.

> The Kaczynski family's partnership with the Justice Department ended on the day of Ted's arrest. Until then, we had worked closely with law enforcement to save lives. After my brother's arrest, however, I watched in dismay and horror as the Justice Department quickly refocused its resources on the goal of taking a human life: my brother's. It didn't seem to concern prosecutors that my brother was mentally ill with schizophrenia, or that executing him would discourage other families from following our example in the future.[21]

David then entered into frantic activity to save his brother's life. David worked tirelessly with his brother's defense team despite the fact that his brother was extremely angry with him. The team's efforts were eventually successful, but they left David disillusioned with the system of capital punishment in our country. David commented, "In the end, my brother's life was spared, not because the Justice Department recognized its error, but because he had great lawyers (the kind of lawyers that few capital defendants ever see)."[22]

David Kaczynski's experiences were not unique. Another brother found himself in a similar situation a few years later. In the early stages of this project, my telephone rang in my office one day, and a man asked if I was the one doing research on families of the condemned. When I acknowledged that I was, Bob began telling me his story. In Bob's case, as in David Kaczynski's, his brother suffered from severe mental illness. He became suspicious that his brother had committed a murder when he found things in his house similar to those described as missing from the victim's home in a local murder. Bob was shocked at first. He did not know what to do and considered a number of options, including buying his brother a bus ticket and sending him out of town. But Bob also worried that his brother might become delusional and kill someone else. He also considered the family of the victim, realizing that they would want to know what had happened. Finally, he decided to go to the police, who seemed very concerned and caring. They promised him that if he would help them apprehend his brother, the death penalty would not be sought and his brother would receive help.

Much like Kaczynski, Bob discovered that what the police told him to ensure his cooperation was not binding. The state sought and obtained a sentence of death despite his brother's history of mental illness. Bob was left feeling disillusioned with the system.

Many years later, his brother was finally executed. During the period leading up to the execution, Bob desperately sought assistance, contacting known death penalty abolitionists for support, including David Kaczynski. Appeals were hard fought, alleging ineffective assistance of counsel. National media were contacted, and millions heard Bob's brother's story. However, nothing changed the outcome.

The difference in these two men's stories is by and large a difference in access to money and power. David Kaczynski and his family were white and middle-class; Bob and his family were African American and working-class. His brother had never even attended high school. Both men had in good conscience gone to authorities out of their concerns for the safety of others, making the agonizing decision to turn their relative in for suspicion of murder. Unfortunately, both families were caught up in the cycle of grief associated with the system of capital punishment.

Although she did not turn in her son, Donna faced issues similar to those faced by David and Bob. She found out from her son that the police were looking for him in relation to a murder. She advised him to turn himself in to them. She believed that perhaps they could get her son some help. Unfortunately, her son's attorney did not agree with her decision. Donna told me, "My son's lawyer said I shouldn't have told him to talk to the police. They were pretty mad at me. I don't know the law. I just told him to tell the truth, and for that I was this bad person." Donna's son was sentenced to death, in part because of his confession. Donna is a religious woman, however, who believes that the truth should be told.

Summary

This chapter has sought to shed light on the experiences of families dealing with capital punishment. A four-phase grief cycle experienced by many family members was described at the beginning of the chapter, with the remainder focusing on the first two stages. The overwhelming majority of the men and women that I interviewed reported experiencing denial and horror when they first found out their relative was accused of a crime for which the death penalty would be sought. Many also reported that they felt that others saw them as guilty by association. In some families, members were divided over how they viewed the accused. Relationships were damaged when some family member supported the accused member while others wanted nothing to do with him or her.

After the initial phase passed, families frequently entered into an intense cycle of bargaining, activity, and disillusionment. This cycle is particularly destructive because of its repetitive nature. Family members would reach the end of the cycle, only to find themselves back at the beginning. How they coped during this phase seems to have had some effect on the impact of the cycle. This second stage often goes on for years, and it takes a severe emotional toll on family members of those facing execution. Those who seek social support seem to fare best during this phase, although they are still harmed.

Families going through an extended battle to save a relative's life are often devastated financially, emotionally, and physically. In Sharon's case, she suggested that being there for her son was her only motivation to stay alive. Other families experienced health problems, divorce, disruptive behavior of other children, and exhaustion of their financial resources. None of the people I interviewed escaped unharmed. Many felt that their lives had been ruined. Most of them had experienced most, if not all, of the aspects of the first two stages of the grief cycle. The following chapters examine the final stages of the cycle, surrender and the aftermath of execution. Most of the interview subjects had not yet reached that stage, but the experiences of those who had are recounted. Chapters devoted to special circumstances follow these two chapters.

Chapter 5 deals with the family members' reactions to the execution, while chapter 6 explores the aftermath. In chapter 7, the focus is on the experiences of family members who believe their relative to be innocent of the crime. In some of the cases, the individual has been exonerated, while in others the family fears he or she will be wrongfully executed. The experiences of these families are like those in this chapter, with the added burden of believing the accused or convicted relative to be innocent of the charges. Chapter 8 explores the experiences of those who are family members of both victims and offenders and their unique experiences. Chapter 9 is devoted to the experiences of those who were not related to the accused or in some cases that married the accused after the death sentence had been handed down.

CHAPTER 5

Facing the End

FAMILIES AND EXECUTION

FOR MANY FAMILIES, the day they fear eventually arrives. Their relative receives an execution date. All appeals are exhausted. Clemency, if sought, has been denied. Hope is gradually extinguished, and the family must prepare to deal with the death. Many family members choose to be present during the execution so that their loved one will see the faces of people who do not hate him or her, not rejoicing in death. The closer the bond between the condemned person and the family member, however, the more difficult this task may be.

EXECUTIONS AS A PUBLIC EVENT

Until the third decade of the twentieth century, executions were public affairs attended by thousands. The death of the condemned man or woman was frequently accompanied by laughter, jeering, and even rioting. To reduce the impact of public executions, the states began moving state-sanctioned killing out of the public eye. The last open public execution occurred in 1936 in Kentucky.[1] Governments also faced the possibility that the public, gathered as a large crowd, might reject the execution and save the condemned. This possibility is forestalled when executions are hidden.[2]

More recently, the issue of public viewing of executions has arisen again, this time with the suggestion of televising executions. During the months prior to the execution of Tim McVeigh, the Oklahoma City bomber, there was considerable discussion of televising his execution. At one point, a major network news team swooped down on my classroom to interview my students about their opinions on televising the McVeigh execution, since our school was less than twenty-five miles from the site of the Murrah Building. The debate about televising executions is complex. On the one hand, some argue that such coverage would desensitize the public. On the other hand, controlling who views an execution may be a way to control the public debate about the death penalty.[3]

Currently, states have varied policies concerning who may attend the execution. The type of witness and the number allowed varies widely. For example, in some jurisdictions up to fifty witnesses are allowed. Some states, like Missouri, allow the prisoner's family and friends to be witnesses,[4] while others do not. However, what remains consistent is that there must be members of the public who witness the execution in order for it to be legal.[5] However, for the family members of the condemned, execution is an intensely personal and painful experience. When they are excluded from being present during their relative's last moment, they may feel cheated of the ability to be there for that person. When they are present, they must endure watching the state take the life of someone for whom they care. Neither option is an easy one. But in either situation, the family member is brought face to face with the inevitability of the death of someone who has been important in his or her life.

Surrender to the Inevitable

Surrender, the third stage of the process, may not occur until hours or even moments before the execution. Family members often hold on to hope that some legal action may stop the process. This is not a totally unrealistic hope, as last minute stays do occur. However, often a last-minute stay is lifted late on the day of the execution, leaving the family members to cope with the sudden reality that their relative is going to die within a few hours. This leaves little time for surrender.

Most of the time, the surrender process begins days or weeks before the execution. If clemency has been sought and denied, the execution of the death warrant is highly likely, and families begin to prepare themselves and their condemned member for the finality of death. The minutes, days, and hours pass rapidly, leading up to the final few hours of the condemned person's life.

Sometimes family members cannot cope with this. One highly publicized case was that of Gerald Bivins in Indiana. Gerald Bivins was executed on March 14, 2001, for the robbery murder of Reverend William Radcliffe at an interstate rest stop ten years earlier. In an unprecedented move, the state allowed his mother to cook his favorite meal, chicken and dumplings, under the supervision of prison staff. Gerald's mother, Jeanne Bivins, spent her final day with her son preparing his final meal at the prison and sharing it with him. She then returned to her hotel room and attempted suicide. She was in intensive care for an overdose at the time of her son's death.[6] Jeanne Bivins did not plan to be a witness at her son's execution but had already said her good-byes earlier.

She was not the only family member who had difficulty dealing with the finality of the death of a loved one. James Chambers was executed in Missouri in November of 2000. His wife, Darlene, was among the witnesses. Darlene refused to believe that her husband would be executed, holding on to the belief that the governor would issue a stay of execution. As her husband died, Ann was faced with the finality of his death. According to an article in a church newspaper, "Darlene beat the glass and screamed in pain. Her two young adult sons tried to help as they patted her and said, 'Mama, don't cry. Mama, we are so sorry.' Finally, she collapsed and was taken to a hospital to be treated for shock and exhaustion."[7]

Jeannette, the mother of another executed man, also reacted to watching her son die, violating the protocol of the execution. As she watched her son's death, she got up and approached the window between her and her son. She was escorted back to her seat by two guards. Her words were haunting. "Please God, don't let this happen to no one else's child. . . . Spare the rest of the inmates, Lord. His eyes might be closed, but he's not gone."

Jeannette was unable to surrender until shortly before the execution because of hopes that her son's life would be spared. There was considerable doubt about whether her son had committed the crime for which he was being executed. At his clemency hearing, the board was sufficiently disturbed about the possibility of his innocence that they unanimously recommended that he be granted clemency. In the state in which this crime occurred, the Pardon and Parole Board makes clemency recommendations but does not make the final decision about granting clemency. If clemency is recommended, the governor then decides whether or not to grant clemency. The governor denied clemency to Jeannette's son, but the defense attorneys requested he reconsider. The final appeal was denied only three hours before the execution, after the prisoner had been served his last meal. Thus, Jeannette had only three hours to accept the reality that her son would be killed. She believed he was innocent of the crime for which he was being killed, and she had held on to the hope that his life would be spared and that he would someday be released.

Tasha, the sister of a woman sentenced to death, also had a very difficult time with surrendering. Her sister's execution received a lot of publicity because a woman was being executed. The condemned sister had been a caretaker for her younger siblings, all of whom were extremely upset and desperate to save their sister's life. A clemency hearing was held, and the family had hopes that their condemned relative would be spared. However, clemency was denied, and the prisoner was immediately led from the room. Suddenly, Tasha began crying and shouting, "I love you, don't go." She leapt out of her chair and ran after her sister and the guards, crying loudly. As the door shut in her face, she began beating on the door, sobbing. She was restrained by the guards and led back to her seat.

Her brother, Bobby, also had difficulty with the clemency hearing. He was seated directly in front of me at the hearing, and as the victim's brother spoke to the board, he became increasingly more agitated. At one point, Bobby jumped up and began yelling at the victim's brother, who then yelled back. Guards around the room began mobilizing. I put my hand on Bobby's shoulder and slowly pushed him back into his seat. His rage was obvious, as was his pain. For Bobby, his mother, and his siblings, the clemency hearing was confusing and pointless. They had come hoping that their sister would be spared. They left with no hope, full of anger but with nobody to blame. They therefore blamed everyone, even those trying to help them and their condemned relative.

Bobby and Tasha, like the rest of their family, struggled with their sister's impending death until the execution. At a church service the night before the execution, Tasha became hysterical outside of the building. Bobby and another brother began making threats against their sister's legal team. Their emotional turmoil continued after the execution and will be dealt with in the following chapter.

Executive clemency is defined as "the power (usually of a president or governor) to pardon or commute the sentence of someone convicted in that jurisdiction."[8] Clemency is not a retrying of a case but instead a request for mercy. According to Chief Justice Rehnquist, it "is the historic remedy for preventing miscarriages of justice."[9] In the pre-*Furman* era, it was not usual to see a governor grant clemency to a condemned individual, with estimates ranging as high as one out of three cases commuted.[10] More recently, because of political pressure, clemency is hardly ever granted. According to the Death Penalty Information Center, only 224 prisoners have been granted clemency since reinstatement of capital punishment in 1976.[11] Almost half of these were the result of Governor Ryan's commutation of all death sentences in Illinois before leaving office in January of 2003. From 1973 through May of 2002, only 162 death sentences were commuted in the entire United States.[12] Thus, the likelihood of having a relative spared through the granting of clemency is miniscule. This does not deter family members from clinging to hope, however. The denial of clemency is just one more step in the repetitive cycle of hope and despair that these families experience.

The pain of family members who witness the execution of their relative is well documented in the National Public Radio special "Witness to an Execution." In the following excerpt from the interview, Associated Press correspondent Michael Graczyk talks with two other journalists about their experiences watching executions in Huntsville, Texas. At the time of the interview, Leighanne Gideon had witnessed 52 executions, while Wayne Sorge had witnessed 162. They had the following to say about the effects of execution on family members who watch.

GRACZYK: I had a mother collapse right in front of me. We were standing virtually shoulder to shoulder. She collapsed, hit the floor, went into hyperventilation, almost convulsions.

GIDEON: I've seen family members collapse in there. I've seen them scream and wail. I've seen them beat the glass.

SORGE: I've seen them fall into the floor, totally lose control. And yet how do you tell a mother that she can't be there in the last moments of her son's life?

GIDEON: You'll never hear another sound like a mother wailing whenever she is watching her son be executed. There's no other sound like it. It is just this horrendous wail. You can't get away from it. That wail surrounds the room. It's definitely something you won't ever forget.[13]

BOTCHED EXECUTIONS

Botched executions are another issue that may have long-lasting effects on family members. Methods of execution have often been violent and painful, including methods such as quartering, boiling in oil, use of implements of torture, beheading, and so forth. The English Bill of Rights barred cruel and unusual punishment, and this was adopted by the United States in the Eighth Amendment to the Constitution. The states have since sought to evade charges of cruel and unusual punishment by changing execution forms over the years.[14] Through the nineteenth century, hanging was the predominant method of execution used in the United States. Hangings, unfortunately, could easily go wrong. The condemned individual could slowly strangle to death if the rope was not the correct length. In some cases, the result was decapitation. Firing squads were another early method. In this case, failure to hit the target over the condemned person's heart could lead at times to slowly bleeding to death. The next method introduced was electrocution. In 1890, the first state death by electrocution occurred. Use of the electric chair quickly spread around the country. The concept was that death was rapid and unconsciousness immediate, making it more humane. Unfortunately, history is rife with examples of botched electrocutions, starting with the first one, the death of William Kemmler in 1890. In the past two decades, Professor Michael Radelet has documented no fewer than nine botched executions, wherein the witnesses reported burning flesh and the need for multiple attempts before the prisoner was successfully killed.[15] Next, officials, influenced by the Nazi death chambers of World War II, initiated the use of lethal gas. Again, there were reports of suffering, and there was additional danger to the witnesses and execution staff.

The quest for a "humane" way to kill the condemned continued. In 1977, Oklahoma became the first state to authorize the use of lethal injection, although the first execution using this method occurred five years later in Texas. Proponents of lethal injection believed that it would be more humane. Three drugs are used in the procedure. The first puts the prisoner into a state of unconsciousness. Next, a drug inducing complete muscle relaxation stops the diaphragm. Finally, a drug induces cardiac arrest. Despite the argument that this is a more humane method, numerous problems have been documented. Many condemned prisoners have histories of drug use, and the execution team often cannot locate a suitable vein. In at least one case, the prisoner finally helped the execution team by placing the needles in his own arm. In another, the syringe came free of the vein and had to be reinserted. A woman had to consent to having the needles inserted in her wrists because no suitable vein could be found. Most recently, a series of cases have challenged this method of execution because one of the drugs used is not authorized in the euthanizing of animals in many states. The argument is that pancuronium bromide, which stops the diaphragm, causes the prisoner to experience excruciating pain and fear as he or she suffocates.[16]

In many jurisdictions, the family may witness the execution through a window in a viewing room, although in other places they may only watch via closed-circuit television. It is not difficult to imagine the trauma that a family member may experience if their relative's execution is botched.

In earlier chapters, the story of Kendra was introduced. Her brother was executed a few months after our initial interview. When I spoke with her subsequent to the execution, she related the traumatic experience of watching him struggle to breathe. He convulsed on the gurney and appeared to be straining against the restraints. Kendra and her mother were horrified. After the execution, Louise broke down and became even more withdrawn. Kendra talked about watching her brother struggle for breath. "He was aware and he was terrified. I was devastated—I wanted to go through the window to help him. And there was nothing that I could do—nothing. I had to watch him suffer. It was the worst moment of my life."

Kendra's experience was exceptionally difficult for another reason as well. Her brother had received an execution date a year prior to his execution. That execution was stayed a few days before it was scheduled to allow DNA testing of some of the evidence. The DNA results came back not supportive of the state's case. They had alleged that the blood on her brother's clothing belonged to the victim, but it did not. Kendra then had to wait months for the courts to decide whether or not that should halt her brother's execution and overturn his conviction. The attorney general argued that the DNA evidence was irrelevant. However, defense attorneys argued that a jury sentenced Kendra's brother to death based on the prosecutor's theory that was proven wrong based on the DNA testing. Finally, the court ruled that there was sufficient other evidence to allow the execution to go forward. However, Kendra still had a last hope. Her brother pursued clemency, and a clemency hearing was scheduled. However, the hearing was not held until the day before his scheduled execution, leaving Kendra and her mother clinging to hope until the last day. When clemency was denied, they had only a day to come to grips with the fact that the execution would go forward.

Reframing the Execution in a Positive Light

Some families cope with the trauma of execution through faith and reframing the death of their family member in a more positive light. The Fowlers did this. They were able to spend much of their son's last week visiting with him, and they were reassured that he had made his peace with his death and with God. Indeed, in his clemency hearing, he had asked the board to consider the effects of executing him on his parents. The day of the execution, the Fowlers told Mark that they would give him a signal if there were a lot of supporters outside the prison.

Mark had originally been unsure about having his father witness his execution. He did not want to put him through that ordeal, and he asked his uncle how one invited people to witness his death. His uncle told him to tell them he did not want to die alone. Jim Fowler never had any doubts that he would be there for the last moments of his son's life. If his son were dying of a disease, he commented, he would be there. This, to Jim, was no different. Jim had not had the opportunity to be present when his other son died, and it was extremely important to him to be there for Mark.

Finally, the hour of execution arrived. The Fowlers were ushered into the room for the family of the offender, along with Mark's uncle. Mark sought his parent's eyes for confirmation, and the family gave the prearranged sign. They began patting the tops of their heads. Ann commented, "The guards probably had no idea what we were doing. Here's this group of people with their hands on their heads." But for the Fowlers, this was their last act of love. They were able to communicate to their son that he had a tremendous amount of support and that many people were outside the prison praying for him. The support of the Catholic Church and the Fowler family's many friends continued to carry Mark and his parents through the moment of his death.

Mark was asked if he had any last words. He began praying a prayer of his youth, "Hail, Mary, full of grace." His family began praying with him. They later commented that they were not supposed to say anything but that they did not care. "Here are these guards at the back of the room, and there's a whole room full of people praying. What were they going to do?"

After the execution, the Fowlers were ushered out of the prison. In Oklahoma, the family members of the victims are allowed to remain inside and to talk to the media in the shelter and warmth of the prison. However, the families of the executed are rapidly taken out of the building. Any comments to the media are made outside. As Jim entered the crowd of friends and supporters, he lifted his fist into the air, shouting, "He finally got away!" Jim coped with the immediate pain by reframing his son's death in a new light. No longer would his son have to live in a small, dim cell, counting the minutes and hours of his life.

Early the next morning my telephone rang. I had been unable to make the long drive to the state penitentiary due to other obligations, and I had told the Fowlers I could not be there. Much to my surprise, I heard Jim's voice on the other end of the line. "How are you doing? Are you OK?" he asked. I was speechless at first. This man had just watched the state kill his son, and he wanted to know how I was handling it. This is the kind of person Jim Fowler is. Ann got on the other line, and they assured me that, while drained, they were both OK. They then described the execution to me.

The family of another man executed in 2001 also reframed the execution in a more positive light. A friend who waited outside the prison with extended family described the family's reaction:

We gathered around the table, holding hands, as I began to pray. (My praying is never very fancy, but God gets the idea. . . .) The cousin/ preacher prayed, and we all ended in the Lord's Prayer. [Prisoner's brother] reported that his stomach felt fine and his head was free of pain. But a sister-in-law said, "You know what I just saw? I just saw an angel, with brown wings!" . . . We continued to pray . . . at 9:15 honking and lights blinking came from my car that does not have an alarm system. I ran to it and did everything I could, as did others, but for five full minutes, it went crazy. Finally it stopped. Guess what! [The prisoner] was pronounced dead at 9:15 p.m. . . . As I left the prison, I saw [prisoner's brother] and his wife at the station gassing up. He said that he was calm and OK. I told them what happened, and they both laughed and we all hugged. We have to remember that with every bad thing, something good comes from it. We have to look for it sometimes, but it is there.

Sometimes the procedures followed by the criminal justice system add to the anguish of the family. Cheryl described the ordeal faced by her family. She, her daughter, and her daughter's two young children went to the prison during the deathwatch period. In Florida, the family is allowed to visit the prisoner every day. However, prior to the condemned person being moved to the prison where he or she will be executed, contact visits are allowed. After the prisoner is placed on deathwatch, the visits are noncontact, except for a one-hour contact visit the final day. Her daughter accompanied her all but one day, allowing her to go by herself two days before the scheduled execution. That day, she couldn't keep her emotions under control. Her husband, who was facing his execution with peace due to his faith, did not understand why she was so upset. She tried to explain her feelings to him, telling him, "In two more days it's going to be over for you. They're going to kill you. I'm going to have to pick up the pieces."

On the final day of her husband's life, the family was allowed a two-hour noncontact visit, followed by one hour of contact. This allowed them to say their final good-byes. Florida also provides a service to family members that may provide considerable relief at a later date. The prison staff takes ten pictures during that final contact visit. According to Cheryl, the guard who took the pictures was a Christian, like her husband and herself. He put great care into taking the pictures, and she is very grateful for them. She talked about the huge smile on his face in the pictures and how that helped her deal with his death.

When she went to the prison the last day, she was told to watch for the birds. Vigil regulars told her that the birds always knew when someone was going to die and showed up outside the prison. After the final contact visit was over, Cheryl gathered her dignity, determined to not break down in front of the prison staff as she left the prison. She reflected, "I can't tell you how hard it was to walk out of there, knowing

I would never see him again. My legs were like Jell-O, but I was determined to not break down."

Florida does not allow the family of the prisoner to witness the execution, so Cheryl had to wait outside the prison. Cheryl explained that it was not that she wanted to see her husband's death but that she wanted her husband to know, as he died, that there was someone who loved him very much and did not want him to die. Because of the protocol, she and her family had to wait outside of the prison with the others holding vigil. As Cheryl walked out the doors that last time, there was a flock of birds outside the prison, just as she had been told.

Like some of the other family members in this chapter, faith helped Cheryl deal with the trauma of having her husband killed by the state. Both Cheryl and her husband were devout Christians and believed in afterlife. Her husband frequently sent her Bible verses because "he wanted to be sure that I joined him in the afterlife." That faith came to her aid during and immediately after the execution. Outside the prison, Cheryl, her daughter, and her two young grandchildren waited for news with the other vigil attendees. The execution was scheduled for 6:00 P.M. A little after the hour, her grandson turned to her and said, "Grandpa is not gone yet." At 6:28 P.M., he said, "Grandpa's on his way to heaven." Then at 6:30, he stated, "Grandpa's gone now." She dismissed his words as the words of a child who did not understand what was happening, until the chaplain brought her husband's ring to her. She then found out that the execution had been delayed and that the timing of her husband's death coincided with her grandson's statements.

Cheryl and her family returned to the boardinghouse where they had stayed that week. They were in a room on the bottom floor, and suddenly a single feather drifted down and landed on the bed. According to Cheryl, absolutely no animals were allowed in the boardinghouse, making it very difficult to explain the presence of the feather. She took comfort in it, feeling it was a final sign from her husband. She still has that feather.

Cheryl and her daughter were in for one final shock. They stayed over an additional day so that they could view her husband's body. They spent much of the day after the execution trying to find out how they could see him. At 4:00 P.M., they finally were able to talk to the man at the funeral home.

And he said to me—you know men down there in the South all refer to women as darling and sweetheart, that's just the way they are—he said, "Darling, there's no way I can let you see this man." When I asked why not, he told me they had done a full cranial autopsy. I was shocked. Nobody had said anything to us about an autopsy.

Viewing the body is to allow the family to have closure. We didn't get that. We were not allowed to see him, not allowed to have any closure.

I asked Cheryl why an autopsy had been done. She had been told that they needed to determine the cause of death. She found that explanation ludicrous. "I mean, they put poison in his veins. That was what killed him. Why did they need to examine his brain? It made no sense."

Cheryl and her family had to go back home to their state without the closure they sought. It was a sad and solemn trip. However, a brief occurrence gave her some final relief on the journey back home. It was a gray, overcast day. Suddenly, a ray of sunshine broke through and shone on the seat between her and her daughter. Cheryl said there was no reason for that one sun ray; the day was extremely cloudy. She felt her husband's presence briefly. A moment later, her grandson said, "I see Grandpa. He's looking down. He's looking at you, Grandma." For Cheryl and her daughter, this was one more sign that their husband and father was now OK.

Dealing with the End

Lisa's experience of her brother's execution was made even more painful by the intense media coverage. Although she lived in a different state, she came back to her home state to be present for her brother's execution.

The media also adds to the false image. Not one word was printed about [her brother's] family, but many articles and interviews were done with her [the victim's] family. There were even rumors that one of her brothers made a comment about killing his sister and nephew. I was actually scared for my life when I came to [the state in which the execution occurred].

The days before his execution were horrible. Every time I turned on the TV or radio, it was everywhere. Every paper had the same headlines plastered with it also. We even ran into her family at the same hotel that we stayed in. We overheard them in the lounge talking about "him frying."

Lisa was so traumatized by what was happening that at the last minute she was unable to enter the prison to view the execution. She collapsed outside and spent the period of the execution crying in the arms of a protester outside the prison walls. She still regrets not being able to be there to support her brother and the rest of her family.

In a recent execution in Oklahoma, the parents of the condemned man were emotionally unable to face seeing their son die. Several siblings made the drive from another state to be of support. I did not interview these family members, as I was no longer collecting stories. It would have been difficult, anyway. They spoke little English. However, the tears the sisters and brothers were shedding at a rally held the day before the execution were evidence of the universal language of grief.

Some family members witnessed the execution because others in the family could not face it. Jane, who witnessed her cousin's execution, had the following to say:

> Her execution is something that is burned into my mind forever. The helplessness of sitting there watching a healthy forty-one-year-old mother of two die—and not even being able to cry because I'd promised her I would not cry. I was there because her mother, father, sisters, and brother said they could not bear to see her killed. I didn't want her to be alone and she asked me to be with her. I describe the execution procedure exactly as it is: OBSCENE. I didn't know the true meaning of the word "obscene" until that night. There is anger, deep sorrow, helplessness—many emotions as you witness someone you love being killed. And you are powerless to stop it.
>
> I have a lot of anger for the state. A state which can murder someone while reading scripture as they die. I remember hearing a sob as she lay dying and looked over and saw a young prison guard crying, tears rolling down his face. Executions don't just affect those on the gurney—they affect everyone in some manner.

In addition to the media, family members of the condemned frequently must face the hostility of victims' family members and victims' advocates. Sitting outside the prison during an execution and frying bacon is one known pastime of some of the victims' rights groups. For family members whose loved one is being executed, this can be exceedingly painful. Usually, those who support the death penalty and those who oppose it do not mingle much outside the prison. However, Judy told the following story to illustrate how these groups may increase the pain experienced by the family:

> Last week a guy named [name withheld to protect family] was executed in Texas. I happened to be visiting my husband during that time so I spent the afternoon with his family at the hospitality house in Huntsville then went and stood in front of the Walls unit while [prisoner] was being executed with the family. [The prisoner] didn't want his family to have to witness his execution. While we were out there, there was a lady by the name of Dianne Clements who is president of a group in Texas: Justice For All. She was standing on the other side of the street from [prisoner's] family. About 6:30 when she thought it was over, she came across the street holding a picture of the two girls that had been killed and put that picture right in [prisoner's] mother's face. His mom handled that with such grace and dignity. She told me her God is not a vengeful or hateful God and would not respond to her. This group makes sure that the guys on DR [death row] have nothing, which means that the families are also being punished.

This story illustrates how the pain of the victims can sometimes result in punishment of the family of the accused. Although the prisoner's mother was guilty of nothing, the victims' rights advocate wanted her to see the picture of the victims, as if she should somehow feel guilty by association for her son's actions. The final comment that Judy made refers to the additional economic burden that families often must shoulder.

SUMMARY

Family members vary considerably in how they deal with the execution of someone for whom they care. Some family members surrender to the inevitable earlier than others, helping them be more prepared for the finality of the death. Others hold on to hope for some miracle to save their relative until the last minute. This latter group often has a more difficult time. Faith and belief in an afterlife or salvation also seems to help mediate some of the pain and trauma, allowing the family member to find something positive in the death. However, regardless of how family members cope, the death is traumatic and painful and has long-term consequences on their lives. In the next chapter, the aftermath of execution is examined.

CHAPTER 6

Aftermath

PICKING UP THE PIECES

AFTER THE EXECUTION, life goes on for the surviving family members. However, trying to find meaning again and let go of the matter that has been the focus of one's existence for many years is not an easy task for most. The days and weeks immediately following the execution of a relative may be overwhelming. The family member often finds it necessary to relive the experience through talking about it repeatedly.

In chapter 3 the different ways of coping were explored, and in chapter 4 we examined the grief process that many experience. The research literature on grief suggests that grief is more complicated when the circumstances are particularly traumatic or painful.[1] Certainly, watching the state kill one's family member in a deliberate and premeditated fashion would qualify as traumatic and painful. The ritual of executions can traumatize family members in many ways. First, it is painful to know that others want one's loved one to die. Second, the artificial atmosphere of the execution process enhances the trauma. The family member cannot touch or comfort their relative. Instead, they must sit quietly behind a window (in those states that allow families to witness the execution) and watch a healthy person die. In many states, they have not been able to have physical contact for many years preceding the death,[2] increasing the trauma. Finally, the assumption of the grief-process models is that the individuals will eventually return to "normal."[3] For family members who have experienced the execution of a relative, this may never occur. The family has been irrevocably changed. Several of my interview subjects talked about replaying the execution in their minds daily.

In American society, we seem to expect, albeit unrealistically, that after a traumatic loss and a period of grieving the bereaved individual will return to a state similar to what they were like prior to the execution. For many of the family members of executed individuals, there will be no return to a prior state. Instead, those with good coping resources may eventually develop a meaningful life despite their loss.[4]

In the remainder of this chapter, the experiences and words of the family members will serve to underscore the feelings after the executions of their relatives. Contrary to media descriptions of executions, many of these people did not view the execution as peaceful, with the offender going to sleep. Instead, it was a painful and traumatic experience. How they dealt with those painful feelings was in part related to the coping styles and resources described in chapter 3.

DIFFICULTY IN GOING ON

In late January of 2001, the telephone in my office rang. As I normally do, I picked it up after a couple of rings stating, "This is Susan." However, after my greeting, there was silence for a moment, and then I heard what sounded like someone softly crying. When the caller finally got her breath and gave her name, I immediately understood. She was the mother of a man who had been executed two days before. Although I had not met her, I knew her name. Laverne's son had been convicted of a particularly vicious crime more than a decade earlier. The evidence suggested that he was seriously mentally ill. He had not sought clemency, expressing remorse over his crime.

I spoke with Laverne for a few moments that day. It was not the time or place to conduct a formal interview, but I understood her need to talk. She said her heart had broken watching her son die. Subsequently, I was able to interview her, but our conversation that first day had the greatest impact on me because of the rawness of her pain. She had witnessed her son's execution so that he would have someone who loved him present, she said. But for her the experience of watching her son die was overwhelming. Now she was haunted by the visual images of the execution. When I interviewed her a few months later, she said that never an hour went by that she did not think about watching her son die. She said she had lost interest in most things, that she stayed home most of the time and did not answer her telephone. Perhaps with the passing of more time, she will be able to regain some interest in living. Although I had not met Laverne before, another interview subject had talked about her frequently.

Laverne was primarily a withdrawer, although she had forged a close relationship with Louise. According to Louise and her daughter Kendra, Laverne was isolated, with little social support.

Laverne was not the only person to make contact with me shortly after execution of a family member. In the spring of 2001, I was part of a panel on capital punishment at a neighboring university. After the presentation, Sharla, a student at that university, came up to me and told me about her uncle's execution. She and other family members had attended the vigil outside the prison. She was tearful but said she wanted to participate in the study. When I called her and left a message, she never returned my call. Then, a professor at that university contacted me stating that she had a student whose uncle had been executed and that she had asked about participating in my research. The young woman had agreed and given the other professor her telephone number. It was Sharla, again. I left Sharla a message but never heard back from her. About a year later, my telephone rang. Sharla identified herself and apologized for not returning my calls. She commented that she just had a hard time talking about what her family had undergone. We scheduled an interview time and met. Sharla did not want to talk about the experience of having a family member on death row. She wanted to talk about the experience of having a loved one executed. She said that her uncle had never denied his guilt, but that she felt that the family of the victim had blamed not only her uncle but the entire family as well. At the clemency hearing, the victim's daughter had told the Pardon and Parole Board members that she wanted Sharla's uncle executed, in part, because none of his family had ever contacted her to apologize for their relative's actions.

> I don't understand. I didn't do anything, but she expected me to apologize? That just doesn't make sense to me. What could I apologize for? What could I say to her? Does she know what it is like to have your relative's name all over the papers, to have people look at you like you are a criminal, too? And then, to know that people hate him enough to want him to die, but you remember the good about him? It made me want to withdraw from life. I am afraid of what people will say if they find out, and I miss him still.

After the execution, family members must deal with the loss of their relative and try to go on with their lives. This is not an easy task for them, and some are less successful than others. Complicated grief is much more likely to result in negative health consequences such as heart and circulatory problems, stress-related mental health issues, and digestive problems.[5] For some of the offender's family members, the stress and trauma resulted in severe health problems and even death.

Louise, Kendra's mother, was unable to successfully pick up the pieces. After the trauma of her son's execution, she became increasingly withdrawn. She died of heart failure within one year of her son's death. Louise was not the only family member whose health was affected. Lisa reported that many of her family members had been terribly damaged.

> My health has been affected. I developed high blood pressure and migraine headaches. . . . The doctors just kept saying it was stress. I was on Prozac for a while. It didn't help much, just helped me sleep a little. I couldn't sleep and sometimes still can't. I go through periods of restlessness. My brain won't shut off. I toss and turn and before I know it, it is morning and I feel like I haven't even slept at all. I am afraid to take any medicine for it.
>
> My youngest niece doesn't hold down a job. All she wants to do is sleep. If anyone says one word to her, she cusses them out and walks off. My sister just drinks all the time now. I am very worried about her. My oldest niece seems to be doing OK, except for her marriage. Myself, I have good days and bad days. I go through spells, especially around the holidays or the anniversary of his death. Sometimes I can't shut it off in my head. It is like a broken record playing over and over and over, but yet the words never change and it always end up where it started.
>
> It is also difficult for me to see my mother suffer like she does. She goes to the cemetery often and sits for hours. Sometimes she won't take off her pajamas nor answer her phone. My brother's room is still like it was when he left. . . . She lives in guilt every day and she is beating herself up for it. She feels totally responsible, and she is punishing herself. Her health is failing fast, and she is going to have a heart attack one of these days.

Although Lisa's brother was executed a decade before the interview, clearly she still suffered, and the rest of her family had been negatively affected as well. Lisa's primary coping response has been withdrawal, and she fears that how others will treat her, based on her experiences, will make it very difficult for her to find support. The family relationships have been damaged, and she reported that when the family got together they were like strangers. She worries about what to tell her children about their uncle and his death when they are old enough to understand. She asked, "What do I tell them? When do I tell them? How do I tell them?" There are no easy answers.

THE ANGER AFTERWARD

Kendra reacted differently once the execution of her brother was over. Her anger at witnessing what appeared to be a botched execution resulted in her investigation of the possibility of suing the state for her brother's suffering. There were rumors that some of the staff, who did not like her brother, had purposely mixed up the order of the medications. According to the rumors, the first medication to keep him unconscious was given after the second, which paralyzes the diaphragm. Thus, he had been conscious, according to Kendra, when he became unable to breathe. Kendra wanted them held accountable. It was not the first time she had been angry at the staff of the prison. Prior to her brother's execution, he had told her about a betting pool on whether her brother would be executed.

> I know there's really nothing I can do about it, and the guards have a pool going on whether he will be executed on his next execution date or not. When he told me that I almost started crying; I said, "You mean they're betting on whether you're going to die?" because he said, you know, one of the guards was mad because when all the stuff was in the media about them trying to get a stay of execution about the DNA. He lost a lot of money—the Supreme Court over-ruled it—and he lost a lot of money and he's been ticked off a lot ever since. Because he's still alive, and it just—that just bothers me, because—who can you tell that to? Can I call the warden and tell him to get onto the guards for betting on my brother's life? It just—it shocked me. It shocked me, it really did.

Similarly, a rumor has been spread that the assistant attorneys general in that state get together on the day of an execution and order the same food as the prisoner ordered for his or her last meal. While I was not able to confirm this rumor with certainty, I did speak with a woman who had left the attorney general's office because she said she was appalled by that practice. Family members often hear this rumor, which adds to their distress. The death of a loved one is always difficult, but when that death is the source of humor for others, the trauma is heightened. In the case of death row families, they have to cope with the fact that their family member was often hated and ridiculed.

Family Relationships and Deaths

Family relationships may also be damaged, even when the family members agree about supporting their relative on death row. Sometimes it is just too painful for the family to remember, and family gatherings are overcast with a gray pall. Jane's family, a close and loving family, has experienced this. Her cousin's execution, although three years prior to the interview, has left the entire family damaged.

> Her execution affected our entire family. All of us. We are a family who loves to get together to have reunions. There is a cloud of sadness over us now. I think another emotion I suffer from is shame. Shame that I could do nothing to help her. The others feel the same.
>
> It will soon be three years since it happened, and it's fresh in my mind daily. Just last week I was cleaning out files and found one of her letters from 1999. She was full of hope that something could be done. She talked of her daughter's wedding and how happy she was for her. She talked of future grandchildren to love. Above all, she held remorse for what the family had to go through because of her being on death row.

Strained family gatherings are not the only negative consequences, however. Jane's aunt, mother of the executed prisoner, died sixteen weeks after the execution. According to Jane, "She had been striving to stay alive for [her cousin], to give her strength." This is eerily reminiscent of Sharon's comments about staying alive to support her son. Jane's aunt was not the only victim. Jane herself has fared well, despite being haunted by memories of her cousin's execution. Jane is a social activist, and she has a tremendous support network. She speaks out against capital punishment at every opportunity.

Children of the Executed

Children are often greatly impacted by the conviction as well as execution of a family member. The negative effects can still affect them as adults. This was brought home very clearly in Jane's story. Jane talked about her cousin's execution. Her cousin had been convicted of hiring a man to help her and her boyfriend murder her husband. Upon her arrest, Jane's cousin was not allowed any further contact with her children. Her in-laws adopted the children after Jane's cousin's parental rights were terminated. The children grew up not knowing their mother, but prior to the execution her daughter made peace with her. She felt that her execution would harm her children the most, and her fears appear to have been prophetic. At her clemency hearing, her daughter pled for her mother's life commenting, "She is all the family I have." Since the execution, the children have not fared well. According to Jane, "Her daughter's a basket case at twenty-one. She was eight when it happened. Her son died last year, age nineteen—riding a motorcycle, slamming into a car at 110 miles per hour. What did he have to live for? Apparently nothing."

Kendra also expressed concern about the effect on her brother's two children. At the time of the first interview, her brother was still alive. However, his children had been severely affected. Their mother was also in prison, so the children lived with Kendra's mother. At least, they were supposed to be living with her mother. The prisoner's sixteen-year-old daughter was out of control. Kendra reported, "[Prisoner's daughter] is a very unruly child. She stays here, she stays there, she doesn't deal with discipline very well. She won't go to school so she won't stay with my mom. . . . I guess his kids, I think, have been affected more than almost anybody."

Kendra's brother has now been executed, and her mother has died as well. The two children were seventeen and twenty at the time of her mother's death. With their father dead, their mother in prison, and the woman who raised them dead, these two young people will quite likely experience ongoing problems.

FAITH AND PICKING UP THE PIECES

Family members who respond to tragedy with faith seem to fare better. Cheryl believes that she and her husband will be reunited in the afterlife. She has dealt well with the loss of her husband, and she came up with a unique way of feeling like he was still with her. Her husband was cremated after the execution. She and her sister-in-law made a decision to divide his ashes between them three ways. Cheryl was to get one-third, her sister-in-law was to get one-third, and Cheryl's daughter was to get one-third. Although Cheryl was very upset by the fact that an autopsy prevented her from seeing her husband after his death, she focuses on positive things. Although it took her sister-in-law several weeks to pick up Cheryl's husband's ashes, eventually two cherrywood boxes with angels on top arrived. Cheryl gave one to her daughter and then thought about what she wanted to do. She likes to travel, and she said that she and her husband had talked about traveling together if he was ever released. So, she sewed his ashes into a teddy bear that travels with her. Now, when Cheryl is on the road, her husband is symbolically with her, which she says brings her comfort. At home, not only does she have the teddy bear watching over her, but also a picture of her husband sits on her dresser. She told me, "I can still feel the love I had for him. I am blessed to have a love like [her husband] and I shared one time in my life."

Despite the fact that Cheryl responded to her husband's death with faith, she has still experienced health problems. Since his execution, she has not had a full night of unbroken sleep. The summer after the execution, she suffered severe depression. After running a lot of tests, the doctor informed her she had developed type 2 diabetes, partly from the stress. Her daughter has also had a difficult time. Cheryl commented, "We are victims just as much as the family of the person that has been killed. Anytime you stop a heart from beating, you have taken him away from the family and the persons that love him."

The Fowlers also responded to their son's death with faith. Before the execution, Jim showed me the box he had lovingly carved for Mark's ashes. Jim is a craftsman, and the box reflected his skill as well as the love he bore his son.

Jim Fowler built the box used to hold Mark's ashes. The top is blue, representing our hope for Heaven. The box is surrounded by eagle feathers representing Mark's living siblings and their children. On the top of the box are five crosses representing the family Mark knew who have preceded him in death. His mother, Carolyn Ann Fowler; his grandparents, Clarence and Monica Gier; Anna Laura "Goldie" Fowler; and his brother, James "Jimbo" Fowler. Donna Nelson of Tulsa made the pall used for the funeral service. Jim Fowler made the cross topping the box, which was given as a gift to his mother while he was in college. During the Entrance Rite, the box will be placed in front of the Easter candle stating our hope in sharing the Resurrection of Christ.[6]

After Mark's execution, a memorial service was held prior to burying Mark's ashes. It was a beautiful late winter day, just north of Oklahoma City. The service was held at the monastery of the Sisters of Carmel of Saint Joseph, a serene and beautiful piece of land, green and windswept. Mark's uncle, Reverend Greg Gier, celebrated the funeral mass, assisted by the bishop, the archbishop, and priests from both Oklahoma City and Tulsa. There were very few dry eyes in the church.

However, the funeral was a celebration of life, and the peace it brought to the family was evident. After the service, the nuns served lunch to the attendees. Although at times tearful, Jim and Ann Fowler mingled with the guests, smiling. Jim commented that he thought Mark would have liked it out there.

In the months following the funeral, Jim and Ann Fowler renewed their efforts to bring about abolition of the death penalty. Jim tirelessly paced the halls of the state capitol building talking with legislators about the need to abolish the death penalty. In his words, he had promised Mark that as long as he was alive he would continue that fight. Jim also wrote letters to the editor that were published in newspapers around the state and country. Finally, the Fowlers reached a point where they decided to pull back from their commitments and made a decision to quit attending abolitionist functions on a regular basis. Health problems and the need to spend more time with family contributed to the decision, but in part they had reached the end of their emotional resources and found that the pain of Mark's execution still was fresh. Ann recently commented to me, "You would think that it would get better, but it hasn't. It is still like it was yesterday."

In respect for the Fowlers, the Oklahoma Coalition to Abolish the Death Penalty voted to make the Fowlers lifetime honorary board members. As Jim said, they had "the perks with no responsibilities. I like that!" Few people have fought harder to abolish the death penalty in Oklahoma than the Fowlers, and few family members have had the faith and the sheer courage to stay as engaged as this couple has. Like Mark Furhman, I have been profoundly affected by their generosity of spirit.[7]

Jim and Ann are still willing to speak to anyone willing to listen about their experiences. I have had them speak to my classes, and few students are unaffected. In their own humble way, they work to change attitudes about capital punishment one person at a time, with great success.

SUMMARY

The majority of the people interviewed for this project had not yet experienced the execution of their family member. A few of the people whose family members had already been executed who wanted to participate in the study were not interviewed. In some cases, I was not able to make contact with them. In other cases, they were not eligible. Lila, the aunt of a woman who had been executed, wanted me to interview her own daughter because of the negative effects of her niece's execution. She had thought it would be cathartic for the girl. I explained to her that I was only allowed to interview adults. She responded to me that adults are better equipped to deal with execution. Her comments were valid, but I was constrained by the original study design to limiting my subjects to those age eighteen and older.

Nonetheless, the stories of those who I was able to interview have several common themes. Many family members were unable to return to a more normal life following the execution. Instead, they were plagued with health issues, depression, and feelings of hopelessness. These consequences were especially pronounced among those who coped by withdrawing. Family cohesiveness was also damaged in several families. The interview subjects talked about the pain of gathering together with the unspoken absence of their relative.

Family members with strong support networks and those who coped through religious faith seemed to fare best, although even these family members have had difficulty at times coping with what they had experienced. Focused anger, like both Jim Fowler and Jane possess, seems to help with postexecution recovery as well. However, one thing appears to be evident for all family members. Having a relative executed leaves an indelible mark. Their lives are not the same, and they experience chronic sadness related to the loss. If the individual does not have strong coping skills and support, then recovery may never occur. Because of the possibility of rejection by others due to their relationship to a condemned person, the risks of negative health consequences are greatly increased. Some of those who have had a family member executed withdraw even more from society, becoming isolated and ill. Others find renewed purpose in continuing to fight against capital punishment. Members of the latter group often develop and maintain a strong network of support in the abolitionist movement. Additionally, because they do not fear rejection related to their relative's crime and death, they are freer to speak about their loss, which may assist them in healing.

CHAPTER 7

"But He's Innocent"

SOME FAMILY MEMBERS have the added burden of believing that their relative is not guilty yet is facing execution. Their concerns are not unfounded. Recent research has indicated that approximately 1 percent of all death sentences are the result of a wrongful conviction with legal innocence later established.[1] Over the past twenty-five years, 112 persons have been freed from death rows around the country.[2] Compelling evidence of innocence has been brought to light in these cases, including DNA evidence in a number of recent cases. This has a strong impact on some families, who believe their relative is innocent.

Wrongful death sentences are not a new problem. In the early nineteenth century, the Boorn brothers were sentenced to death for the murder of their former brother-in-law. Seven years later, they were released. The supposed victim was not dead, it was discovered, but had merely left the state.[3] A century later, convicted murderer Bill Wilson was released after his victim also turned up alive and well.[4] However, in the past twenty-five years, the number of exonerations has increased at an alarming rate.

Wrongful convictions occur far more often than some find comfortable, leading to examination of the sources of these errors. Although DNA analysis has led to the identification of some innocent persons, all cases do not present the opportunity for this type of testing. Many persons on death row are sentenced based on less conclusive evidence. Eyewitness testimony,[5] false confessions, jailhouse informants,[6] and junk science[7] are frequent sources of error.

FAMILIES AND EXONERATION

The advent of DNA testing has been instrumental in the release of some wrongfully convicted death row prisoners in recent years, leading to intensive media coverage. Proponents of capital punishment claim this is evidence that the system works. For those who have spent years on death row and their families, however, these words have a hollow ring. First, exonerations frequently occur because of the efforts of dedicated individuals outside of the criminal justice system, such as journalism professor David Protess and his students. Second, and more germane to the current project, considerable damage has been done to the wrongfully convicted individuals and their families. Third, in many cases, no DNA evidence exists. Since many convictions are obtained through such questionable tactics as the use of criminal informants or unreliable eyewitness testimony, repudiating the evidence is difficult. Finally, despite legal exoneration, the cloud of suspicion often continues to hang over the head of the exonerated individual.[8]

Consider the story of Sandra, whose brother spent almost five years on death row before his conviction was overturned. Two more years passed while the district attorney struggled with the decision of whether or not to retry the case. Then, in 1993, a second trial was held. After the prosecution presented its case and rested, the judge took an almost unprecedented position. He instructed the jury that the prosecution had failed to present a case and gave a directed verdict of acquittal. Turning to Sandra's brother, he stated, "You are free to go." All is well that ends well, right?

Unfortunately, the answer is a resounding, "No!" Sandra, her brother, and their family had been through a terrible ordeal, beginning with the murder of her sister-in-law eight years earlier. It had taken a toll on the entire family. Sandra was not in the United States at the time of her brother's trials, so she felt isolated from the support of her family. Her husband provided little support, fearing the case could have an adverse impact on his career. Sandra reflected, "It has been real hard because with us being in the military I was kind of by myself. . . . I didn't have anybody there for me you know and then when my husband didn't want to discuss it—to this day does not want to discuss it—it just made it real hard. I just felt so isolated because, you know, I couldn't be there, and I wanted so badly to be there for my parents."

Sandra's entire family was affected by the charges. Her parents were stressed and worried. Her younger sister was overwhelmed. Other relatives also were harmed. "My dad had one brother who is a federal judge, actually. . . . He found it to be a tremendous embarrassment to his name because when it is all over the headlines and stuff. . . . My grandparents were just devastated—I mean, just devastated. It was horrible. I mean, here they were at the time up in their eighties . . . and you know they just, my grandmother just cried every time [her brother's] name was brought up and that was real hard."

Her brother, whose wife had been the victim, was left the single parent of two very young children, ages four months and fourteen months at the time of their mother's death. Following her brother's arrest, Sandra's parents took the children. Sandra and her husband had been transferred overseas, and her younger sister was also not able to take them. The family believed that the situation would be shortly resolved. After her brother was sentenced to death, the family made a decision. Her parents were too old to raise two small children; no other family members were in a position to take custody of them. So, they located a foster family through the church. "That was just devastating to my parents. I was in Germany with my two children, which were the only other grandchildren. And now, [her brother's] children were living with someone else. . . . Fortunately, the foster family was very, very cooperative as far as allowing us to spend as much time as we wanted to with the girls, but still it just tore the family apart," Sandra stated.

The trial was difficult for all family members. Sandra was still overseas and had to wait for news. She had no support; her husband would not talk to her about it, and he did not want her talking to others there because of concerns about his career. Her aging parents, especially her mother, had to locate attorneys and do all the work because her sister became too upset to do anything. "My dad, he just was pretty much nonfunctional through all this. . . . It was just so hard for him. And my mother was a very strong person and very aggressive—not aggressive, but . . . she sees something that needs to be done and she goes after it. My dad just kind of retreats into himself and just can't do anything."

Sandra had to wait until the end of the trial to find out what was happening halfway around the world because the cost of telephone calls was too high for daily updates. The telephone call came one evening when she, her husband, and his parents had gone out to dinner. Her baby-sitter relayed the message to call her parents, and she went into her bedroom, alone, to call them.

I didn't even tell my husband because I didn't know how he would react. Took the phone in the bedroom and got my dad, and I said, "Well, what happened?" Then he said, "Well, honey, I have bad news . . . they found Greg guilty." . . . I said, "I just can't believe it." He said, "Well, honey, it is worse than that . . . they sentenced him to death." And I just sat in this bedroom in Germany by myself, you know, and he said, "Your mom is just too upset to talk to you. I will have to have her talk to you later." . . . I mean, it was just the most devastating—it was just horrible.

My husband did come in, and I told him what had happened, and he said, "Why don't you just stay in here and I will make your excuses." And being the good hostess that I am, I said, "No, let me just splash some water on my face." So I went back out.

The family was also financially devastated. At the time of his arrest, her brother had owned his own home, two cars, and a boat, making him ineligible for indigent counsel. The family hired two attorneys who wanted her brother to plead guilty and did nothing to prepare for the trial. Three weeks before the trial, the family discharged those attorneys and hired another attorney who had once been a top criminal attorney. Unfortunately, he no longer was. Sandra then described their experiences.

He was a chronic alcoholic who had brain damage. He had been sanctioned by the bar association to not even practice law because they had had so many complaints against him. But they [her parents] didn't know any of this.

I just kept making trips back and forth from Germany. My parents—they had paid, I want to say, I am pretty sure it was $30,000 to the first attorneys who did absolutely nothing and they got none of that back. Then they turned around and paid probably that much again to the second attorney, who, as it turned out, did absolutely nothing. And my parents are not wealthy people by any stretch of the imagination. And so, you know, financially for them it was very difficult.

The family sold her brother's possessions to help defray the cost, but that provided only a small portion of the money spent. It did, however, ensure her brother's eligibility for a publicly paid attorney to take over his appeals. That turned out to be fortunate, as the attorney was able to get the conviction overturned due to ineffective assistance of counsel.[9]

Sandra and her family believed wholeheartedly in her brother's innocence. Fortunately for this family, the case was overturned, retried, and her brother acquitted. However, the problems still exist. Although this is not a usual practice, her brother was released on bond while awaiting his new trial. However, he found it difficult to get work and could only find temporary jobs. Upon acquittal, he was free, but his and his family's lives were destroyed. His children were now part of another family. His parents had spent most of their savings for retirement on his attorneys. He was also unable to work steadily. The years on death row had taken a toll, leaving him with emotional problems that interfered with his stability. He has received no compensation from the state for the ordeal that he and his family had undergone. Although he hired an attorney to file a lawsuit, he allowed the statute of limitations to expire, making her brother's suit ineligible. He now lives on Social Security Disability. Sandra continues to worry about him.

Verna is also the sister of a man who spent years on death row before being exonerated. On the hearth in her home, she has a picture of her brother taken before the ordeal began. A handsome young man with an engaging smile looks out of the portrait. When I commented on how handsome he was, she laughed and said, "He had his pick of the ladies— young ones, married ones—and they were all after him."

Her brother had been a charming young athlete with much promise. He was drafted by a major sports team but injured early on, ending that career. He also began exhibiting symptoms of bipolar disorder, starting a long pattern of alternating stability and hospitalizations that continue until the present. At the time of his arrest, they lived in a small college town. Public sentiment about the murder of a young woman ran high. Due to the testimony of jailhouse informants, her brother and a friend were convicted of the murder. The friend received a life sentence. Her brother was sentenced to death.

Living on death row, her brother's mental illness progressed, although he was treated off and on. Eventually, the appeals process reached an end, and his execution date was set. Verna received a letter of instructions for claiming her brother's body. He was moved to deathwatch cell, and he screamed for hours on end. "I did not kill [the victim]!"

Fortunately for this family, someone did believe him. A stay of execution was ordered while the forensic evidence was tested one last time. By this time, DNA testing was available. The results were shocking. Not only were both her brother and his codefendant exonerated, but the DNA test also indicated that the crime had actually been committed by one of the key prosecution witnesses. Both convicted men were finally released.

Release brought a new set of problems. Never stable, her brother now required a lot of assistance. Penniless and mentally ill, he was awarded disability income and moved into a series of halfway houses and cheap apartments. In order to deal with the trauma of incarceration, he began drinking more heavily, creating still worse problems.

The appellate attorney who had achieved his release filed lawsuits in his behalf, resulting in a multimillion-dollar settlement. At least, his sister reasoned, there was now money to care for him. She was appointed his guardian and handled his finances. She moved them both to a larger city where she had other relatives to help her with him. A home was purchased for him near her as well as close to an Alcoholics Anonymous group he started attending.

However, the money brought with it further problems. Her brother resented Verna's control over his money, and at times he found ways to get around her efforts to keep him from going through money that was supposed to support him for the rest of his life. Bright and charming, he was able to convince the bank to give him money out of the guardianship fund. He gave several thousand dollars to a new "friend" and spent many thousands on tips for exotic dancers.

His sister was able to tighten the reins on his spending, paying his living expenses and giving him a generous allowance. He responded with rage. One evening, I spoke with her on the telephone. She played for me almost thirty messages he had left on her answering machine. Most were brief, cursing her in both Spanish and English. As the messages ended, she began crying softly, telling me she did not know what to do and just couldn't go on like that. "I just don't know what to do anymore. I can't take much more of this. He's killing me."

Verna ended up calling the police and committing her brother yet again to a psychiatric facility, where he was detoxified and his medications regulated. After he was stable, she located a group home in a rural area for him. Perhaps the most painful thing, she said, was seeing how unhappy her brother was. Recently, she had read a statement by her brother about his wrongful conviction and exoneration. In it, he stated he wished he had never been born. Tearfully, Verna commented, "It just breaks my heart to hear those words. I hate that he feels that way. That's what the death penalty has done to him—and to me."

Behind her, the picture of her brother sat on the hearth as she wiped away her tears. It was a picture of a handsome young man with his whole life ahead of him. The man her brother had become bore little resemblance to the man in the picture.

Both Sandra and Verna were more fortunate than many other family members. Their relatives have been exonerated and released, although their lives are far from perfect. Most family members who believe in a loved one's innocence are not that fortunate.

Believing in Innocence When the Family Member Remains on Death Row

In chapter 3, the story of Jim and Sharon was introduced. Their son's death sentence has been overturned twice, and his conviction has been overturned once. Three times they have sat through his trials, three times they have heard his death sentence pronounced.

According to Jim, who is retired from the military, at the beginning of their ordeal he had complete faith in the justice system. But after almost twenty years, he feels differently today. From his perspective, the trial was a sham. Jim reported, "They got the kids to testify that [his son] was near the scene of the crime in his Volkswagen—that they had to push it. And we knew that wasn't true because [victim] was killed in December of 1982 and the car wasn't bought until September of 1983. . . . I felt like we were accused as well."

The prosecutor suggested they could have falsified the papers. That was just one problem that this couple had with the trial. Their son was not arrested until more than two years after the crime occurred. The first trial was riddled with errors. One juror slept through significant portions of the trial. Although they were not supposed to be in the courtroom because they were witnesses, the victim's family members sat in the judge's chambers with the door open so they could hear all of the testimony.

Embattled police chemist Joyce Gilchrist provided testimony that later became the subject of a judicial warning. In this case, the evidence used to convince jurors that Jim and Sharon's son was present included a hair found on the victim's body. The chemist went beyond the boundaries of good science, testifying that the hair definitely belonged to their son and proved that he was in close and violent contact with the victim. Absolute identification based on hair examination is not possible, as experts know.[10]

The hair evidence was quite contradictory. At first, their son was eliminated as a suspect on the basis of a hair. Later, the same hair was used as conclusive evidence that he had committed the crime. Gilchrist explained this as a typographical error that she had overlooked. Her notes included a handwritten change made in a color of ink that was different from that used to make corrections at the time of testing. The hair has now disappeared from the evidence room.

Another problem in the case was the use of a jailhouse informant, who claimed that he had heard Jim and Sharon's son discussing committing the murder while in jail for a traffic charge. Perhaps not so coincidentally, the same informant claimed he had also heard Kendra's brother admit that he, not his codefendant, was the perpetrator in the murder for which he has since been executed. In Kendra's brother's case, there was no question of whether he was involved in the robbery that resulted in the murder of an elderly woman. However, other than the informant's testimony, no evidence existed that he participated in the murder. Based on one purportedly overheard conversation in the dayroom of the jail, the prosecutor was able to obtain a death sentence for him as well as for another young man. Hearing this story, I tried to visualize two young men casually discussing the details of two unsolved brutal murders with witnesses all around them. According to Sharon, "The snitch testified that he had overheard [their son], [Kendra's brother], and I think there was two more guys sitting at this table in the cell talking about their crimes. And he said he heard [their son] confess to the murder—oh, and he was also going to go after the daddy. He recanted his testimony. But then, from what I understand, he said the same thing again. See he was in jail and he got out of jail as soon as he testified against [their son]."

This was not the only informant evidence used in this case either. Jim and Sharon showed me a letter they had received from an inmate who claimed the prosecutor had tried to get him to testify their son had admitted the murder to him. Visibly upset, Sharon reported, "And we've got a letter—he wrote us a letter—it's around here somewhere,——has the original. He wrote us a letter—how he got our address I'll never know—he wrote us a letter saying that [the prosecutor] tried to get him to testify against [their son] and [Kendra's brother]."

Recently, their son's attorneys were able to get DNA testing of some of the evidence in the case. With new evidence now being considered, Jim and Sharon are once again cautiously hoping that their son will be released. DNA evidence has suggested that the conviction may be false. However, these parents are almost as concerned about the possibility of release as they are of execution. Reflecting on this, Sharon stated, "I just don't know what [her son] will do if he gets out. He is so angry. He [the victim's father] may just come after him himself. It is just a mess."

No easy solution or perfect outcome exists for this family. This family's son has spent almost all of his adult life on death row. He is not equipped for life in the twenty-first century, and he has years of anger at a system that he says convicted him unjustly. He missed his daughter's childhood, although he has as good of a relationship with her as one can develop talking through shatterproof glass windows. His parents, meanwhile, have to deal yet again with the uncertainty of his situation, fearful that a son they believe to be innocent will become a victim of the system of capital punishment. His mother summed up her concerns, saying, "I am having a terrible time with depression, it seems like nothing we do is ever going to help him. As they execute more and more I feel so bad for the inmate but it's the families that are left suffering for the rest of their lives."

The daughter of a death row prisoner is extremely angry at what she considers to be a corrupt system that conspired to convict her father of a crime that he did not commit. Misty claimed she was with her father the day of the crime, shopping in another state. "The Wal-Mart videotapes were conveniently lost . . . stolen. Then the DA turned a couple of stupid little boys, who had never seen my father in their lives, into eyewitnesses. But the make and color of the car they saw, or said they saw, was nowhere near the appearance of my dad's car. The DA investigator blatantly lied about finding blood in my father's car. Even the lab technician on the police force proved the investigator to be a liar."

This young woman is angry and disillusioned. Her family's testimony about being in another state was discounted in the courtroom.

Her mother was initially arrested and charged with being an accessory to the crime in a failed effort to get her to testify.[11]

Denise believes in fighting the system. Denise's brother is convicted of a murder in Texas. Her initial reaction was not panic, however. She believed that the system would recognize its mistake and free her brother. "At first I blew it off because where I'm from, if a crime is committed, they harrass [*sic*] every black man within fifty miles of that place."

However, she quickly realized that this was serious, and she fell apart. Pregnant at the time, she could not stop crying. She dropped out of college because she couldn't concentrate, and she quit attending church, angry at the situation. Denise commented, "I felt like I didn't want to serve a god that would let this happen to my brother. He let them take away the only person that I felt close to."

The family was also devastated financially and has still not recovered. Denise and her mother have both developed severe health problems. Denise developed asthma, migraine headaches, and bulimia. Her mother has panic attacks, diabetes, asthma, lupus, and depression. Adding to the family's stress, her mother has threatened to kill herself if Denise's brother is executed.

Denise's self-confidence has been damaged, and she comments that initially she became a racist, although she has learned to separate her feelings about the criminal justice system from her feelings about whites. She has given up many activities she greatly enjoyed before her brother's arrest, including volunteering at elementary schools and running.

Perhaps the worst damage of all has been the effect on family relationships. Her brother was convicted solely on the testimony of a cousin's husband. That alone would create a rift in the family, but additional issues exist. Denise's brother was the eldest child, "the glue that held us together." With him not there, the other siblings blame each other for what happened, and Denise refuses to go back to "that racist town they choose to stay in." Instead, Denise lives in Austin and has networked with death penalty abolitionists. And she continues to reach out to media and the public for help. Dozens of Web sites are devoted to her brother's case.

Another mother, Sarah, wrote about her son's death while on death row for a murder he did not commit. A clothing store robbery resulted in two young men being tried for capital murder. The other man admitted that he alone had committed the robbery and murder, but prosecutors did not drop the charges against her son. Her son was outside the store in an automobile at the time of the robbery and did not know until afterward that a murder and robbery had occurred. Evidence in the first young man's trial was excluded from her son's trial as hearsay. The evidence would have exonerated him. Sarah told me, "We knew [her son] was innocent, and they already had the guilty boy, and even after he told many people that [her son] took no part in the crime, he was still given the death penalty."

This mother lost virtually everything. She sold everything she had and even wrote checks with insufficient funds to be able to hire an attorney for her son. She took his infant daughter to raise, fleeing from the law for a brief period of time.

Sarah and her family had believed in the criminal justice system. Her son turned himself in willingly and gave his statement to the police. He was told that he did not need an attorney present, and the interview with the police was not recorded. The issues in his case have affected the entire family.

> This whole thing ruined our lives. . . . For the past twenty-odd years, I've only existed for my son. . . . My youngest son who went for years on drugs and alcohol because he hated the system so much . . . the kids in school who were not allowed to play with him. [Her convicted son]'s daughter whom I adopted had to hang with the wrong kids growing up because the others were not allowed to play with her. . . . She had to have a lot of counseling over the years.

After twenty years living on death row, Sarah's son had a heart attack in 1999. The guards refused to get him medical attention until it was too late. This mother continues to fight the death penalty and has authored several books about her son's life and death. In her opinion, the state murdered her son, and she is active in Murder Victims' Families for Reconciliation. She eloquently parallels the experiences of families of the condemned with those of families of victims. "I think the public should know that after they murder our loved one, we feel the same pain and rage at the system as the family of a murder victim. I would tell them that there is no difference in a mother's pain at the loss of her son . . . by the mother of a child who's been murdered on the street or the mother whose son was executed. The pain is the same."

RELEASE BEFORE TRIAL

Another mother, Beverly, tells of the ordeal that she and her family experienced when her son was wrongfully arrested. From the moment she found out about his arrest, her life was thrown into turmoil. "I spoke to my son only an hour before the arrest. I went out to his house and he was painting a boat, and we stood out in the yard talking about what he was doing. . . . I first became aware of his arrest an hour after I got back to my home. His wife called and was screaming that the police had his face down in a burn pile and a gun to his head. I asked to speak to an officer, and he told me my son was on his way to death row for Capital Murder."

This family's story is particularly poignant because the son's arrest occurred as he was trying to help police solve the case. He had taken in a boarder to help pay expenses. The boarder started talking about having killed a store clerk. Beverly's son and his wife notified authorities, and her son agreed to wear a wire to help police gather evidence. However, when the boarder and another accomplice were arrested, they pled guilty to the robbery but accused her son of being the actual killer. Her son was arrested and charged with capital murder. He was held without bond for seven months before evidence proved that due to a disability, he could not have acted in the way the two codefendants suggested. Beverly said that after seven months of desperate attempts to help her son, all charges against him were dropped. Her son was never tried, and he has been vindicated. The actual killer confessed six days before the trial. Unfortunately, the effects of the arrest did not disappear. According to Beverly, "The ordeal nearly ruined our lives. I ended up in the hospital twice with what the doctors said was a heart attack, but it was a broken heart. I can assure you. My son would tell me behind the glass to forgive him, because he was going to kill himself rather than let the state kill him for something he didn't do."

The emotional pain has subsided some, but not completely. Her son has not laughed out loud since his release. His wife divorced him. He and Beverly stay in close contact, not only because the ordeal made them realize how much they cared for each other but also because they are still fearful. "He lives only twenty-four miles from me and we visit or talk on the phone every day. Before the arrest, we didn't see each other so often or talk so often but after, it's like I have to be near him and know where he is at all times, and he feels more secure doing so," she commented.

However, the relationship between Beverly and her closest sister was destroyed. She has been able to maintain her marriage and a relationship with another sister. Although things are better now, Beverly has never completely recovered her health, saying, "I feel the whole ordeal took twenty years off my life. I don't have the strength to do anything anymore."

The family also has suffered in other ways. Close friends stopped coming over or calling. She was even asked to leave her church. Beverly was not the only one in the family who felt isolated. Her son's children experienced painful ridicule at school. Beverly reacted by taking them out of school and homeschooling them. They still have not returned to public school. Beverly's church contacted her after charges were dismissed against her son, but she has not returned to church. And she found herself the object of intense scrutiny at times. According to her, "People all around me acted different about us. When I went to the post office, people turned their heads. Wouldn't look at me. In stores people would see me in an aisle and turn around and go the other way."

Beverly and her husband also experienced severe financial burdens. Their savings were wiped out, they sold everything they could to pay for legal expenses, and they mortgaged their home. Although she had enjoyed crafts prior to her son's arrest and sold them in crafts malls, she did not have time for them and has never regained interest in them. Like Sharon and Jim, Betty is now disillusioned with the criminal justice system as well as with the public. She considers herself wiser but sadder.

> What the police and prosecutors did was so very wrong. They did not care about getting to the truth at all. The prosecutor told me over the phone she didn't care whether he did it or not, he was the one going down for it. People are not aware of really how often this is happening. I will never feel the same about our judicial system again. It frightens me to no end to think that they can get away with this. And, to execute an innocent person is so easily [*sic*] to overlook for them.

Beverly deals with what happened to her family by fighting the system that she now despises. While her son was in jail, she wrote over twenty letters every day to anyone she thought might listen. She urges others to do the same. Today, she wants others to know what the system is like and to "fight it with everything they have." The prosecutor feels differently and has been reported to comment, "Am I ever going to apologize to [Beverly's son]? No. The system worked for him. He's got no complaints."[12]

This case also suggests that even vindication does not restore a family to the way it was before the original charges were filed. Beverly, her husband, her son, and her grandchildren have to live with the damage. Her son, although vindicated, still lives under a shadow. The police detective who originally brought the charges against him still believes that he was involved in the crime, despite the fact that the three men involved in the crime have confessed and admitted that they lied about his participation.

INNOCENCE AND OTHER SENTENCES

Earlier in the book, I introduced Paula, the mother of a sixteen-year-old charged with capital murder but ultimately sentenced to life without parole. Paula continues to maintain that her son is innocent, and the evidence clearly suggests that her claim has merit. Her son was passed out miles away from the crime. All involved agree that he was not present.

Although the trial and sentencing of her son occurred years ago, Paula has not given up her efforts to have her son released. She is working on a book about her experiences and her son's case, hoping it will help finance future legal battles.

Paula's response to her son being incarcerated is different from that of most family members, however. First, she stresses that if her son was truly guilty, she would not be fighting to free him. On the other hand, she feels relief to know he is innocent. "It used to eat me alive that he was in prison and innocent. . . . I would pray about it and think about it all the time. Truly obsessed! Not that I feel any differently, but it totally dominated my mind. Then one day God gave me the peace I needed. . . . What if he was guilty of such a crime? How would you feel then? Wow! . . . I thank God he is innocent, because I would hate to think my child was capable of such an act."

Paula goes on to acknowledge that guilt would not affect her love for her son. However, she would not be fighting to have him released if she thought he was guilty.

QUESTIONS OF INNOCENCE

Inconclusive evidence does not prevent juries from voting to convict, according to several of the people interviewed. Martina's brother had been on death row for about a year at the time of the interview. In his case, there was no confession or statement made. The victims all had foreign DNA on their bodies; there were more than fifty unknown fingerprints. According to Martina, her brother was railroaded for a crime that he never committed. Evidence exists, she suggests, that the killings for which he was sentenced to death were actually committed by a serial killer. Her brother went to the home of one of the victims and found the girls covered in blood. One was still barely alive, and when he tried to help her, she scratched him. That was the sole evidence against him.

The entire family has suffered as a result. Martina's elderly parents have been devastated by their son's convictions. Her brother also left behind a young daughter who now must deal with her father's death sentence. Martina must deal with her anger at the system.

Another mother, Doris, believes that her son allowed himself to be convicted because of his fear of retaliation if he told what he knew. He tried to protect her and the rest of the family and as a result was sentenced to death. Doris reflected, "I believe my son to be innocent of shooting both of the victims and that his friend shot both—and he is paying the price for someone else's crime. . . . Also my son feels he is protecting us from possible retaliation from his friend's brother. . . . Too many innocents are on death row who believed in the justice system and refused to accept a plea believing a trial by jury would set them free."

Several of the interview subjects talked about a slightly different type of innocence issue. Their family members had been involved in the crime during which the murder occurred, but they believed their relative was innocent of the killing.

Gloria's nineteen-year-old son was definitely present at the time the murder occurred and later participated in an attempt to hide the crime. The victim's body was rolled up in carpeting, dumped on a country road, and set on fire. Gloria's son participated in the dumping of the body, and he admits to being in the house when the murder occurred. However, there were also two young women present in the house, and one of these women may have been the killer. In the all-too-familiar pattern, the young women turned themselves in to authorities in exchange for a deal. They would plead guilty to a lesser charge, mutilation of a corpse, in exchange for testifying that Gloria's son committed the crime.

I had known this family many years earlier in another state. When I first interviewed her, the sparkling and vivacious woman I had known had disappeared. Gloria sat curled up in a chair, barely able to speak. She had been working as a bartender, but since her son's arrest she had not been able to go to work. Her energy was focused on how to help her son.

Fortunately, this murder occurred in a jurisdiction where the district attorney was not interested in adding another notch to his belt by getting a death sentence. Although there was public outrage about the burning of the corpse, he considered that to be a separate offense rather than an aggravator. He also acknowledged that there was a question about the participation of the two young women. Although he had originally expressed a plan to seek the death penalty, he ultimately decided to try the case as a noncapital case. He sought and obtained a life sentence, with a possibility of parole at some future date.

Gloria is doing better now, but her life and her younger son's life were permanently changed. She lost the job she had at the time of the arrest, while her younger son became withdrawn. The family's limited financial assets went to her son's defense. Her other son has experienced both being ignored and having to be even more available to his mother. Gloria indicated that she knew she didn't have much time for him because all her thoughts and energy have been focused on the son who was arrested, especially in the months prior to his trial. She also expressed finding herself emotionally dependent on her younger son. "I want to know where he is—I don't like to have him away from me. I am afraid for him and afraid for me. Even though [her son in prison] didn't live with me, I could talk to him whenever I wanted. Now, I have to wait for him to call. I don't know what I would have done if I hadn't had [her younger son] to depend on."

Her ex-husband refused to have any contact with his son, expressing anger and shame. The paternal grandparents contributed much of their retirement savings to legal fees. The paternal grandmother was particularly devastated, and her already shaky health became worse. They are relieved that the district attorney did not seek a death sentence, but the months before he made his decision were, in the grandmother's words, "a living nightmare."

DEGREE OF CULPABILITY

One county north of the crime involving Gloria's son, another crime had a very different outcome. The case involving Kendra's brother was eerily similar. The victim's body was burned, but in that case the victim was still breathing, justifying the prosecutor's decision to seek the death penalty. Two young men were convicted of that crime, and both were involved in the robbery. However, Kendra harbored doubts about the degree to which her brother had been involved in the murder. Part of the evidence in the case had been blood on a pair of pants. Kendra's brother's execution was stayed to allow time for testing of the blood on the pants. The tests came back indicating that testimony during the trial was incorrect. The forensic evidence used to obtain the conviction was tainted, but the higher court ruled that there was enough other evidence to make this a harmless error. That was not the only problem with the evidence. The codefendant's brother had turned in Kendra's brother and his codefendant for reward money. He alleged that Kendra's brother had raped the elderly victim. Medical evidence indicated that the victim had not been raped, and her brother was acquitted of that charge. Nonetheless, in the months leading up to the execution, the prosecutor made frequent public statements about the victim being raped.

> And I have come to find out the media prints, you know, what they want to print. This reporter for the [local newspaper], I've left him messages and . . . they reported that [her brother] was convicted of raping the victim as well. And some people think—well, he was convicted of killing her so what's the deal about raping. . . . I mean this is a very horrible deal. I mean, in my mind this was a very elderly woman. And the fact that [her brother] was found not guilty of it. Just because [the DA] said it occurred—he keeps putting it in the paper. . . . I walked up to him and introduced myself and said, "Do

not put that in the paper again." I said, "I will fax you a copy of the transcript of the trial where he was found not guilty. But don't put that in there again." And the article—the very next day he had it in there again. . . . It's like they need something to inflame the public.

Kendra is left still wondering whether her brother actually committed the murder or just the robbery. She is also left with the reality that many people believe her brother raped an elderly woman. She says she will always wonder whether he would have been executed without that allegation.

The Fowlers also faced this situation. Their son was convicted and sentenced to death for a grocery store robbery in which three employees were taken into a back room and killed. Their son, Mark, took part in the robbery with another young man, Billy Ray Fox. Both young men were using drugs, and they wanted money to buy more. Fox had been an employee of the grocery store and said he thought he knew how to get the money. The two devised a plan for Fowler to go into the store preparing to be a customer. Fox was to wait outside until the employees were distracted. However, according to Fowler's statements, Fox entered the store with the shotgun and was recognized by an employee. He herded the employees into the back room, where he shot two, then clubbed the third with the rifle. When Fowler rushed in, all three were on the ground. Almost all the evidence supported this version of the events.

However, the testimony of police chemist Joyce Gilchrist again became instrumental. District Attorney Bob Macy asked to have the two trials joined. In testimony similar to what she gave in the trial of Jim and Sharon's son, Gilchrist placed Fowler at the murder scene with hairs found on a victim's shirt and one found on the gun. These hairs, she asserted, proved he was in close contact with the victim. A defense expert pointed out that hair analysis is not definitive, that the hairs were as similar to those of the victim as they were to Fowler's. But the jury appeared to accept Gilchrist's version of the events. Fowler and Fox were both convicted and sentenced to death.

By joining the trials together, the prosecutor was able to prevent each defense team from placing blame on the other defendant. In the words of Sarah, "The prosecutors know when to sever a trial and when to try two defendants together. In [Sarah's son's] case, if they had been tried together the jurors would have heard all the evidence, but since the prosecutors wanted the jury not to hear how [her son] was not guilty, they had two separate trials where evidence heard at the first trial was not admissible in his trial."

In the Fowler trial, the opposite was true. By joining the trials the prosecutor was able to effectively neutralize any claims of lesser guilt. According to Jim Fowler, this sealed his son's fate. He told me, "They tried really hard to get them separated but—didn't work out. . . . I don't believe that Mark was guilty of being there. I believe he'd have been found guilty, regardless of who tried him or where, ah, maybe he wouldn't have got the death penalty. But to try people together just does not seem right."

Ann commented that she had hoped that the joining of the trials would be considered an error, leading to reversal. "We thought that would be grounds for another trial, but it wasn't." Although higher courts found no reversible error, one court did note that the district attorney improperly linked Fowler to Fox's confession and that Gilchrist's testimony was outside the boundaries of acceptable scientific evidence. Jim and Ann Fowler believe that Mark, while guilty of robbery, never killed anyone.

While that makes Mark's execution seem pointless and unfair to the Fowlers, it also brings them some relief. Family members who believe their relative innocent of the crime of which he or she was convicted seem to find some measure of solace in believing that their relative did not commit a brutal crime. Several of the interview subjects stressed their belief that their family member was not capable of such an act.

Summary

Belief in their relative's innocence makes facing his or her possible execution even more painful, and family members tend to fight the system, often wrecking their own health. They also become disillusioned with the criminal justice system, with law enforcement personnel, and often with the political process. The latter occurs when they believe that the district attorney, sheriff, or judge makes decisions based on their political career rather than on justice.

Some recurring themes are reported by family members who believe their relative was wrongfully convicted. In particular, relationships with other relatives, friends, and others are often damaged. This is most likely to happen when other family members do not believe the accused person is innocent.

CHAPTER 8

Double Losers

BEING BOTH A VICTIM'S FAMILY
MEMBER AND AN OFFENDER'S
FAMILY MEMBER

THE POLICY OF FOCUSING on the "needs" of victims' family members for some kind of resolution ignores the fact that many of the victims' families are also family members of the offender. According to the Federal Bureau of Investigation, nearly 13 percent of murders that occurred in the United States in 2002 were murders of family members.[1] Actually, this number minimizes the relationship between victims and offenders because the relationship is not included in the data in over 40 percent of the cases. Perhaps it would be more accurate to state that in the 8,039 cases where the relationships between victim and offender were reported, over 22 percent of the murders were committed by family members. In other words, close to one in four homicides occur in families. These statistics relate to homicides overall, and only a small fraction of homicides result in a death sentence. However, many families may find themselves related to both victim and offender. Indeed, I found this relationship in several of my interviews.

Those who are related to both victim and offender find themselves in an appalling situation. While they maybe bitter and angry toward the perpetrator for killing their loved one, they also may have vestiges of affection for the perpetrator as well. A death sentence, then, could add to their losses. Family members reacted to this situation in varied ways. In some cases, they wanted nothing to do with the offender. In others, they found themselves fighting to prevent his or her execution. In both situations, the family member's pain was increased by the potential of yet another death.

TO FORGIVE OR NOT FORGIVE:
MURDER IN THE FAMILY

One of the people that I interviewed had a cousin on death row for the murder of his mother. Martha lives in a medium size city more than a thousand miles from where her aunt was brutally murdered by her cousin. He actually was an adoptive cousin, but she considered him to be like a blood relation until the murder. Martha said that initially she was full of rage and hatred. She felt that her aunt had tried to help this young man and he had repaid her kindness with murder. She wrote her cousin off and had no contact with him for many years. She reflected, "For a long time I made a big deal that this man was adopted, that he was not genetically related to them."

When I arrived for the interview Martha was prepared. She had a large box full of letters, documents, and newspaper clippings about her cousin and the case sitting in her living room. As we talked, she went through the box looking for relevant papers. Martha told me, "When the people started sending these clippings and copies of clippings to me, I just picked up a box and started sticking them in there. And when I ran across anything that seemed to pertain to it, like those letters, I just stuck them in there."

The story Martha related was a sad one. Her aunt and uncle did not have children, so after ten years of marriage they adopted her cousin. They were an active couple, enjoying the outdoors. They hunted, and they took their young son with them. From his parents, he learned not only how to kill but also how to butcher the kill. Years later he would use that skill to dispose of his mother's body.

Martha's aunt, uncle, and cousin lived in Arizona. By the time of her aunt's murder, her uncle had already passed away, leaving mother and son closer to each other and dependent on each other. Her cousin had a troubled childhood, with frequent skirmishes with the law, but at the time Martha did not think he would become violent. He had learning disabilities in addition to his emotional problems. He attended a school for disabled children, but he was expelled from that school. Martha said she thought it had something to do with molesting another student, although she wondered if it had been consensual sex. Martha described her cousin as inept in social situations and a bully while growing up. He picked on other children and put his hands inappropriately on other children.

As he grew into adulthood, his behavior continued to get him into trouble. He was arrested for petty crimes, and he frequented prostitutes. Eventually, however, his crimes became more serious. In 1972, he abducted an eight-year-old girl. Fortunately, she was not harmed. His car broke down and he eventually turned himself and the girl in to the authorities. He was given a sentence of nine years to life. At this time, his family remained supportive. They wrote him letters and sent pictures. Then, he said he had put a contract out on another family member. Martha and her family quit writing to him.

While in prison, he got involved with another inmate who was running a scam from the prison. According to Martha, the other prisoner probably found out that her aunt was wealthy and instigated the murder. "I think [her cousin] probably did a lot of bragging although he shouldn't have. He probably told everybody. His mother had $300,000 and therefore she was fair game. And, of course, the people he was associating with—not the really honest kind of people that you want knowing your business."

Her cousin murdered his mother apparently for financial reasons. He was given a brief furlough from the prison to visit with his mother. A young friend of her aunt's apparently forgot that he was taking her to the motel to visit her son, so she took a bus and was there unaccompanied. On Friday night, she was murdered. Martha's cousin then dismembered the body, hoping to hide the murder.

Martha found out about the murder when another aunt called her husband. Martha and her family went to Arizona to take care of arrangements for her aunt's service. Officials there met with them and took a family history, then accompanied them to search her aunt's home. The story she learned about her cousin's behavior was sad.

I think he believed he'd probably get away with it. When we were driving to Flagstaff, I kept saying to myself, "Why did he hang around the hotel? Why didn't he take her money and go across the border into Mexico? And why did he behave like he did?" And then I thought, well I know why. He expected to get away with it. I think he thought if he put those different body parts in different dumpsters that they would be picked up and discarded, gone, and he was telling people that we encountered that she had left to not come back. She had disappeared. She had gone to visit somebody, I believe he said, and hadn't shown up. But it's hard to think that he thought he could get away with it, like his efforts were so poor.

In the years following the murder, Martha was angry enough to not have any contact with her cousin. She said that her aunt had been planning to leave Arizona and return to Oklahoma to be nearer to family. Perhaps, she suggested, this was what triggered her cousin's violence. Martha remembered, "She had been talking about moving to Oklahoma City, and she'd told her Avon lady she was leaving. And it could have been that day she told [her cousin] that she was thinking of moving away, and I think some people thought maybe she was going to be changing her will. But he was probably feeling abandoned, and they got into an argument and fought."

Not only did her cousin end his mother's life, but in Martha's perspective, he ruined his own at the same time. Martha missed her aunt, but she also felt sorry for her cousin. "She was there for my birth and had been fairly close, but I think if she'd just died, I could have dealt with that. But she did so terribly. And he hurt himself. The money he hoped to get was denied him. The freedom, whatever other things he wanted from life, was denied him," she reflected.

Martha talked at length about how the family dealt with the tragedy. Martha and her children were opposed to his getting the death penalty, although she assured me that was not due to sentimentality as much as it was due to pity. Martha said that her reasons for not having any contact with her cousin were varied. She felt that she was not the right person to give him support. Additionally, she was unsure about her feelings toward him or how much she could trust anything he had to say. But her brother did stay in contact with her cousin, writing and visiting. Then her brother died a few months before the interview, and Martha found herself thinking a lot about her cousin and his fate. In 1991, he had an execution date set, but his execution was stayed. Now he was getting near the end of the line. She found herself thinking about his life in a different light. As she talked about him being expelled from the school for disabled children, she commented that was another loss he had suffered.

"But you know, after I talked to you, I was thinking this man suffered a lot of loss at this time. He was very young. He lost his mother. Consequently, he also lost his father. And I don't know what kind of losses he went through in school, but I'm sure there must have been some rejection that he experienced. He lost his father [her uncle] and he lost his freedom and finally he lost his mother, he'd killed her with his own hands."

Martha's brother, the major support person, was now another loss for her cousin. She began wondering what she should do. To further complicate her feelings, she was seriously ill as well. She had had two heart attacks and nearly died from the complications. Coming face to face with her own mortality and vulnerability, she began looking for healing in her relationships. She also worried that her cousin, when his execution date came, would be alone. She talked at length about her brother's struggle with his own impending death as well as that of their cousin on death row. In her words, he wanted closure. Before he died, he was able to forgive his cousin without accepting that it was OK that he had killed his own mother.

Martha opposes the death penalty, as do her children. That has made dealing with her cousin's death sentence even more difficult. She expressed concern that people on death row were unable to make any kind of contribution to society. While she thought many of them needed to stay separated from society, she felt that they also had good in them and were deserving of forgiveness, including her cousin. She expressed the opinion that if they were allowed to make a contribution, they would feel better and perhaps seek forgiveness for what they had done that put them on death row. At the time of the interview, she was grappling with the question of whether or not to contact her cousin. A few months later, I received a message from her that she had written to him, starting the process of forgiveness.

When Children Are Involved

Along with the emotions surrounding having a relative charged with the murder of another family member, other problems frequently must be faced. When the murder involves a husband and wife, there may be young children affected, as we have seen. Families in this situation are faced with three issues with which they must deal.

First, they are faced with the loss of the murder victim. Family members of homicide victims experience not only grief but also shock and trauma. When the murder has been particularly brutal, they may experience posttraumatic stress disorder. In addition to confusion and stress, the family member of a homicide victim may suffer rage and anger. In nonrelative homicides, the family member may focus on finding somebody to blame. However, when the person charged is also a family member, this can create a conflict in the individual. The family member of the homicide victim also may face public reaction.[2] Blaming the victim is common among individuals in the community, in part to deal with their own feelings of vulnerability. This is compounded when the person charged with the murder is also a relative. As we have seen in earlier chapters, family members of those facing a potential death sentence may be seen as guilty by association. The family member of both victim and offender may become both "vicarious victim"[3] and "vicarious offender." They may find themselves socially isolated at a time when they most need support.

Second, the family member experiences the potential loss of their relative who is facing a potential death sentence for the crime. These dual relationship family members experience fears of loss similar to those whose relative has been charged with killing someone not in the family. However, the feelings and reactions to this potential loss are clouded by the feelings associated with the loss of the victim.

Finally, the family may have to find a solution to placement of children. This is not an easy situation. In the case of a married couple, one set of grandparents may take the children. If anger and hostility toward the other family are present, the children may be kept away from those family members. This may be particularly true when the victim's family takes the children and also wants to see the offender executed. Occasionally, no family members are in a position to take on the responsibility of the children. Then, foster care or even adoption becomes a potential solution. This could result in additional trauma for children, as children may be separated from not only their parents and other relatives but even from each other.[4] The children as well as other family members may face this additional loss.

When Jane's cousin was arrested and charged with hiring someone to murder her husband, both sides of the family were traumatized. Jane and her relatives experienced the loss of their brother-in-law, the long-term loss of Jane's cousin, and the more immediate loss of Jane's children. Jane's cousin had never been in any legal trouble prior to being charged with her husband's death. She and a female friend had grown close in the year or so prior to the murder. They spent a lot of time talking about their marital problems, and her friend eventually suggested that Jane's cousin should have her husband murdered so that she could get his life insurance. Jane's cousin became involved in an extramarital affair with a man that was introduced to her by this friend. She and her lover were convicted of paying a third man to murder her husband. The children were in the house when the murder occurred. After her arrest, Jane's cousin's parental rights were terminated, and her husband's parents took the two children. He said that he and his wife had been too old to be parents to small children, as they were unable to engage in sports and physical activities like younger parents would have been able to do.

The murder created considerable anguish in the two families. Her cousin's sister-in-law, who wanted to see Jane's cousin executed, still had feelings for her. According to her, they had been a close family. She and her husband had often played dominoes with Jane's cousin and her husband. The murder had been a tremendous shock.

By the time Jane's cousin was scheduled to be executed, the children were adults and able to visit her. She was able to reconcile with her now-married daughter, although the relationship with her son remained strained. Her daughter, however, pled for her mother to receive clemency. Her father's parents and sister, however, asked for the death sentence to be carried out. While this did not create a rift with her father's family, it had to create some emotional pain, knowing that her family wanted her mother to die. Since the execution, she has experienced emotional problems.

In the book *Not in Our Name*, MVFR member Felicia Cook has spoken out about growing up as the family member of both victim and offender. When she was eleven years old, her father murdered her mother and grandfather.

> For twenty-three years of my life I walked around with a black cloud hanging over my head, always knowing that one day I would have to face my father's execution.

From day one it made me sick. I never received one moment of peace knowing my mother's and grandfather's killer would be executed. After the tragedy of losing a loved one to murder we should seek healing and peace, rather than vengeance. The judicial system underestimates the hearts of victims. They expect we want vengeance and death for the murderer, and when we don't, they consider us bad victims.[5]

The story of Dr. Sam Sheppard was immortalized through the television series and movie *The Fugitive*. Sam R. Sheppard was a small child when his father was convicted of murdering his pregnant mother. Sam has described the impact of a potential death sentence on his family.

What does the death penalty give us? What did the threat of executing my father for the alleged murder of my mother do for me and my family when I was a young boy? It added more terror to an already horrific situation. It created stress and heartbreak that led to my grandfather's failing health, two suicides by immediate family members, several lives wracked by alcoholism, and other relatives unable to cope. For me, it led to symptoms of post-traumatic stress that I must still live with to this day—over forty years later.[6]

The family frequently does not have time to deal with the grief of having a relative murdered before they are faced with the additional burden of having another relative charged with the crime and facing potential execution. In Sandra's case, her sister-in-law was murdered, leaving her brother with two young children. The entire family was affected by the murder. Sandra was very close to her brother and his wife. She and her family were living about two and a half hours away from them, having been transferred there about three years before the murder. "So, we had been back for three years, and during that time is when he and [her sister-in-law] had met and gotten married. Had both of their children, and so we had really spent a lot of time together, you know, because of the family things. So we were probably closer then than we had been for a while. At the time [her sister-in-law] was killed, we were very close, and we were very close to [her sister-in-law]."

Now the family was faced with a second loss. Her brother was charged with the murder a few months later, leaving his children parentless. The family, believing in his innocence, at first did not see this as a long-term problem. However, when it became evident that there was not going to be a quick resolution, they had to make extremely difficult decisions about the children. They eventually decided to put them in a foster home. This family has been somewhat fortunate under the circumstances. Sandra's brother selected the family that took his children. That family has been extremely supportive, allowing the children and their relatives, including their father, to stay in contact. Today, those relationships remain intact.

DOUBLE LOSERS: MULTIPLE CRIMES

In some cases, families may experience both sides of the death penalty from unrelated crimes. This occurred in the Fowlers' lives. Their story has been presented in earlier chapters, but it is pertinent in this one as well. Mark Fowler was convicted of a triple homicide in 1986. Just a few months after he was sentenced to death, Jim Fowler's mother was brutally murdered, and Rob Miller was sentenced to death for this crime. Years later, Miller was exonerated by DNA evidence. Then the DNA implicated another man who was already in custody of the Department of Corrections. There would be yet another trial. Meanwhile, the execution date for Jim's son was rapidly approaching.

The Fowlers's mental health as they faced these crises is testimony to their strength and inner resources. They faced multiple losses, a factor that put them at risk for grief-related problems. Indeed, the Fowlers experienced many of the risk factors that are associated with complicated grief, including loss of an adult child, ambivalent relationship with the deceased,[7] stigma associated with Mark's conviction, the violence of Jim's mother's death, and concurrent crises.[8] Furthermore, the new set of charges against Ronnie Lott for the murder of Jim's mother created some divisions in his family. Jim's siblings wanted to see his mother's murderer executed. Jim, on the other hand, had reevaluated his stance on capital punishment after Rob Miller was freed, realizing that there were problems in the system. While his siblings did want Mark to be spared, they were strongly in favor of capital punishment, while Jim was strongly opposed.

This led to differential treatment by law enforcement and prosecutors. Jim found himself excluded from many of the discussions about prosecution of Lott, while the rest of the family was invited to planning and strategy talks. This extended to the trial itself, wherein his siblings were allowed to talk about the impact of his mother's death on them and their desire for vengeance, but Jim was only allowed to say that he did not want Lott executed. Family members of victims who oppose a death penalty frequently find themselves at odds with the system, their voices disenfranchised.

In one of the most unusual cases to occur, a wrongfully convicted man on death row lost his brother through a murder.[9] Kerry Max Cook spent over twenty years on death row, becoming the family member of a victim while he was under a sentence of death himself. Although Cook has since been exonerated, his family has been destroyed. His only brother was murdered while Cook was incarcerated, and his father died from cancer. Cook had to grapple with his own desire for retribution, but ultimately decided he did not want his brother's killer executed. Cook lost his mother, too. She still lives in east Texas, but she will not speak to him. "She accuses me of killing my brother and father," he says, looking down at his hands. "She knows I didn't rape, mutilate, and kill that girl, but she says that I brought shame on the family by hanging out with the wrong people. She has no love for me at all. She said I was executed and I can't come back."[10]

In one case, the family members were affected by both murder in the family and separate homicides. Brenda tells the story of her husband's family. She describes what her mother-in-law has experienced:

> [Her mother-in-law's] experiences are so intriguing because she lost both of her sons to violence. He eldest son was murdered on the street of New York. Just five months later, her youngest son killed his girlfriend and the mother of his daughter. [Youngest son] has been on death row for sixteen years. His first death sentence was overturned. For five years [prisoner] was in general population until he had a second sentencing in 1995. Once again, the jury returned a death sentence. The entire family was devastated, including his oldest daughter, who literally flipped out in the courtroom and verbally attacked the jury.

In this family, not only were there two separate murders—one of the eldest son and one of the girlfriend of the youngest son—but also the family members were on both sides in the second offense. The victim was the mother of one of the offender's children. Thus, the daughter lost both her mother and father as a result of the crime. She now has contact with her father, who sells cards he has designed to help build a college fund for her as a way of making restitution.

SUMMARY

The individuals whose stories are in this chapter are only a small number of those finding themselves on both sides of the death penalty. However, their stories illustrate the situations in which these individuals find themselves. While being family of both victim and offender may be more common in family murders than in unrelated homicides, both do occur. Given the number of death sentences issued in this country and that more than one in five are family members, hundreds of individuals may find themselves related to both victims and offenders. Furthermore, nonfamily homicides, as is true of most crimes, frequently occur in the neighborhood of both victim and offender, further increasing the odds that a family might find itself on both sides. Family members who are on both sides of the death penalty are faced with special issues. They not only deal with the emotions surrounding having a relative facing a death sentence, but also face the same trauma as other family members of homicide victims. On the one hand, they deal with shock, disillusion-ment, and desperation associated with having a family member facing a possible death sentence. On the other hand, they deal with the trauma and rage associated with being the family of a murder victim. This is further compounded when the victim and offender were parents of chil-dren. These children have lost two parents abruptly, and finding appro-priate placement for them can be difficult. Furthermore, families in this situation may be divided. Some may want the offender sentenced to death, while others may want to show mercy. This may be even more pronounced when the two crimes that place the family members on both sides of the death penalty are unrelated, as in the cases of Kerry Max Cook and Jim Fowler. Regardless of the characteristics of the indi-vidual situation, however, these double losers can experience significant stress and trauma.

CHAPTER 9

Family after the Fact

FICTIVE KIN AND DEATH
ROW MARRIAGES

NOT ALL DEATH ROW PRISONERS have family actively involved in their lives. For example, Scott Allen Hain, who committed his crime at age seventeen, had minimal contact with his parents during his years on death row. Until the week of his execution, he had neither seen nor spoken to his parents for ten years. Letters were infrequent, averaging about one each year. His parents did come to visit him but did not stay for the execution. If he had not had the support of his legal team, he would have been alone. Hain is not unique in being abandoned by family. In an online request for a pen pal, Fredrick Paine, a Nevada death row prisoner, had the following to say. "I won't bore you and mention how my family and so-called friends have deserted me through this trying time because that's pretty much a given to anyone who's on death row."[1]

Families break off contact for several reasons. Of course, some death row prisoners have not had contact with family for years prior to their offenses. In other cases, anger at the offender leads to rejection. Anger at her brother for his actions caused both Lisa and her sister to withdraw from him for years. Even the Fowlers did not visit their son his first year in prison. Other family members, like Martha, had unresolved feelings that led to severing contact. Sometimes family members end contact because it becomes too painful. Visitation is difficult in the best of situations, and for families that are at the end of their emotional and financial resources, it may simply become overwhelming. Dan, whose story is described in earlier chapters, commented, "I think people need to know that it's probably the most painful experience they'll ever go through and that they should try, they should keep in contact with the person. Because, the worst thing—of course you see that a lot with a pen pal—

the worst thing is to abandon somebody in that kind of situation, and there are a lot of people that don't have family to visit them."

At times, family members of other death row prisoners reach out to men and women on death row. As we saw earlier in the book, Jim and Sharon send birthday cards to all the prisoners on death row with their son, wanting none to feel totally abandoned. Dan and Carol also try to provide support to other prisoners by writing and sending cards for birthdays and holidays. Carol told me, "We used to send Christmas cards to everybody—that was another thing that fell by the wayside. I couldn't do everything. We write to five or six others around him . . . but not every month. You know, we try to write at their birthday, and usually, many times, we'll get a note back saying, you know it was my birthday and it was the only birthday card I got."

Likewise, the Fowlers continue to stay in touch with Mark's former cell mate. They worry about him because he has little support. Mark had been his primary support until his execution. Now, they occasionally send him letters to let him know he is not alone. Cheryl sent holiday cards to the prisoners on death row with her husband, until his last appeal was denied. The cards she had addressed the day she found out are still sitting on her dresser.

Family members of other prisoners are not the only ones who befriend men and women on death row. Some individuals become involved with an offender after he or she is sentenced to death, filling a void in the prisoner's life. This may occur in a number of ways. A number of organizations help death row prisoners find pen pals. Others meet the condemned person through prison ministry or volunteer work. Still others develop relationships with the condemned men and women through their work. In particular, attorneys and other members of the legal team may become attached.

This chapter is devoted to those who became "fictive kin" to death row prisoners. They become family members in principle if not by blood ties, often the only family left to a death row prisoner. When family is still involved with the prisoner, pen pals and other fictive kin often befriend the prisoner's family as well.

Pen Pals

When families break off contact, prisoners are left with virtually no support. Many of them turn to abolitionist groups, seeking pen pals.

LifeLines, the Canadian Coalition to Abolish the Death Penalty, Reprieve, and the Campaign to End the Death Penalty are some of the most active sources for finding death row pen pals.[2]

Developing a friendship with a death row prisoner can be both rewarding and painful. Jan Arriens, founder of LifeLines, describes what it is like for him to have a pen pal executed. He wrote, "It's so strange to wake up at six in the morning and know that a person you have been writing to is at that very moment being strapped into the electric chair. . . . You sit in bed and watch the second hand of the clock sweep around and you know that it is all over. One minute there was a fit, able-bodied person, the next minute they are dead in the name of the state."[3]

Arriens also describes some of the problems faced by pen pals. He explains that while most death row prisoners are male, most people willing to write to them are female. Many of these men have never had a nonsexual relationship with a woman, making it challenging to develop one. Furthermore, they may eventually open up to their pen pals enough to describe their crimes, which may be devastating and shocking to the pen pal, who has come to know a kinder, gentler version of the prisoner than the one who committed the offense.

The Canadian Coalition to Abolish the Death Penalty maintains a Web site about being a pen pal to prisoners. Here, a number of individuals share their experiences. One writer talked about wondering what to say to someone on death row. "My first thought was 'what can I say to him? What can we have in common to talk about?' Well, Bobby and I have been the best of friends for three and a half years now," she wrote.[4]

Another shared her experience and offered advice to those considering becoming pen pals to a death row prisoner. This woman harbored no illusions about the ability of prisoners to be manipulative on occasion, but she also saw the redeeming qualities.

What we normally suggest—is drop them a line saying where you saw their advert, just introducing yourself. If you're married—say so from the first, just in case they have more of a wife in mind than a friend. Never mention your financial situation. If an inmate is asking about your financial situation from the first—the chances are that he's looking for "funding." . . . Treat them with respect, and DON'T ask about their case. That's up to them to tell you about it when they're ready—even if we know that most cases can be looked up on the Net. Don't make promises you can't, or don't intend, to keep. It's the most worthwhile thing I have ever done in life, apart from having my kids—and it's been a life-changing experience. Because now—I can see beyond the act to the person—and some of them are tremendous people. . . . Sadly they only learn to find the people they can be, once they're in that dark place.[5]

I interviewed some pen pals to explore how they are affected. Vanessa, who is a pen pal to several Texas death row prisoners, became interested in the plight of those on death row several years ago. She watched the story of Carla Faye Tucker unfold from her home in England, and she is interested in death penalty reform. She reflected, "It is a terrible business, and one which sickens me to the stomach. I am living in England, where capital punishment does not exist. I have lost pen friends from Texas's death row, and those deaths took their toll on my emotions, and my life. As a result, I can understand how families feel. George Bush has become the Bogeyman in my nightmares."

Dolores developed her friendship with a prisoner by writing to him. She knew the circumstances of his conviction, but felt that it was not her role to be judgmental or to ask him about his offense. Her life has changed as a result of their relationship.

My relationship with family members has become strained since they do not understand a friendship with someone on death row. They say "they still love me," but try very hard to pretend I'm not involved. . . . My answer about my family was the same at work. Today, my friends are all people I have met through anti-d/p activities and other women who have loved ones on death row. We understand and support each other.

Thank God for my roommate. Her husband is on death row with [her friend]. Thank God for the internet. . . . I belong to a support forum that is private and only has persons on it across the country who have friends/relatives on death row.

You live two lives . . . one for the outside world and one with a very limited number of people who understand.

Like the family members in other chapters, Dolores's life has been greatly affected by her relationship with someone on death row. She no longer sleeps well. "It's as if the sentence of death is looming over me. It is never completely out of my mind no matter the distraction," Dolores commented.

Two of the women I interviewed talked about the frustration they dealt with on a regular basis. They are reminded daily that their pen pals are not free. Katrina expressed her sadness, stating, "When you feel the wind on your face, how couldn't you think to him who is locked in a very small cell, 23 hours per day, 5 days per week and 24/24 the other two days. Each of your joys in life have now a bittersweet taste."

Dolores speaks to her friend at least once a week and visits him at least twice a month. However, she missed being able to speak to her friend whenever she wanted. Visits, while important and rewarding, had a negative side as well. Doris related, "I am very frustrated. For instance, sometimes I just want to pick up the phone to hear his voice, but . . . not to be. I can become very depressed, especially after a visit. . . . It is so very hard to see him handcuffed, shackled and chained and I walk out free."

She believes that the public should understand that despite the crimes some of them have committed, the men and women on death row are human. The public also needs to understand the pain that is being inflicted on those who care about the prisoner. "This loved one may have made devastating choices and those that were hurt cannot have their loved one back and are indeed victims. But to turn around and forget that this man is also a human being and he too has a family and loved ones that care about him and that they will become victims. Why do they want to inflict the same pain on another set of families? So now we have two sets of victims. Can't anyone see this?"

Katrina lives in a European country. She writes to several prisoners in Florida, Alabama, Louisiana, California, and Texas. With most, she exchanges one or two letters a month. One has become closer, however. They correspond a couple of times each week. Over time, they have developed a family-like relationship.

When you start to write to an inmate, most of the time you are far to realize what it means, because, slowly, he becomes your brother, your friend, your family. His need to be comforted will sort of suck the lifeblood from you. Because when a sincere and deep relationship is built, you will have to handle his fears, his hopes, his calls for tenderness . . . it is very hard. You will have to handle also his anger, even wrong words because he needs a "punching ball." Your own stress is following you each hour of each day because you are helpless and so aware that hope is so thin.

Katrina also talked about what it was like when she did not hear from her pen pal. She then reflected on actually meeting him face-to-face. "You wait for his letters, when it takes time, you scare 'is he ill, is he locked down, what happened. . . .' When you go and meet him—it's such a joy for him and for you—such a pain, also, because you will have to wait eleven months before coming back when you live on the other side of the Atlantic Sea. You scare also because you pray all the time not to have to cross the ocean 'before' the holidays for a very last visit."

Pen pals are not immune to rejection by others as a result of their decision to befriend someone on death row. Additionally, like family members, they find that the relationship with the prisoner often interferes with other relationships. Katrina reflected, "Your life is another life since he entered it. . . . Your family, husband, children, even friends will have to accept that involvement. You lose so-called friends because they cannot accept what you do. You have to face rejections, even in your own family, you have to hide your own stress . . . it is not easy! But you know also that nothing is more important."

Many Europeans write to death row prisoners, and they often will try to come to the United States to visit them. This has led to difficulties recently in Oklahoma, with noncitizens being turned away from the prison in McAlester without getting to visit their pen pals. Prison authorities have indicated via correspondence that they are simply enforcing existing policies due to security concerns. It appears that no security clearances are available for Europeans visiting the prison. However, it also appears, from the following excerpt of a letter, that the prison administration does not approve of relationships between prisoners and women from Europe.

In response to your correspondence, please be advised, there is no new policy regarding background checks for visitors: it is simply being enforced. Policy has always required background checks on visitors prior to being granted permission to visit. When it was learned that Interpol would not conduct background checks, some foreign visitors were allowed to visit without the required background checks. When this was discovered, the permission to visit was terminated. There is no document that the visitor can present that will result in permission to visit since the background check must be received directly from the agency preparing the document.

The other issue that has caused concern is the number of women requesting to visit men on Death Row. In most cases they have never met the men and are unaware that the men are corresponding with several women, often indicating that they want to marry each of them. It is not uncommon for inmates to do this and there is eventually a request for money or some other favor from the women. I have explained this to some of the women who have contacted me and they refuse to believe that an inmate would attempt to exploit them.

There are no plans at this time to allow foreign visitors, especially persons unrelated to the inmate, to visit. I trust you understand our position in this matter.[6]

Unfortunately, several pen pals had come to Oklahoma's death row to visit a pen pal, only to be turned away. Although the prison administration insisted this was not a "policy change," it was definitely a change in practice.

Although some death row prisoners may indeed be simply seeking someone to manipulate for money or other assistance, others are just lonely and isolated, seeking a friend. After years of isolation, writing letters is the most human contact many will have for the remainder of their lives. The intense sharing that occurs between some death row prisoners and their pen pals can at times develop into something deeper than friendship.

The relationship between a death row prisoner and an outside supporter at times develops into a romantic relationship, and the couple may marry, where law allows. In these cases, the prisoner often acquires not only a wife but also stepchildren as a result of the marriage. In the state of Florida alone, over ten death row marriages have been documented since 1997. Death row marriages have been documented in other states as well, including Texas, California, and North Carolina.[7]

I was able to interview six women who had married a prisoner that they met after his conviction and sentence. In most cases, they met the prisoner through writing. However, in one case, the wife worked in the prison. They describe getting to know a person on death row as an individual, finding the humanity in these men. Judy described a journey that eventually led her into a relationship that she never anticipated. She did not enter into a pen pal relationship easily, thinking about the pain and responsibility involved in befriending someone on death row. The man that she eventually chose was executed almost immediately after she had written him the first time. He passed her name on to another prisoner, the man she eventually married.

> A couple of years ago someone approached me about writing someone on death row. We talked about three months before I took that step. He told me that it wasn't an easy task and starting to write someone then stop is more cruel than not writing at all. So, the first person I picked was [executed prisoner]. At first I didn't know he had a date, then as I read more, I realized he had only a couple of weeks left. At first I decided not to write, then I thought to myself that if I didn't write then I was doing what the rest of society was doing and write him off. So I wrote him. I did get one letter back, which changed my life from that day on, the things he said about life. I didn't know though that the night before he was executed, he sent my letter to [her husband] to see if maybe he would like to write me. I received [her husband's] letter five days after [prisoner] was executed. We connected from the very first letters.

Judy has done a lot of soul-searching about her relationship with a death row prisoner. Having been in two abusive marriages, she questioned whether she became involved because it was "safe." However, she came to the conclusion that she married him because she loved him. Their relationship is based on sharing of deep and intimate thoughts and feelings.

> You know, they say you should marry your best friend, well I did. He isn't one of those guys that is innocent. He is guilty of what he was convicted of. He has never lied to me or kept anything from me. I have total access to all court records, to his lawyer, his family

and am involved in every part of his life. A young kid (eighteen) high on drugs, drinking, grew up on the streets. You know the story, just a different face. It took him a year to actually speak out aloud what happened that night. When he did finally face the reality that he took a life, it about devastated him. I have told him things I have never told anyone else, the same him with me.

Over time, he taught me to be free and strong. He allows me to talk and has never told me to shut up or what I thought was stupid, he never laughed at my fears or made fun of my dreams. He never has asked me for money or anything else but my love. In fact, he has sent me money to help with food at times. It is sad that I have to find God's actual unconditional love behind prison walls and not inside Church walls. The first time I visited him, he started our visit out with prayer and ends our visits in prayer. Two years later, he still does. Is it wrong to love someone on death row? Maybe it is, maybe it is crazy like everyone says. Maybe I am "desperate," maybe I am with him because he's "safe." All I know is that when I receive his letters I do nothing but smile. When I'm with him I do nothing but laugh.

Cheryl described her marriage in similar terms. She wrote to her husband four years before they were married. Her only regret, even though her husband has now been executed, is that she did not marry him sooner. She reflected on how she had viewed relationships like hers prior to falling in love with her pen pal. She said she clearly remembers watching a talk show with a woman guest who had married a man on death row. "It didn't make sense." Today it makes more sense to her.

Everything has not been easy for Cheryl, however, She works in a steel mill. She has been careful to keep her personal life separate from work because of her concerns about reactions. She and her daughter attended a protest in another city, and her picture was in the newspaper. A man at her work put the picture on a bulletin board, and Cheryl found herself the target of ridicule. She remembered, "All that does is put more pain and hassle on me as a victim. I lost my husband and they ridiculed and made fun of me. If he had died in a car crash, I would have gotten sympathy."

Cheryl's adult daughter has also struggled since the execution. She found papers in Cheryl's husband's belongings that indicated he was planning on adopting her. For her, being adopted by him would have fulfilled a hope. That hope will never be realized now that he is dead.

Cheryl was not the only wife who expressed concern about public perceptions of women married to death row prisoners. One woman's concern about public perception translated to a concern about a book on families. She commented, "I am a bit leery of your proposed book because some have been written in the past which portrayed death row wives, widows as pitiful, lonely, unattractive kooks. I don't think I am any of those things."

Like other families, these "new" families sometimes have better outcomes than most. Loretta's husband had his sentence commuted to life after spending eighteen years on death row. They had been married for ten years at the time of the interview. Most people have been supportive of her, in part because she is an upbeat person. Loretta told me, "I feel that people may very well think I am strange or confused or even slightly nuts, but I am the type of person that people like when they get to know me, so after they get to know me, when they ask, what does your husband do, or some such question, then I tell them."

Her employer has a tendency to dismiss her when her husband has problems. Loretta said her boss would consider a coworker's spouse having surgery as more important than if her own husband had surgery. But Loretta is not one to allow herself or her concerns to be pushed aside. She commented, "But I will be assertive and tell him that MY husband is as important as HIS wife, like it or not! He has not fired me at least!"

Although Loretta is fairly happy with her life overall, there have been negative effects. She still doesn't sleep well, and she doesn't take care of her own health as well as she thinks she should. However, her frustration with public perception has been the most difficult thing of all. She commented, "It can happen to anyone. When you meet families of men and women on death row, they are not typical of what one would expect, they are next door neighbors, they are friends, they are people you encounter in church and at the mall. If anyone thinks that no one in their family could ever be convicted of a crime or be on trial, they are wrong. It can happen to the nicest families, the best of mothers."

Loretta knows what bothers her about public opinion, and she also knows what she believes the public should know. She sees capital punishment as a waste of productive lives, by not allowing the prisoner the chance to redeem himself and to contribute to society. "Knowing what a good man my husband is and knowing that a lot of people only look at his crime, not at him and how he has changed and habilitated himself. . . . When I look at my husband and the good that he is doing right now and has done for years, I am so thankful that he got off death row, and if people could just see him, listen to him, know him, they would know that a man can change. He is living proof."

When the condemned man marries a pen pal or someone he met after he arrives on death row, he may acquire children as well as a wife. For some wives, this affects their children Brenda described the effects on children, both hers and his from before the marriage. She talked about what had been the most difficult for her in the situation.

> Seeing our children suffer. Hearing [her daughter] tell me she wants to sit on Michael's lap when she visits him at the prison and is separated by bars and glass. Hearing our eldest grandchild say the same. Seeing the fear in [another child's] face and knowing that much of the anger she has inside is a result of her shame at having a dad that society finds worthless enough to want to eliminate, despite her love for him. The death penalty is so cruel and confusing to these children who have parents on the row.
>
> It has been very difficult for [her husband's] children. I cannot imagine what [his daughter] is going through. She lost her mom to murder and now the State may take her dad, who she loves dearly.

For Brenda, there has been considerable support from both her mother and her husband's family. Her sisters do not mention her husband much. Brenda was a law student when she met her husband. This has led to some interesting experiences when she began seeking a position. She reflected, "What is interesting to me is how people react when they find out I am married to someone on death row. Interviewing at law firms was a riot when they asked me what my husband does!"

Brenda reflected on her experiences. For her, the experience has been worth the stress, but she does not minimize the pain. "There are no words to describe what it feels like to love someone who has been sentenced to death. I imagine it is analogous to loving someone who has a terminal illness that lingers on for ten to twenty years. You are always waiting . . . for something . . . for good news or for bad. Without my faith in God, I do not think I could be married to [her husband]," she stated.

The last wife met her husband through her work rather than as a pen pal. She worked at the prison, and when she realized she was developing feelings for the man that was to become her husband, she went to the warden to explain her conflict of interest. She left her position for a year and then returned in a different capacity. Tanika has received support from both her family and her husband's family, but it has made her relationships with some of the correctional officers strained. Most people that she works with keep their opinions to themselves, however.

Tanika's husband was executed after the interview. Tanika was always aware of her husband's offense. She had never planned on becoming involved in a relationship like theirs. The most difficult aspect of the relationship for her was the stress.

> It puts a strain on every aspect of your life because you do the sentence with your loved one. . . . . Loving someone and never knowing when you may lose them. Always feeling that death is looming over you.
>
> My husband's appeals put me under enormous stress. I found out when I went to the doctor that I have Hep C and one of the main concerns with Hep C is stress because it makes the situation worse. I have also gained fifty lbs. in the past two years because I eat when I am stressed.

Tanika wanted the world to know that the death penalty is not fair. She also wanted the public to understand that it affects both the victim's and the offender's families. She asserted, "It does not bring closure to the victim's family and the offenders' families are the unseen victims and treated as if they committed the crime."

OTHER FICTIVE KIN

Friends, pen pals, and women who marry death row prisoners are not the only fictive kin affected by capital punishment. Anyone who gets close to a prisoner risks emotional pain when he or she is executed. Attorneys and other members of the legal team are frequently at risk. They often become very close, especially those working on the last stages of the prisoners' appeals. I have become privileged to become acquainted with several attorneys and investigators during the course of this project, many of whom have shared their difficulty with continuing in a career that brings them close to people who are then executed. One woman, who had been a defense investigator for many years, finally found a position with another agency that was not so intense. Another man indicated to me that he was unsure how much longer he could do that kind of work.

One attorney, Steve Presson, has given me permission to repeat some of what he said in different e-mail messages. Steve Presson has worked on many cases and had nine clients executed. Several of his cases have been extremely high profile, including two men who were juveniles at the time of their executions (Sean Sellers and Scott Hain). After the 2003 execution of Scott Hain, Steve sent a message to the various groups and individuals who had supported him in his efforts to save Scott's life. In the message, he provided a poignant description of the relationship between himself and the prisoner.

> As we talked, it became apparent to me that Scott was devastated that his parents would not witness his death, did not want his remains, and did not want his property. We spent the time talking about what he could have been had he been fortunate enough to be born to other parents.
>
> Scott knew that I'd recently married, and he often asked me if Jean and I planned to have children. He brought the subject up again, and I said we did. He said, "You'll be a good father. Your kids won't turn out like me." We talked a little bit about kids and teens. The topic then turned to my honeymoon.
>
> Jean and I had spent our honeymoon in Hawaii. Scott wanted know which Islands were the prettiest, and which one Jean and I like the best. He also wanted to know if we were going back. I said of course we were. Scott asked if it would be too much trouble for me to spread his ashes on Kaua'i, which Jean and I thought was the prettiest island. He didn't want to burden me with this, but just was thinking out loud, he said. I told him about our visit to Charles Lindbergh's grave on Maui, on a cliff overlooking the Pacific, surrounded by trees and in a constant gentle breeze.

Scott, his voice choking, asked me whether I could spread some of his ashes around Lindbergh's grave, and the rest over the cliffside near the ocean. . . .

The last thing he said to me on Wednesday night was that I had been more of a father figure to him than anyone else in his life.

This was not the only time that Steve developed a family-like relationship with a person condemned to death. On the evening of Dion Smallwood's execution, Steve sent another e-mail, stating, "Dion Smallwood, my client, my friend, my brother, will most likely be executed tonight at 9:00 P.M. I visited him yesterday afternoon in McAlester, hugged several times, cried a few times, said our goodbyes. . . . Forgive any typos; my eyes are too bleary to see very well."

Steve is an idealistic, ethical, and committed attorney. He is deeply bothered by what he sees as the inequities in the system. On one occasion, he spoke about a 1983 murder case. A parent of the accused came to court every day and cried. The judge in the case admonished them not to be emotional in the courtroom. The wife of the victim, however, was allowed to cry in court.

Steve has not always been an attorney. Before deciding to pursue a career in law, he was a police officer. Then, the wife of a close friend was murdered; his friend was harassed. Steve realized that he needed to make a contribution to a system with which he was growing disenchanted.

He is not the only member of his family to become fictive kin to a prisoner. In the documentary *The Execution of Wanda Jean*, the viewer is privy to the close relationship between Steve's brother, David Presson, and the condemned woman. In the film, we are shown her taking on a sisterly role and telling him he needs to eat right.[8]

Bob, spiritual advisor to a number of death row prisoners, wrote about his first experience with being a witness to an execution. He was saddened and angered by the experience.

First of all, as [prisoner's] Spiritual Advisor, I want to thank all those of you who have given me much support (both emotional as well as spiritual) in recent weeks as we approached [prisoner's] execution.

Two hours prior to his scheduled execution, I was escorted to [prisoner's] Death Row holding cell where I was able to minister some final prayers, scriptural sharings, and goodbyes to him. He appeared slightly nervous, but prepared to the inevitable and assured of his eternal destiny.

The entire staff that I was confronted with at the Oklahoma State Penitentiary were very courteous to my wife and I during our many visits there this past week. It is my belief that a "Smiling School" ought to invite the lady guard who mans the reception desk at the H-Unit facility. Her facial attitude expressions seem to make the visitor feel like we are the violent perpetrators which she is guarding the public from. The chaplain extended hospitable courtesies to the both of us. However, he left me feeling that he is somewhat insensitive towards inmates as he labeled all of them as "GAME PLAYERS." I cannot feel that at some point in the past, the Oklahoma State Penitentiary needed a Chaplain but got a COP instead.

Bob has been wounded by his experience. However, this does not deter him from reaching out to other prisoners on death row, offering them friendship and faith.

Two of the fictive kin were very unlikely people to befriend someone on death row. The first was someone who had viewed the prisoner as "family" prior to the offense. In January of 2001, Oklahoma executed eight prisoners in thirty days. Wanda Jean Allen was one. As my class discussed the case, one of my students revealed that Wanda Jean had been his baby-sitter at the time of her arrest. Ron said that his family found out about her arrest from the television coverage. He was saddened by the situation, and he said he had loved her. He did his paper that term on capital punishment and mental retardation.[9]

Juanita is a teacher in another country. In 1992, her students began writing to a prisoner on death row in the United States. She thought it would be instructional for them to write to someone condemned to death, since her country does not have capital punishment.

It was a big surprise and an event strange when we had his first answer. The girls and boys decided to go on to write him. They wrote him all the problems and interests in their lives. [Prisoner] answered to each one and had right words for each one of my pupils.

I lost the pupils because they went to other schools. I know that someone of them go on to write to [prisoner]. The correspondence with [prisoner] was kept on by me. We became friend. . . . Now my life is very changed because I always think to [prisoner]. I can't be happy; I have a lot of fear about him. I feel me not able to save him and I ask how can I draw upon him again the public attention, but the media spoke about a prisoner only if there is the terrible date for me of execution. I'm desperate. Each day I think: another day of life for [prisoner], but how much other again?

Despite the language barrier, this schoolteacher, who thought it would be instructional for her students to write to someone on death row, has been deeply affected. Some of the students have quite likely also been affected. One has gone on to study law, in hopes of helping the prisoner her class befriended.

Two women who provided emotional support to the person who had murdered their family members are the final two subjects of this chapter. Their relationships with the two offenders were quite different. Sue Norton ended up developing a deep friendship with Robert Knighton, who was convicted of murdering her father and stepmother. Deeply religious, Sue believed that her Christian faith required her to forgive him. She made contact with Knighton, whom she called BK, immediately after his trial. After he was transferred to the prison in McAlester, they developed a friendship. They exchanged letters, and Sue visited him when she could. Like other family members, Sue was appalled at the expense of telephone calls from the prison. Sue commented, "Do you know that each fifteen-minute phone call to another state is $18, plus charges, averaging $22 each. I had I think six calls in the last month here at home and it was $168. That is awful! But it cost $3.80 or something like that to get a call in McAlester."

I met Sue about two years before BK was executed. When I first met her, she was vivacious and happy. Then, in the months before the execution, the stress began to wear on her. She was often tearful, and she worried about how she would pay for his funeral expenses. She discovered that being "next of kin" and agreeing to take BK's remains had hidden costs that appalled her. At one point, she jokingly threatened to pick the body up herself rather than pay to have it transported to the funeral home.

Do you know about the Bill of $138. that the McAlester hospital is now sending to the families of the executed? We don't even know what it is about, but think it is for overnight storage! They will not allow the mortuary pick up the body that night and keep it until 9 A.M. I refused to pay it.

It has been a bit of a morbid humor in our more dire moments, that I tell BK that I am going to haul him out of that dungeon in my own car, and take him on a last tour of where I have been traveling the past twelve years as I came to see him. AbaGayle [a friend] has promised to sit in the back seat and hold him up! Of course we are praying for this one time, to be pulled over by the law, so we can tell them that this is the body of the man that was just murdered by the state!

Sue wondered what she could do to keep the state from killing BK. As his execution approached, the stress became even more apparent. Sue testified at the clemency hearing, asking the state to spare BK's life, but clemency was denied. Sue's stress level increased. She reported, "I am just trying to maintain. . . . I bawled all the way home the other day and Gene [her husband] listened to me talk for two hours. He has been so good. I have not been out of the house since. I was supposed to go to the store and do some errands this morning, but did not go. I hate leaving the house alone."

When BK was executed, Sue was his witness. Afterward, she received his personal effects. She reflected on this, commenting, "Received the ashes yesterday and it sure feels odd to have a 7.5 pound box and know that is all that is left of BK. Also finally got up the nerve to open his property boxes. Two big boxes very loosely packed, with a TV, radio, fan, and various ointments, toothpaste, soap, and some legal papers and his recent letters. Otherwise that was all that the man had."

Sue is very fortunate because her husband has been extremely supportive of her friendship with BK. Prior to BK's execution, Sue made frequent trips from Kansas to Oklahoma to see him. She has also developed a strong support network. She became active in MVFR and is currently the national secretary of the organization. She is active in abolitionist organizations both locally and nationally. Sue speaks at schools, churches, and civic groups about her reasons for opposing the death penalty. By befriending her parents' killer, Sue believes that she has been able to get a completely new perspective. She learned about BK's life before his crime, and she has come to believe that those on death row deserve understanding. While the sad personal histories do not excuse their crimes, they do merit compassion and forgiveness. Above all, she wants the world to know that all victims' family members are not focused on retribution. She represents a different approach, one of mercy.

> I cannot afford to have a replay of what happened to Johnnie Carter, and have the media not focus on the victims of the offender and of the execution. My sister and Virginia's family members will probably be there, and for years they have wanted to get in the lime light, so I don't doubt that they will be there.
>
> If you remember how I felt as I was facing BK's execution, you know that I was concerned with the "Mothers and Fathers" of these men and women being executed. I did not know how they could face their child's fate, it hurt that bad for me with "just" a friend. Without MVFR and my other friends, I could not have gotten by.

Johnnie Carter was a witness for her granddaughter's murderer. Seven-year-old Kathy Busch was murdered in February 1990. Her body was discarded in a dumpster. The perpetrator, Floyd Allen Medlock, turned himself in to police the following day. Johnnie initially reacted with anger. However, by the time Medlock was tried in 1991, she had sought help from a minister to deal with her pain and rage. She was no longer as angry, although she was still heartbroken, and reached the belief that she needed to forgive the perpetrator in order to heal. She became an outspoken opponent of capital punishment, eventually chairing the Oklahoma Coalition to Abolish the Death Penalty. Eventually, she made contact with her grandchild's murderer. "In August 2000 I started writing to Medlock. This was a young man who was very, very remorseful. He told me he admired what I was doing—that is, trying to put an end to the death penalty—but that he was very thankful it would not happen in his lifetime. He wanted to die. But I didn't want to see him die. I believe that God gives us life and only He can take it away. I don't think we have the right to do that to ourselves or to other people. When we execute someone, we do the same thing that murderers do."[10]

On a cold winter day, Johnnie showed me a letter she had received from Medlock. In it, he requested that she attend his execution as his witness. Johnnie was very upset and under tremendous stress due to the upcoming execution. She struggled with Medlock's request, finally deciding that she needed to attend.

> I wound up going to Medlock's execution. He asked me to, and I wanted him to see that I really did forgive him. But I had to go for myself, as well. It's something I can't explain, but I needed to go.
>
> On January 16, 2001, Floyd Medlock was executed by lethal injection. This is how it works: A curtain goes up and the person who is being put to death is lying there in front of you on a gurney with a sheet pulled up to his neck. The warden is there and the doctor and the minister. There's no dignity to it. It's cold. It's impersonal. It's a barbaric ritual, sanctioned by the state.[11]

I spoke with Johnnie shortly after the execution. She was still very upset about the execution, saying, "It took my breath away." While Johnnie did not condone what Medlock had done, she nonetheless believed that he deserved support. He had been willing to answer her questions about Kathy's death. In turn, she had been willing to be present for him when the state took his life.

Johnnie's story is important for another reason. Because she was Medlock's witness, she was no longer a victim in the eyes of the state. Following the execution, the victim's family members who supported Medlock's execution were escorted into an area of the prison for a press conference. Johnnie, however, had to go outside into the cold, rainy night. In the eyes of the state, she was on the "wrong" side.

The men and women who become fictive kin differ from family members because their experiences begin after the accused man or woman is sentenced to death. Ron was the only subject of this chapter who had a relationship with the offender prior to conviction. These fictive kin, therefore, do not experience the initial shock and horror of having a relative facing a possible death sentence. They also often escape the beginning stages of the BADD cycle. However, once they do become involved with the offender, their stories become very similar to those of other family members. They repeatedly experience periods of hope, followed by despair, only to have their hopes lifted again. They develop stress-related illnesses, and their relationships with others are often damaged. On the other hand, fictive kin are far less likely than other family members to withdraw. Instead, they are joiners. As they become more isolated, many fictive kin become active in groups that are supportive of their decision. Indeed, some of them become involved with the offenders because of their participation in abolitionist groups. Overall, they tend to fare better than many of the family members described in earlier chapters because of their connection to strong support networks. Their lives, however, are irreparably changed by their relationship to someone on death row.

CHAPTER 10

The Death Penalty and
Families, Revisited

The worst fear every mother has is losing her child.
Every day I have lived with that threat for the past
eight years. . . . This is the true torture of the death
penalty.

THE FAMILIES OF PERSONS facing the death penalty face
many challenges and fears, ultimately including the death of a relative.
While many family members do not have contact with the condemned
relative, even those individuals are not always immune to the effects of
capital punishment. One has only to recall the fears of Jason, whose
brother had been executed, that others might find out and reject him.
Likewise, Lisa and her sister have suffered greatly over the years despite
the fact that they went for years with no contact with their condemned
brother. Martha, who had made no contact with her cousin since he had
murdered her aunt, agonized over whether or not she should write to
him. Thus, it can be a mistake to assume that all family members who are
not in contact with the person facing death are unaffected.

However, most of the subjects of this book are individuals who are
(or were until execution) in contact with their family members facing a
death sentence. Furthermore, they are family members who were willing
to talk about their experiences and who could be identified and located.
So, this book has been about the experiences of what is quite likely a
nonrepresentative sample. Does that mean their voices should not be
heard? I do not believe that to be true. I am reminded of the parable of
the boy walking along the beach and throwing one starfish back into the
ocean. When it was pointed out to him that it was a useless task, that he
could not save all the starfish, he responded that his efforts mattered to
that starfish. Similarly, while the stories and experiences portrayed in this

book of family members of those facing a death penalty may not represent those of all the family members, they matter to these individuals and many more like them. They deserve to be heard.

Several common themes have been running through these stories. In chapter 2, families of those facing death were compared and contrasted with families of homicide victims as well as families of other prisoners. Based on what we know about these other two groups, I argued that there were both similarities and differences in the experiences of families of those facing death and families of both victims and other prisoners. I did not interview members of the other two groups, so the conclusions that I have reached are based on comparisons of what my subjects expressed to what other researchers have reported about the others. As I anticipated, families dealing with the death penalty are both similar to and different from both of the other groups.

VICTIMS IGNORED BY THE SYSTEM

Families dealing with the death penalty often compare themselves to those of homicide victims. They report experiencing a similar initial shock and trauma when they first find out their relative is being accused of a potentially capital offense. In addition to the shock, however, they often grapple with trying to understand what is happening. Alice, whose son is on death row, summarized the reaction she and her husband had, saying, "The night we got the call, we both went into shock. Capital murder, what does that mean!!"

The accused's family members are not faced with the immediate loss experienced by family members of murder victims. Instead, they are faced with a protracted grief process more similar to that faced by families of military members missing in action or families of those dying of AIDS. Pauline Boss discusses how "ambiguous loss" such as that faced by families of those facing a death sentence can lead to what she terms "frozen sadness."[1] The person experiencing this is often in a cycle of hope and despair, due to the uncertainty of the situation. The repetitive nature of this cycle is particularly destructive, in part because of its long-term nature.

When a loved one is murdered, the family experiences severe trauma. It can be difficult to find meaning, and the shock of the loss coupled with the horror of how the person died can cause severe problems, including nightmares, suicidal thoughts, and chronic illnesses.[2] In the book *Dead Man Walking,* Sister Helen Prejean describes hearing the experiences of victims' family members at meetings of the group Survive, which provides assistance to primarily lower-income victims' families in New Orleans, and of the group Parents of Murdered Children. She reminds the reader of the plagues that visited Egypt, the worst of which was the loss of firstborn children. At the meeting of Parents of Murdered Children, Sister Prejean was struck by the pain and sorrow expressed by the members. Some had little support from friends or from the system, as was the case with the family that was told to write to Ann Landers when they went to apply for assistance from the victim compensation fund. Others talked about the destruction to their lives that the murder had created, including lost jobs and divorce. Mainly, the members provide support to each other by sharing common experiences and feelings, reassuring each other that their experiences are not unique.[3]

At the Survive meeting, the family members' pain is also palpable. This group, which Prejean helped start, serves a different population, primarily indigent minorities. The pain from their losses is no different from the pain expressed by the members of Parents of Murdered Children. Sister Helen wrote, "Some talk of considering suicide, of staying in bed and sleeping, of numbing the pain with alcohol or drugs. They talk of confusion and bewilderment."[4]

The family of a murder victim is often further traumatized by the criminal justice system. This is particularly true if the victim's family is poor or members of a minority group. Although almost half of the murders in this country were of black victims, these murders all too often do not result in prosecution.[5] Even when prosecution occurs, the family is often a tool used by the prosecution to get a desired conviction or sentence. Family members who represent the "right" kind of victim may find themselves courted by the district attorney's office, while others find their telephone calls unreturned. The latter group often interprets this as a lack of validation of the importance of their loss.

The family members whose stories are told in this book experience pain similar to that of victims' families, although their pain is not one of immediate loss. Instead, they experience immediate horror and a long, slow loss. Furthermore, they are frequently treated as if they are also guilty. When asked what they would like people to know, they overwhelmingly indicated that they were victims and yet they were treated as if they had committed the crime themselves.[6]

Although Sarah's son was not executed, dying in prison instead, she felt the loss keenly. Sarah and her family were treated as if they had committed the crime. She felt that the public should be better educated about this. Sarah wrote, "I think the public should show a little bit of compassion for the families of those who have a loved one in prison or on death row. After all, they did not commit any crime and yet they are made to feel like they did. They are looked down at by the public as if they were scum, as if they were trash who had no right to live and were beneath them."

She also expressed the belief that the pain the offender's family experiences at execution is no less than that experienced by the victim's family. If anything, it is made worse by the fact that others celebrate the death of someone they love.

> They laugh at the families whose loved one has just been exterminated outside the prisons. They party, laugh and sing and cheer in front of a grieving family who loves their person no matter what he had done.
>
> I think the public should know that after they murder our loved one, we feel the same pain and rage as the family of a murder victim. I would tell them that there is no difference in a mother's pain at the loss of her son . . . by the mother of a child who's been murdered on the street or the mother whose son has been executed. The pain is the same, and the public wants to exact the same pain on the perpetrator's family as the victim's family experienced.

Sarah wanted the world to know what the offenders' families go through. They not only experience the grief over the death of their family members, but also face rejection and hostility. She told me, "We are human beings, we feel, we cry, we laugh, and we feel the pain of losing our children, too, yet there is no sympathy for us. For we are hated as much as the one who did the crime."

Donna also talked about being treated as if she herself were guilty of a crime. The trial of her son was made even more difficult by the actions of the victim advocate. "I think the public should not treat the family like they commit a crime. I never been in jail, and when we went to the trial the victim person kept bringing the family in our face like we were not feeling their pain," she said.

Some family members felt that the victim's family's desires to end their own pain contributed to the pain of the offender's family members. Dana expressed this opinion, believing that the focus on revenge was the true problem. "They think that, of course, they are affecting the convicted family and that they are going to get even. . . . They think that they are getting even because they have him on death row and he will be put to death for doing his crime. They don't care. I mean, we didn't do anything, but they don't care. They see that it is going to make their sorrows go away. I mean, it is never going to go away. . . . It is hard. It is not just hard on them. It is hard on everybody. It is not the way to go."

Loving the Offender

Family members also stressed that there was much more to the person facing death than the one act leading to the possibility of execution. Lisa, whose brother was executed several years earlier, talked about the fact that her brother left behind a family, all of whom were innocent of the crime. She told me, "I want everyone to know that [her brother] has a mother, two sisters, three nieces, two nephews, and lots of aunts, uncles, and cousins. We didn't do anything so don't point your bitterness at us. We are mourning our loss as well."

Similarly, Kendra wanted people to realize that the families of those on death row were facing terrible loss. While she understood sympathy for the victim's family, she felt that the media excluded any understanding of the offender's family. Furthermore, media representations tended to be one-sided, presenting only the worst thing that the accused had ever done, ignoring all the good things.

> I think that something I'd really like the public to know is that . . . I think that in general anytime any of them see something terrible on TV, it's very easy to sympathize with the victim's family. I think that's just part of human nature—you're going to sympathize with the person who is hurt or injured.
>
> I just wish that people would consider, you know, and think about it for a moment. . . . I would really like for people to step in the other shoe a moment. What if it was my family member, my son,

my brother, my uncle, my father that was accused of doing these crimes, how would I approach it then?

I guess when you see those people on TV, you don't know about them. You don't know if they're married, or if they have children or . . . how close they were with their family or—you just don't know any of those things. But . . . they have a family—I mean, they do. And they have people that love them and care about them as well.

I guess that's it—just try to envision the defendant as somebody you love, just for a minute. I'll never stop loving [her brother] because of what he is accused of—never! And yes, I'm aware of the fact that he is my big brother and I grew up with him and it's not going to be any other way. Again, I would say, just try to envision that your loved one was the person accused of committing this crime. You might look at it a little bit differently.

In addition to remembering that the offenders were more than just their offenses, some family members wanted the public to remember that the crime may have occurred in part because of a situation that got out of control. Linda wanted the public to know this, to know her husband was not all bad. When asked what she would want people to know, she told me, "Look at the people that are up there as humans. . . . Sometimes people get mixed up in things they wouldn't normally get mixed up in. That is society's biggest problem. There are different types of people that are on death row."

Jim Fowler stressed the similarities in the experiences of these two sets of families and the fact that the accused's family is forgotten. Nobody is in a better position than Jim to realize this, as he has been on both sides.

I'd like to let the whole world know that we hear in the media and the papers about the victims of violence, and they're always referring to the parents of the person who was killed or raped or whatever the damn problem was. We're all victims. We're all in the same terrible bucket. I don't know how to explain it any stronger than that. That we've all suffered a terrible loss. Our loss is that we lost Mark the day that he was arrested for that terrible crime. And we've been going through a fifteen-year period of—of hell. And we're so help-less. We're just on the other side of the fence. We're both victims of the same terrible tragic night.

Repeatedly, the men and women that I interviewed stressed the effects on their own families. Their sadness and desperation often came through in their words. Donna was one of those who seemed to be at the end of her ability to remain emotionally healthy. Her whole life had become focused around her son's case. She found it particularly painful because her son was diagnosed with schizophrenia as well as bipolar disorder, making it difficult for her to understand why he should be executed.

> My health is so-so. I been sick a little but I can't sleep to [sic] good and I get nervous when I heard about things on the news or some-times just depressed, but I don't say anything because I don't think people understand.
>
> Our relationship was sort of shaky because he was diagnose [sic] with schizophrenia and manic depression, and when he came home in the state I live in they don't have good mental health programs . . . so he was without his meds most of the time and he started self-medicating (street drugs).
>
> I think that if a person has some mental background that they should get them help.
>
> I guess I'm all right but I feel guilty sometimes because [her son] has a chemical unbalance and I never knew about it even though I took him for regular check-ups.

Some family members talked about the way the death penalty had put their own lives on hold. Over the years, the whole focus of their lives has become the person on death row and whether or not he or she will be executed.[7] For Alice, the protracted nature of having someone on death row was the worst aspect of all. Unlike the family members of murder victims who are faced with immediate loss, family members like Alice are faced with years of waiting for the state to kill their loved one. She commented, "I think the hardest part is the waiting . . . why don't they reverse the sentence or get on with it. . . . We have no life, we are waiting."

Family members often know another side of the accused. They may struggle with the public perception of their loved one. Carla's daughter was convicted of a murder that has resulted in considerable media cover-age, including a book. For Carla, the descriptions bear little relation to the daughter she loves.

The books that have been written describing my daughter as a monster, even though I know how loving she really is. I feel I've become very hard hearted toward the system and have no respect for justice. The crying never ends!

Her death will be terribly painful to me, but I believe the death penalty is wrong. Not just for [her daughter] but wrong for all of us. Her death will be just as painful for her family and friends as if she were found in a field or killed in an accident and no less.

Kathy has a brother on death row with multiple disabilities. She spoke eloquently about what the family members experience.

I see families, who, like us, live with not only the sorrow and pain of what their loved one has done, but with an agony and profound sense of dread as we wait our loved one's executions. We know down to the last detail how they will be killed; we just don't know the "when." We know that we are powerless to stop it, and we wonder if we will have the strength to bear it. I've heard it said that those who are on death row will die a thousand deaths while waiting for their execution. We know that we will also die a thousand deaths before our loved one is executed. We know that the weight of this punishment will be borne by those of us who will go on living . . . those of us who saw their value and knew that they were not just garbage to be thrown out.

HEALING RELATIONSHIPS

For some families, however, the years of having a relative on death row allowed the family to heal their relationships. This occurred for the Fowlers. Mark was able to mature into a caring man after he was incarcerated and off drugs. They were not the only family that experienced healing of relationships. Lisa also talked about her brother becoming her best friend after she finally made contact with him. This is one way that families of those facing death differ greatly from families of victims. For the victim's family, there will never be an opportunity to strengthen relationships. Their loved one is irrevocably gone.[8] There will be no more letters, phone calls, or visits. In this way, families of offenders are more fortunate. However, the opportunity to rebuild relationships can be a double-edged sword. It means that the person who is eventually executed is not the same person who committed the offense. It also means that when that person is finally killed by the state, the loss may be even more deeply felt. Laura's son was executed shortly after I interviewed her. She spoke of "the sadness and the loss of such a superb young man." Her description of the relationship she had built with him while he awaited death was poignant, as were her comments about what the family experiences.

> I have a son on death row. When I think of him the past is all I have. . . . Since my son has been on death row he has found a new way and a new life. He has found God.
>
> We have become so close; since he found God he is my best friend and the joy of my life. We were this close when he was small.
>
> What possible good could come from trying to right one wrong with another. I will forever be in mourning for my son, who corrects that wrong?
>
> Who tries to ease the pain for the parents of the condemned? Who tells us that they are sorry and remorseful for the death of our child? Does the State consider we the family of the condemned as victims? No, they do not, but as surely as I live and breathe we are.
>
> The death penalty is cruel and not just to the offender but to all those who love him. I believe that it lowers us all as human to a baser level.

Lisa, whose brother was executed in the early 1990s, talked about missing her brother. She also felt the public should realize that the crime can be punished without killing the offender. Like Laura, Lisa developed a strong and close relationship with her brother while he was on death row.

> We wrote letters two to three times per month and he called me on every holiday. Our relationship grew and developed into more than it ever was growing up together. . . . What is most difficult for me is missing [her brother]. I miss him as a friend and confidante. I only wish I could have grown up with the [her brother] that he had become, due to faith. We would have had a wonderful family if that were the case. . . . It is also difficult for me to see my mother suffer like she does. She goes to the cemetery often and sits for hours. . . .

BUT, if you would only believe me that death row is worse than dying.

LACK OF SUPPORT

Support for these two types of families is also different. While difficulties with the type of support provided to victims' families exist and support is not always given equally, some support is nevertheless available. Most states have some type of victim's assistance program. These programs may provide financial assistance and emotional support. Additionally, support groups for victims are found throughout the country. The families of those accused of the crimes, however, have few places to turn for support.[9] They are left to deal with their grief alone, often losing the support of friends, extended family, and community organizations. They may not only lose support but actually find themselves the target of media coverage and retaliatory actions. This happened to Paula and her children. Furthermore, no compensation funds exist for offender's families. Indeed, as Linda noted, although her husband is permanently removed from the family, her children cannot receive Social Security or other assistance.

The family members of the accused are aware of their needs but often do not know where to turn for support. Their grief and desperation is often not seen as valid. Well-meaning friends and family members may counsel them to just forget the offender. Some churches, traditionally a source of support, may ask families members to leave the congregation. Because they are spread out geographically and small in number, it is difficult to organize a support group. Lisa summed up these problems faced by family members, stating, "I think that families of death row inmates need to know where to get help. Education needs to be more than what it is. We are just out here on our own. More sensitive media coverage should be approached as well."

Along similar lines, another subject brought up something mentioned earlier in the book. Judy talked about the movement toward mediation between offenders and victims' families across the country.[10] Noting that families of offenders have nowhere to turn, nobody telling them they are sorry for what had been done to their relative, she suggested developing a mediation program between families of offenders and the state. "There are groups that offer mediation between victims and the offenders, but there isn't anyone that the families of those executed can meet with. How do they come to terms with what has happened. So, here is my thought. I would like to start a mediation program that would be able to allow the families to confront the government, i.e., the governor, or someone on the clemency board, a judge. Someone that would be able for them to vent their frustration and anger and come to terms with what society is doing."

Unfortunately, the likelihood of the state supporting that type of mediation program is virtually nonexistent. Families of those facing death are not given the opportunity of confronting those they hold responsible. Perhaps this is why a number of family members that I interviewed have become active in abolitionist groups. Those groups provide not only support for family members but also an outlet for expressing their pain and anger.

The feelings expressed by the families in this book were in many ways similar to those of victims' families. Like the families of victims, the families of those facing a death sentence experienced grief and loss. Unlike the victims' families, however, they also faced blame and condemnation. They were also more fortunate than victims' family members because they had the opportunity to restore damaged relationships.

FAMILY MEMBERS AND CONTACT

Death row families can also be compared to the families of other prisoners. Again, I found both similarities and differences to what previous research describes about families of those not facing death. The concerns of these families differ greatly, with families of other prisoners focusing more on getting loved ones moved to a prison closer to home and helping them achieve parole. While the families of the condemned often spend considerable energy to get the death sentence overturned, few expect the prisoner to be released. Additionally, each time that an appeal is denied, the family may experience the trauma of having a relative face death all over again. Frequently, they commented that the experience was like dying slowly—like dying a little every day.

The amount of contact with the prisoner is another major difference in the experiences of these two types of families. Families of noncapital prisoners do experience many problems in maintaining contact. However, the issues are both similar and different. Both types of families face problems with exorbitant costs for telephone calls. Additionally, both types of families may have to travel considerable distances to visit their relatives.[11] However, the contact between family members and the offender may also vary greatly for these two groups. The majority of states with the death penalty do not allow contact visits, while most states do allow contact with offenders not sentenced to death.[12] Tanya talked about how this affects families.

> The reason I am speaking out is because of my mother. For all the mothers of death row inmates. I have seen the pain and suffering that my mother has been through over the last several years. A mother of a Texas DR inmate will never touch their son again. There is no human contact allowed. I can't even imagine how that must feel. . . . There was a special mother that begged to hold her son one last time before his execution and she was denied. They then let her hold her son's still warm but lifeless body. Don't they see that they are sentencing the family as well?

Additionally, some death row visitation policies may create hardship on family members. For example, in Oklahoma, the visiting area is very uncomfortable. Furthermore, the area has no rest rooms. Once family members leave the immediate visitation area, they may not return. Several of my interview subjects talked about how this had affected them. Ann and Jim Fowler described visiting H-Unit, where Oklahoma's death row is housed.

ANN: I'll never forget the first time that we went down to . . . down to McAlester. It was the most degrading feeling to walk into that place. In the first place, they don't know you. They don't know what your relationship is. Oh, they may know this mother, this is father. But they don't know you personally. And you're treated as if you were as bad as the person they've locked up in the prison. And you feel—unclean.

This H-Unit, in your visiting station—this building is built half underground. Solid concrete. And the visiting area is about as wide as this room here is. Maybe not quite as wide. There are four stations, two feet square with windows. Quarter-inch glass with steel wire reinforcing it in—in that glass. On [the prisoner's] side of this glass, there are six one-inch bars in this window, with two cross-pieces of steel, this wide and that thick, that these bars go down through. Anyway, and then you talk to him on the phone—he's in a little cubicle over there about three and a half feet wide and eight feet long. No air, no ventilation comes into this room at all. And it's blocked off, and so, in the hot part of the summer, his shirt will be just wringing wet. So we've cut our visits short sometimes just so he can get out of there and get some fresh air. We're on the outside here and we're sitting on—

And he can't open the door to get fresh air in there. They lock it once he gets in.

JIM: And then there's this pedestal that we sit on—steel pedestal bolted to the floor. . . . And it's got a two-by-twelve block of wood that the corners have been mitered off of so that you don't have any sharp corners. That's what you sit on. That's the only seating in this whole visiting area. So, there's no physical contact with him, no touching at all. And now I can't wear a hat in the prison!

ANN: (laughs, then starts crying)

JIM: I've worn a hat all my damn life. It's just little things that they do to you there. They—they try to dehumanize everything. They're in a position to make uncomfortable, to make life miserable for anybody and everybody that they want. Why do they want to do that? It's just their mentality.

ANN: This is another thing. You go down there and a lot of those people come from great distances when they come to visit. And so, you want to spend the full amount of time with them that you can. . . . But there's no reason I can think of to make that—to make those rooms so uncomfortable for them to sit in. Uh, there are no rest rooms. So, if you—and I have a colon problem—I never know when I'm going to have to go to the rest room. And one day, we hadn't been there thirty minutes—and I had to go out and I could not get back in. Once you go out, you cannot get back in.

The Fowlers were not the only ones to describe the harsh visitation policies on death row. Dan and Carol also commented about it. To them, one of the repercussions is that families give up.

CAROL: We drive so far, and you know, it's kind of an upsetting trip and it's emotional. I mean, I got sick going down one time and after you get there, you aren't guaranteed a visit after you get there if they're busy. I mean, we haven't had that happen, though we've had to wait an hour and a half once we got there. But I had diarrhea once, and I wasn't sick enough to warrant not trying to go visit. But I mean, I really needed to go to the bathroom every once in awhile. Pretty much, your visit's over if you have to leave to go to the bathroom. And they search you and you can't leave the building. The bathroom's right there—it doesn't make sense.

DAN: And another thing—the only seats available are for the person— but if someone else is with you, they either stand up or sit on the cold concrete floor.

CAROL: And it's cold. The seats are real weird—but the counter—hits me right about here so it's not comfortable to go, and the seats are too high, but your feet can't fit flat on the ground, they kind of dangle off. So, there's just no comfort at all, you know, it's almost like they anticipate—I mean try to make it as difficult as possible.

DAN: Have you ever been there and seen how it is? You go up a stairway and they lock you in this stairwell and the stairwell is like this big hallway and there's four pods.

CAROL: You die a little every day—every day I come to see [her son]. And people don't realize what the visitation is like for people. And a lot of people finally can't go anymore. There's no reason why they couldn't have—you know, there's these little cubicles. There's no reason why you couldn't have contact with him.

DAN: And you know, it's very uncomfortable visiting the same week that there's an execution, because, you know, it brings it back to reality.

Certainly, visitation in any prison is difficult. Visitors face rules about what they can bring, rules about what they may wear. Even where contact visits are allowed, there are rules about contact. Still, for the family members of those who live in states where death row prisoners are not allowed contact, this seems to be one of the most difficult issues. Linda expressed her feelings, saying, "Just to be able to touch his hand one more time." Several mothers talked about the pain of not being able to hug their child. This type of visitation sets up an artificial atmosphere. Families that have been demonstrative in the past now must make do with paltry substitutes.

The heightened security of death row makes visitation even more humiliating. Sandra talked about visiting her brother for the first time. She dressed carefully in order to give a good impression—an impression that was wasted on the prison staff.

> I couldn't believe it, kind of like one of those out-of-body experiences. I just kept thinking, "I am not really doing this." They make you leave your car keys and your driver's license. . . . When you are going to death row, you walk all the way down this sidewalk, and then you get up there and you go through a couple of clanging gates, and then you have a body search where they shake you down, make you take your shoes off . . . then you go and sit now in these little chairs and the other side of this glass and wait for them to bring them in. . . . I looked at him walking in and sitting down at this telephone, and I thought, "This may be where he will spend the rest of his life." I mean, it just really hit me then because I was so sure all along that this would not happen. . . . I just thought, "This will be what he will do for the rest of his life. No physical contact, no nothing, sitting behind this glass." That was an experience that was just burned into me. I don't think I will ever forget it.

For Sandra, visiting her brother in prison brought home the greatest difference between families of death row prisoners and families of other prisoners. Not only could she not touch her brother, but she also realized that this was final. Fortunately for Sandra and her family, her brother was eventually freed. In most cases, that does not occur.

Both types of prisoner families deal with emotional upheaval and financial devastation. For the family of the death-eligible offender, that financial devastation may be threefold. Many families talked about their fears of having a state-appointed attorney represent the accused. Most non–death penalty cases are plea-bargained, but when the state seeks the death penalty, a trial is likely. If the family has any assets, they may sell or mortgage them to raise money for a private attorney. Few families have the kind of resources needed to pay for the kind of defense that is needed, and they end up feeling betrayed by both the system and their own attorneys. Additionally, some families lose the income of the prisoner, as was the case with Linda and her son. The health and mental health of several family members were so severely affected that they were unable to continue working, creating a third source of financial strain.

The stories of the family members make it clear that the experience of having a family member facing a death sentence is incredibly traumatic. Like any families dealing with loss, they experience emotional pain and trauma. However, these families face additional burdens. First, the may lose social support at a time when they desperately need it. Second, they may find themselves treated as if they were in some way responsible for the offense. Third, because of the uncertainty surrounding whether or not the offender will be executed, they experience a long-term grief process that may repeat a destructive cycle many times. Thus, these family members are quite likely to experience stress-related illnesses and complications in their lives.

CHAPTER 11

Conclusion

IT IS DIFFICULT to do research of this nature and to maintain complete neutrality at the same time. When the idea for this project first started to emerge, I had not thought a lot about capital punishment. I knew that I opposed it in principle, but my opinion was not strong, nor was it well supported. The preparation for my class started me on a journey of learning more about capital punishment. In turn, the class led me to this project. That journey and this research have changed my life. I now find myself engaged in the type of "sociologically informed activism" described by Michael Radelet.[1]

My path has followed Professor Radelet's in some ways. Research and teaching led me to seek a deeper understanding of the issues surrounding the death penalty. I began learning more about it, and the things that I learned led me to want a more personal understanding of the subject. That in turn led me to a desire to use my scholarship to effect social change.

My earlier research with the families of prisoners had been a more quantitative approach, using surveys administered to prisoners. That allowed me to maintain a level of detachment. While I was concerned about these prisoners and their families, I did not get to know any of them on a personal level, nor did I spend hours listening to their stories. However, the study that culminated in this book was very different from the beginning. It required me to sit down face-to-face with people with heart-wrenching stories. I watched parents and siblings brush away tears as they answered my questions, waited when their voices became choked with emotion.

Eventually, I became curious about the men and women on death row, and I began corresponding with three prisoners. One has died of natural causes, but during our correspondence he taught me to see the basic humanity of those facing execution. They are men and women with hopes and dreams, much like the rest of us. However, they have also committed terrible crimes, resulting in their death sentences. I began developing a deeper compassion for the victims of crime as well as for the offenders and their families. It is impossible to spend much time studying the death penalty or those on death row without developing a sincere horror at some of the crimes they have committed. My belief in the futility of capital punishment also increased, however. I could not see how the deaths of the offenders would fix anything. Instead, a new set of victims would be created, their families and those who loved them. My research has led me to agree with Amnesty International. Capital punishment is indeed cruelty to the families of those sentenced to death.[2] They are not guilty, yet they suffer as much as the families of the victims.

I met many inspiring men and women as I conducted my research, and I corresponded electronically with many more. I was amazed by their willingness to share their pain in order to educate the public about the ways in which the death penalty affects families and friends of those facing execution. Many of the men and women that I interviewed kept in contact with me after the interviews, keeping me apprised of their loved ones' situations. Several have become friends. This, in conjunction with my opposition to capital punishment, opens me up to criticism for lack of neutrality. The criticism is misplaced. I believe that I can accurately and objectively report what my research discloses and still have my own opinions and friendships. What this requires of me is the willingness to report everything, including data that do not support my position.

I had expected to hear the family members talk about being "blamed" for the accused individual's actions. Although a few alluded to this, none of my subjects talked about being maligned in the trial. Some did report people suggesting that they must have failed in some way, but none of them reported being described as abusive or in some way creating a "monster." Perhaps this did not occur in any of the cases related to this research, or perhaps the family members simply chose not to discuss this with me. I can only speculate about this; I have no answers.

At the beginning of this project, I was not sure how the family members would feel about capital punishment. Some of the subjects of this book do not oppose the death penalty. However, their stories are just as important as the stories of those who do. Subjects like Eugene stated that they supported the death penalty in principle but were disturbed by how it was applied. Others supported the death penalty but believed that their relative should not face it. The majority of the subjects opposed the death penalty, although many had supported it prior to their family member's arrest. The fictive kin, however, all opposed capital punishment prior to becoming involved with a prisoner, with the exception of Ron. Since Ron was a child when his baby-sitter was charged, he had not really considered the death penalty. For the other fictive kin, opposition to capital punishment had led them into the relationships with persons on death row.

I was surprised to hear from a few family members who had broken off contact with the offender. Their reasons for doing so varied from fear of being identified as relatives of a murderer to anger at the offender. These are not the only reasons that families have no contact with prisoners, of course. In many cases, contact ended long before the crime. I was not able to locate any family members in this category, and their experiences may be very different from those reported by my subjects. The greatest limitation of this project is the inability to create a representative sample. It is virtually impossible to get a representative sample of this population due to its hidden nature. Some accused and convicted prisoners have no family with which they are in contact at the time of their offense or subsequent to their offense. Thus, this book should be viewed as exploratory in nature.

Despite its exploratory nature, the book does illuminate experiences common to many families. Negative reactions from others, ostracism, and shame were not uncommon. Family members frequently reacted to the initial news with shock and disbelief. Alternating periods of hope and despair were described by most. The execution itself was extremely traumatic, and many family members withdrew for a period of time afterward. Health problems, difficulty sleeping, and problems with being able to hold a job were common.

I took the position that the effects of dealing with the death penalty begin at the time a family member is first facing a possible death sentence. The stories of my subjects indicated this is true. Some of their relatives have been exonerated, and others have received lesser sentences. But the families went through similar pain and trauma, regardless of the outcome. The theme of being viewed as guilty by association reverberates throughout the book. Family members shared many examples of this, ranging from the reactions of friends to the reactions of prison personnel when they visited their loved ones.

One final anecdote about the research may help illustrate the reactions that these families face. When I initially submitted my proposal to the Institutional Review Board for Research with Human Subjects at my university, I was met with a reaction that illustrates the "otherness" of these families. In order to have the project approved, I was told that I would need to obtain a federal certificate of confidentiality, in case these family members disclosed to me their own criminal behavior. It was clear that even some academics viewed them as guilty by association. The unspoken belief was that any family that produced someone capable of committing a capital offense must be different from other families. I obtained the certificate of confidentiality, but I was disturbed by the requirement. Most of the family members that I interviewed were law-abiding citizens. Most had believed in our criminal justice system until they had experiences to make them develop other opinions.

My research ended, but the problems faced by families facing execution of a loved one continue to occur. As I was writing the last few pages, I had the opportunity to witness one more family undergoing the stress related to a pending execution. That experience changed the way I wanted to end this book. Hung Thanh Le, a Vietnamese man, was scheduled to die in Oklahoma on February 26, 2004. A rally was held the day before the scheduled execution, and his brothers and sisters came from Ohio. As I stood in the cold wind, I watched his two younger brothers. One held the flag of the United States, the other the flag of South Vietnam. As they listened to different speakers, their eyes frequently filled with tears. Hung Thanh Le's sisters stood beside them, also with tears in their eyes. His parents, speaking little English and unable to face watching their son die, had remained in Ohio. The family's pain was palpable. I found myself thinking about what they must have experienced over the past decade as well as what they were facing. Le's attorney spoke about her efforts to save his life, asking the governor to reconsider his decision to reject clemency. She has spent countless hours working on this case, often sleeping at her office. She often describes the offender as a wonderful person, and she began crying when she read a message from him to his supporters. She has become fictive kin.

Almost as if to provide further support to my description of the BADD cycle, a last-minute stay of execution was issued just moments before lethal injection was to commence. This family, in less than two days, faced all the elements of the BADD cycle. At the rally, many prayers were offered for a last-minute reprieve. Certainly, the rally of almost two hundred people constituted activity. Hung Thanh Le's brother-in-law spoke to the crowd and to the governor, asking for mercy. The governor's office issued a statement that there would be no stay, leading to disillusionment and despair. The family went to McAlester to witness the execution. Then, at the last moment a stay was granted. Hope was renewed, but it was tinged with an element of desperation. A new execution date, less than a month away, was simultaneously set. I tried to imagine what these family members were feeling. They had driven hundreds of miles, and they will quite likely need to do so again in a few weeks. Emotionally, they had prepared themselves for the death of a beloved relative. Now, they had a measure of renewed hope. And so, the cycle continued. Hung Thanh Le was executed on March 23, 2004. The family went through the cycle of hope and despair once more, with nothing changing.

Another family was slightly more fortunate. Osbaldo Torres was scheduled to be executed on May 18, 2004. Due to questions about his degree of culpability as well as an International Court of Justice ruling that his case should be reviewed, he received a recommendation for clemency from the Pardon and Parole Board. On May 13, the governor commuted his sentence to life without parole, shortly after the Oklahoma Court of Criminal Appeals granted a stay of execution to allow an evidentiary hearing. Like the family of Hung Thanh Le, the Torres family had participated in a large rally at the state capitol, pleading for mercy. His sister emerged as the family spokesperson, attending press conferences and speaking out to international media. However, despite Torres receiving clemency, the emotional ups and downs are not yet over for this family. Torres and his attorneys must decide whether to accept the life without parole sentence or to pursue the evidentiary hearing in hopes of a new trial. The family members want him to get a new trial, but that would start the cycle over, as the state could again seek the death penalty.

Other family members in this book find themselves once again hoping for miracles. Misty's father is fast approaching execution. However, recent advances in science have bolstered his claim of innocence. It will be up to the state to decide whether or not his claim of innocence has merit. I have not spoken with Misty since the news broke, and I wonder how she is handling the roller-coaster ride.

Likewise, Jim and Sharon have renewed hope. New DNA evidence and accusations of prosecutorial misconduct have led to yet another hearing next fall. Sharon, however, is afraid to hope. Furthermore, their son wants to end his appeals process, saying he doesn't want to continue living on the basis of a false hope. Sharon commented that six months is a long time for them. She is not sure if her health will allow her to live that long, and she fears her son's death. After almost twenty years and several trials, this family has suffered more than most. Although the hearing must occur by October, it is quite likely it will not occur before then. The attorney handling the case is overloaded and will not have time to prepare for court for several months.

The judge, in his order for a new evidentiary hearing for their son, commented that the implications of the case are far-reaching. He suggested that if the allegations were true, it would undermine public confidence in capital punishment.[3] For those families affected by questions about prosecutorial misconduct and new evidence, it does something else. It places them again in the cycle of hope and desperation that is the subject of this book.

This book is dedicated to the family and fictive kin of persons charged with a capital crime. In particular, it is dedicated to all of those who were willing to share their pain, experiences, and hope with me. Your stories are important, and I hope that my efforts help bring the experiences of family members of those facing death to the attention of the public. I know that by combining the stories of many, I have left out many details that may be important to you. I humbly ask you to forgive this, knowing I could never do justice to your stories.

Appendix A. Death Row Visitation Policies

Social/Family Visits

Contact	Contact in Some Cases But Not in Others	Noncontact	No Information Available
Alabama (194)	Arkansas (41)	Arizona (127)	Georgia (116)
Indiana (39)	California (625)	Colorado (6)	Virginia (29)
Kentucky (38)	Florida (380)	Connecticut (7)	
Missouri (69)	Illinois (7)	Delaware (19)	
New York (6)	Louisiana (92)	Idaho (21)	
	Nebraska (7)	Kansas (7)	
	Nevada (88)	Maryland (15)	
	New Mexico (2)	Mississippi (69)	
	Tennessee (105)	Montana (6)	
		New Hampshire (0)	
		New Jersey (15)	
		North Carolina (214)	
		Ohio (207)	
		Oklahoma (110)	
		Oregon (31)	
		Pennsylvania (241)	
		South Carolina (77)	
		South Dakota (4)	
		Texas (423)	
		Utah (11)	
		Washington (12)	
		Wyoming (2)	
		Federal Bureau of Prisons (26)	

SOURCES: Major Daniel Hudson, *Managing Death-Sentenced Inmates: A Survey of Practices*, 2nd ed. (Lanham, MD: American Correctional Association, 2000); Criminal Justice Project of the NAACP Legal Defense and Educational Fund, *Death Row U.S.A, Summer 2003*, http://www.deathpenaltyinfo.org/DEATHROWUSArecent.pdf.

NOTE: Number of prisoners on death row as of July 1, 2003, in parentheses following state.

Appendix B. Interview Schedule for Initial Interviews

Much attention has been paid to family members of murder victims, but little has been written about families of offenders. I would like to hear in your own words how having a family member either facing prosecution for a capital offense or on death row has affected your life. I would like to begin with a few questions about you before asking you about your family member.

1. How old are you? What is your marital status? With whom do you currently live?

2. What is your relationship to the person we are talking about? How close would you say you and ___ were at the time of his/her arrest? [Probe] When was the last time you had seen ___, talked to him/her on the phone, or received a letter from him/her? How often were you in contact before the arrest? Has that changed? How? [Probe] Do you have contact with ___ now? How often? [Probe]

3. How did you first become aware that ___ was charged with a capital offense? What was your initial reaction? Please say as much as you want.

4. Did _____'s arrest affect your relationship with other family members? In what ways? [Say as much as you want] How are those relationships now? [Probe]

5. Initially, did the arrest or finding out about the arrest affect any other areas of your life? How about church, work, finances, school, social life? Tell me about any effects on your life. Has that changed? In what ways?

6. I would like to know ways in which your relationships with friends, coworkers, and neighbors may have been affected. Tell me about how you felt other people reacted to you when they found out. How about today? [Probe]

7. Are there some people that you feel have been supportive of you? [Probe for details] Are there any people who you feel are unsupportive of you? [Probe for details]

8. Do you have any hobbies or sports that interest you? Have those been affected in any way? [Probe for details]

9. Have any other family members also been affected, in your opinion? [Probe]

10. Tell me what has been most difficult for you.

11. What would you want the public to know about dealing with a family member's death sentence?

12. Is there anything that I haven't asked you about that you think is important? [If yes, probe for details]

Appendix C. Demographics of Interview Subjects

I. Face-to-face interviews in Oklahoma[1]

A. Kendra: Sister (white, thirties) of man on death row executed after first interview. Reinterviewed following execution.

B. Verna: Sister (white, fifties) of man formerly on death row but exonerated by DNA evidence. Multiple interviews.

C. Sandra: Sister (white, forties) of man formerly on death row but exonerated by DNA evidence. Multiple interviews.

D. Matt: Brother (white, thirties) of man on death row. Interviewed twice.

E. Dana: Sister (white, twenties) of man on death row (she was a teenager at time of offense).

F. Tasha: Sister (black, twenties) of woman on death row subsequently executed. Her brother Bobby was present during part of the interview. His comments are included, but he is not treated as a separate interview subject.

G. Carol: Mother (white, late forties) of man on death row approaching execution. Interviewed twice. Her husband, Dan, participated in the interview as well. (Same case as subject E.)

H. Sharon: Mother (white, fifties) of man on death row who has had multiple trials. Currently exploring question of innocence and possible new trial. Multiple interviews.

I. Jim: Father (white, fifties) of man on death row. Husband of subject H.

J. Jeannette: Mother (black, fifties) of man executed. Interviewed shortly before and shortly after execution.

K. LaVerne: Mother (white, sixties) of man executed. Initially contacted me less than a week after execution. Interviewed later.

L. Lydia: Mother (white, eighties) of man given death sentence that was later commuted to life. Multiple interviews.

M. Gloria: Mother (white, early forties) of man charged with capital offense but death sentence dropped before trial. He received a life sentence. Her other son was present during the interview and contributed some comments.

N. Lynette: Mother (white, forties) of two men charged with capital offense (they are both mixed race).

O. Jim Fowler: Father (white, seventies) of man on death row subsequently executed. Interviewed multiple times before and after execution.

P. Ann Fowler: Stepmother (white, sixties) of man on death row subsequently executed. Interviewed multiple times before and after execution. Wife of subject O.

Q. Naomi: Mother (Hispanic, fifties) of man executed shortly before interview. He was half Hispanic, half Native American.

R. Andrea: Mother (early fifties) of man given death sentence subsequently commuted to life without parole due to mental illness.

S. Linda: Wife (white, thirties) of man on death row

T. Lynn: Daughter (Hispanic, twenties) of man on death row (white) who died of natural causes subsequent to initial interview. Reinterviewed once.

U. Misty: Daughter (white, twenties) of man on death row.

V. Martha: Cousin (white female, sixties) of man on death row. No contact at time of initial interview with prisoner since conviction. Second interview.

W. Jane: Cousin (white female, fifties) of woman on death row subsequently executed.

X. Sharla: Niece (African American, nineteen) of man executed shortly before interview.

Y. Nedra: Grandmother (African American, seventies) of man on death row whom she had raised.

II. Electronic interviews[2]

A. Denise: Sister of man on death row whom she believes is innocent.

B. Lisa: Sister of executed man. She had not had contact with him until shortly before execution.

C. Sonia: Sister of executed man. (Same case as subject II B.)

D. Paula: Mother of juvenile charged with capital offense who received life sentence.

E. Eugene: Uncle of man on death row.

F. Bob: Brother of executed man.

G. David Kaczynski: Brother of man charged with capital offense who ultimately pled guilty and received life sentence.

H. Mandy: Sister of man on death row.

I. Laura: Mother of man who was executed shortly after interview.

J. Jason: Brother of a man who had been executed (interviewed by postal mail at his request).

K. Kathy: Sister of man on death row who is developmentally disabled as well as mentally ill.

L. Melinda: Niece of executed man.

M. Tina: Sister of man on death row who is claiming innocence.

N. Judy: Mother of mentally ill man on death row.

O. Alice: Mother of man on death row.

P. Tanya: Sister of man on death row.

Q. Doris: Mother of man convicted of capital offense.

R. Donna: Mother of mentally ill man on death row.

S. Marissa: Common-law wife of executed man.

T. Karen: Mother of man on formerly on death row, sentence commuted.

U. Carla: Mother of woman on death row.

V. Doris: Mother of man on death row.

W. Margaret: Mother of man currently on death row.

X. Beverly: Mother of man charged with capital offense but charges dropped after one year.

Y. Marie: Grandmother of man on death row.

Z. Sarah: Mother of man who died of natural causes on death row.

AA. Lila: Aunt of executed woman. Interviewed after execution.

BB. Martina: Sister of man on death row who is arguing innocence.

III. Fictive kin interviews include postconviction spouses and pen pals

A. Vanessa: Pen pal to several death row prisoners.

B. Katrina: Pen pal to several death row prisoners.

C. Dolores: Pen pal, close relationship with one death row prisoner.

D. Juanita: Teacher in South America who has established relationship with man on death row.

E. Ron: College student whose baby-sitter when he was a child
was executed.

F. Steve Presson: Attorney and friend to several death row prisoners.

G. Bob: Minister to several death row prisoners.

H. Tanika: Wife of death row prisoner.

I. Cheryl: Wife of man already executed.

J. Judy: Wife of man on death row.

K. Brenda: Wife of man on death row.

L. Cindy: Wife of man executed in the 1980s.

M. Loretta: Wife of man formerly on death row whose sentence was
commuted.

N. Sue Norton: Victim's daughter who befriended perpetrator.

O. Johnnie Carter: Victim's grandmother who provided support to
offender at his execution.

Notes

Preface

1. Fox Butterfield, "Killings Increase in Many Big Cities," *New York Times*, December 21, 2001, http://www.nytimes.com/2001/12/21/national/21CRIM .html.
2. John F. Galliher, Larry W. Koch, David Patrick Keys, and Teresa J. Guess, *America without the Death Penalty: States Leading the Way* (Boston: Northeastern University Press, 2002).
3. Craig Haney, "Mitigation and the Study of Lives: On the Roots of Violent Criminality and the Nature of Capital Justice," in *America's Experiment with Capital Punishment*, ed. J. R. Acker, R. M. Bohm, and C. S. Lanier, 351–384 (Durham, NC: Carolina Academic Press, 1998); D. O. Lewis et al., "Neuropsychatric, Psychoeducational, and Family Characteristics of 14 Juveniles Condemned to Death in the United States," *American Journal of Psychiatry* 14, no. 5 (1988): 584–589.

Chapter 1 Introduction

1. David L. Altheide, *Creating Fear: News and the Construction of Crisis* (New York: Aldine de Gruyter, 2002); Ray Surette, *Media, Crime and Criminal Justice: Images and Realities* (Belmont, CA: West/Wadsworth, 1998); Nicole Rafter, *Shots in the Mirror: Crime Films and Society* (New York: Oxford University Press, 2000); Leonard Beeghley, *Homicide: A Sociological Explanation* (Lanham, MD: Rowman & Littlefield, 2003).
2. Altheide, *Creating Fear*, 134.
3. Todd Clear, *Harm in American Penology: Offenders, Victims and Their Communities* (Albany, NY: SUNY Press, 1994), 119; Samuel R. Gross and Phoebe C. Ellsworth, "Second Thoughts: Americans' Views on the Death Penalty at the Turn of the Century," in *Beyond Repair? America's Death Penalty*, ed. S. P. Garvey, 7 (Durham, NC: Duke University Press, 2003).
4. Galliher et al., *America without the Death Penalty*.
5. Rafter, *Shots in the Mirror*, vii, 40.
6. John Grisham, *The Chamber* (New York: Doubleday, 1994).
7. Austin Sarat discusses the role of movies, including those mentioned, and popular culture in the death penalty debate in great detail in chapter 8 of his book, *When the State Kills: Capital Punishment and the American Condition* (Princeton, NJ: Princeton University Press, 2001).
8. *The Life of David Gale*, Universal Pictures, 2003.
9. In three recent polls, the OU POLL (Oklahoma University Public Opinion Learning Laboratory) found that over 80 percent of the subjects interviewed

believed that an innocent person had been executed. The first poll, conducted in August and September of 2001, was of a nationally representative sample. The second and third polls, conducted in 2003, were conducted with Oklahoma residents, stratified by age, sex, and race. Additional information about declining support for capital punishment can be found in the Public Opinion section of the Death Penalty Information Center (http://www.deathpenalty-info.org). Recent studies show declining support for capital punishment, particularly when compared to support for alternate punishments such as life without the possibility of parole.

10. Federal Bureau of Investigation, *Crime in the United States: Uniform Crime Reports, 2001,* sec. 2, 19 (Washington, DC: Federal Bureau of Investigation, 2002).

11. M. Watt Espy and John Smykla, *Executions in the United States, 1608–1987: The Espy File,* machine-readable data file (Ann Arbor, MI: ICPSR, 1987); Robert M. Bohm, *DeathQuest II* (Cincinnati: Anderson, 2003).

12. Hugh Adam Bedau, *The Death Penalty in America* (New York: Oxford University Press, 1982).

13. Eric Prokosch, "Death Penalty Developments," in *The International Sourcebook on Capital Punishment,* ed. W. A. Schabas, 66–80 (Boston: Northeastern University Press, 1997); William A. Schabas, ed., *The International Sourcebook on Capital Punishment* (Boston: Northeastern University Press, 1997).

14. *Furman v. Georgia,* 408 U.S. 238 (1972); Bohm, *DeathQuestII.*

15. *Woodson v. North Carolina,* 428 U.S. 280 (1976).

16. *Gregg v. Georgia,* 428, U.S. 153 (1976); David R. Dow, "How the Death Penalty Really Works," in *Machinery of Death: The Reality of America's Death Penalty Regime,* ed. D. R. Dow and M. Dow, 11–35 (New York: Routledge, 2002).

17. Death Penalty Information Center, 2004, http://deathpenaltyinfo.org.

18. Stephen B. Bright, "Legalized Lynching: Race, the Death Penalty and the United States Courts," in *The International Sourcebook on Capital Punishment,* ed. W. A. Schabas, 5–29 (Boston: Northeastern University Press, 1997); Dow, "How the Death Penalty Really Works."

19. Carol Steiker and Jordan M. Steiker, "Judicial Developments in Capital Punishment Law," in *America's Experiment with Capital Punishment: Reflections on the Past, Present and Future of the Ultimate Penal Sanction,* 2nd ed., ed. J. R. Acker et al., 55–83 (Durham, NC: Carolina Academic Press, 2003).

20. Governor George Ryan, speech at Northwestern University, January 11, 2003. See also Steiker and Steiker, "Judicial Developments," 55.

21. *Pulley v. Harris,* 465 U.S. 37 (1985).

22. *Callins v. Collins,* 510 U.S. 1141 (1994).

23. Bedau, *Death Penalty in America;* Stephen Nathanson, "Does It Matter If the Death Penalty Is Arbitrarily Administered?" in *Punishment and the Death Penalty: The Current Debate,* ed. R. M. Baird and S. E. Rosenbaum, 161 (Amherst, NY: Prometheus Books, 1985).

24. Oklahoma Statutes, title 21, chap. 24, sec. 701.12, 1981, (4) and (5).

25. Mark Costanzo, *Just Revenge: Costs and Consequences of the Death Penalty* (New York: St. Martin's Press, 1997); Gross and Ellsworth, "Second Thoughts," 7–57.

26. Jonathan Simon and Christina Spaulding, "Tokens of Our Esteem: Aggravating Factors in the Era of Deregulated Death Penalties," in *The Killing State:*

Capital Punishment in Law, Politics, and Culture, ed. A. Sarat, 81–113 (New York: Oxford University Press, 1999).

27. Marian J. Borg, "Vicarious Homicide Victimization and Support for Capital Punishment: A Test of Black's Theory of Law," *Criminology* 36, no. 3 (1998): 537–567.
28. Costanzo, *Just Revenge,* 148.
29. Costanzo, *Just Revenge,* 148–149.
30. Sarah Rimer, "A Father Feels the Weight of His Son's Sins," *New York Times,* April 29, 2001, http://www.nytimes.com/2001/04/29/national/MCVE .html (accessed April 29, 2001).
31. Death Penalty Information Center; Tracy Snell, *Capital Punishment, 2001* (Washington, DC: U.S. Department of Justice, Bureau of Justice Statistics, 2002); Criminal Justice Project of the NAACP Legal Defense and Educational Fund, *Death Row U.S.A., Summer 2003,* NAACP, http://www.death-penaltyinfo.org/DEATHROWUSArecent.pdf (accessed October 28, 2003).
32. Costanzo, *Just Revenge.*
33. Franklin E. Zimring, *The Contradictions of American Capital Punishment* (New York: Oxford University Press, 2003).
34. T. R. Miller, M. A. Cohen, and B. Wiersema, *Victim Costs and Consequences: A New Look* (Washington, DC: National Institute of Justice, 1996); Rachel King, *Don't Kill in Our Names: Families of Murder Victims Speak Out against the Death Penalty* (New Brunswick, NJ: Rutgers University Press, 2003); Beeghley, *Homicide,* 2003; M. A. Cohen, T. R. Miller, and S. B. Rossman, "The Costs and Consequences of Violent Behavior in the United States," in *Understanding and Preventing Violence,* vol. 4, ed. J. Roth and A. Reiss, 67–116 (Washington, DC: National Academy Press, 1994).
35. Federal Bureau of Investigation, 2002.
36. Mark D. Reed and Brenda Sims Blackwell, "Families of Homicide Victims: A Review and Recommendations for Current Research and Practice," paper presented at the American Society of Criminology meetings, Chicago, November 2002; Beeghley, *Homicide;* E. K. Rynearson, "Psychotherapy of Bereavement after Homicide: Be Offensive," *Psychotherapy in Practice* 2 (1996): 421–428; Catherine M. Sanders, *Grief: The Mourning After* (New York: John Wiley & Sons, 1999); A. W. Burgess, "Family Reaction to Homicide," *Journal of Orthopsychiatry* 45 (1975): 391–398; R. I. Mawby and S. Walklate, *Critical Victimology* (Thousand Oaks, CA: Sage, 1995); Uli Orth, "Secondary Victimization of Crime Victims by Criminal Proceedings," *Social Justice Research* 15 (2002): 313–325; Deborah Spungen, *Homicide: The Hidden Victims: A Guide for Professionals* (Belmont, CA: Sage, 1997).
37. Margaret Vandiver and Felix M. Berardo, "'It's Like Dying Every Day': The Families of Condemned Prisoners," *Families, Crime and Criminal Justice* 2 (2000): 339–358; Margaret Vandiver, "The Impact of the Death Penalty on the Families of Homicide Victims and of Condemned Prisoners," in *America's Experiment with Capital Punishment,* 2nd ed., ed. J. R. Acker et al., 613–645 (Durham, NC: Carolina Academic Press, 2003).; Pauline Boss, *Ambiguous Loss: Learning to Live with Unresolved Grief* (Cambridge, MA: Harvard University Press, 1999); Margaret Vandiver, "Coping with Death: Families of the Terminally Ill, Homicide Victims, and Condemned Prisoners," in *Facing the Death Penalty: Essays on a Cruel and Unusual Punishment,* ed. M. Radelet, 123–138 (Philadelphia: Temple University Press, 1989).

38. Vandiver, "Impact of the Death Penalty"; J. O. Smykla, "The Human Impact of Capital Punishment: Interviews with Families of Persons on Death Row," *Journal of Criminal Justice* 15 (1987): 331–347; Rachel King and Katherine Norgard, "What about Our Families? Using the Impact on Death Row Defendants' Family Members as a Mitigating Factor in Death Penalty Sentencing Hearings," *Florida State Law Review* 26 (1999): 1119–1173.

39. Reed and Blackwell, "Families of Homicide Victims"; Vandiver, "Impact of the Death Penalty"; Vandiver and Berardo, "'It's Like Dying Every Day.'"

40. Clear, *Harm in American Penology; Booth v. Maryland,* 482 U.S. 496 (1987); Sarat, *When the State Kills.*

41. Oklahoma Country District Attorney 2002, [online], http://www.oklahomacounty.org/districtattorney/da2.htm.

42. *Daily Oklahoman,* January 16, 2001.

43. Costanzo, *Just Revenge;* Robert Renny Cushing and Susannah Sheffer, *Dignity Denied: The Experience of Murder Victims' Family Members Who Oppose the Death Penalty* (Cambridge, MA: Murder Victims' Families for Reconciliation, 2002); King, *Don't Kill in Our Names; State ex rel. Lamm v. Nebraska Bd. of Pardons,* 260 Neb. 1000, 620 N.W.2d 763 (2001).

44. King and Norgard, "What about Our Families?"; Vandiver and Berardo, "'It's Like Dying Every Day.'"

45. Vandiver and Berardo, "'It's Like Dying Every Day.'"

46. King and Norgard, "What about Our Families?" 1138.

47. Smykla, "Human Impact of Capital Punishment."

48. King and Norgard, "What about Our Families?" 1138; Bruce Arrigo and Christopher R. Williams, "Victims Vices, Victim Voices, and Impact Statements: On the Place of Emotion and the Role of Restorative Justice in Capital Sentencing," *Crime and Delinquency* 49 (2003): 603–626.

49. Rev. Jesse L. Jackson Sr., Rep. Jesse L. Jackson Jr., and Bruce Shapiro, *Legal Lynching: The Death Penalty and America's Future* (New York: New Press, 2001); Arrigo and Williams, "Victims Vices"; Sarat, *When the State Kills;* Edna Erez and L. Roeger, "The Effect Victim Impact Statements Have on Sentencing Patterns and Outcomes: The Australian Experience," *Journal of Criminal Justice* 23 (1995): 363–375; Clear, *Harm in American Penology;* Paul Wright "'Victims' Rights' as a Stalking-Horse for State Repression," in *Prison Nation,* ed. T. Herivel and P. Wright, 60–65 (New York: Routledge, 2003).

50. Cushing and Sheffer, *Dignity Denied.*

51. Mark S. Umbreit and Betty Vos, "Homicide Survivors Meet the Offender Prior to Execution: Restorative Justice through Dialogue," *Homicide Studies* 4 (2000): 63–87; Mark S. Umbreit, "Restorative Justice through Victim-Offender Mediation: A Multi-Site Assessment," *Western Criminology Review* 1 (1998), http://wc.sonomo.edu/v1n1/umbreit.html.

52. Cushing and Sheffer, *Dignity Denied;* King, *Don't Kill in Our Names.*

53. Todd Clear, "Backfire: When Incarceration Increases Crime," *Journal of the Oklahoma Criminal Justice Research Consortium* 3 (1996): 7–17; S. W. Daniel and C. J. Barrett, "The Needs of Prisoners' Wives: A Challenge for the Mental Health Professionals," *Community Mental Health Journal* 17 (1981): 310–322; L. T. Fishman, "The World of Prisoners' Wives," in *Long-Term Imprisonment: Policy, Science and Correctional Practice,* ed. T. J. Flanagan (Thousand Oaks, CA: Sage, 1995); Katherine Gabel and Denise Johnston, *Children of Incarcerated Parents* (New York: Lexington Books, 1995); John Hagan, "The Next Genera-

tion: Children of Prisoners," *Journal of the Oklahoma Criminal Justice Research Consortium* 3 (1996): 19–28; Creasie Finney Hairston, "Family Ties during Imprisonment: Important to Whom and for What?" *Journal of Sociology and Social Welfare* 18 (1991): 87–104; Creasie Finney Hairston, "The Forgotten Parent: Understanding the Forces that Influence Incarcerated Fathers' Relationships with Their Children," *Child Welfare* 77 (1998): 617–630; Denise Johnston, "Effects of Parental Incarceration," in *Children of Incarcerated Parents,* ed. K. Gabel and D. Johnston (New York: Lexington Books, 1995); C. Kampfer, "Post-Traumatic Stress Reactions in Children of Incarcerated Mothers," in *Children of Incarcerated Parents,* ed. K. Gabel and D. Johnston (New York: Lexington Books, 1995); Christopher Mumola, *Bureau of Justice Special Report: Incarcerated Parents and Their Children,* BJS Publication No. NCJ 1832335 (Washington, DC: Department of Justice, Bureau of Justice Statistics, 2000); Joan Petersilia, "Prisoner Reentry: Public Safety and Reintegration Challenges," *Prison Journal* 81 (2001): 360–375; Susan F. Sharp, "Mothers in Prison: Issues in Parent-Child Contact," in *The Incarcerated Woman: Rehabilitative Programming in Women's Prisons,* ed. S. F. Sharp, 151–165 (Upper Saddle River, NJ: Prentice-Hall, 2003); Sharp et al., "Gender Differences in the Impact of Incarceration on the Children and Families of Drug Offenders," in *Interrogating Social Justice,* ed. M. Corsianos and K. A. Train, 218–246 (Toronto: Canadian Scholars' Press, 1999); Susan F. Sharp and Susan Marcus-Mendoza, "It's a Family Affair: Incarcerated Mothers and Their Families," *Women and Criminal Justice* 12 (2001): 21–49; Jeremy Travis and Joan Petersilia, "Reentry Reconsidered: A New Look at an Old Question," *Crime and Delinquency* 47 (2001): 291–313; Ralph A. Weisheit and J. M. Klofas, "The Impact of Jail: Collateral Cost and Affective Response," *Journal of Offender Counseling, Services and Rehabilitation* 14 (1989): 51–65; Marsha Weissman and Candace M. LaRue, "Earning Trust from Youths with None to Spare," *Child Welfare* 77 (1998): 579–590.

54. Nell Bernstein, "Relocation Blues," in *Prison Nation,* ed. T. Herivel and P. Wright, 106–111 (New York: Routledge, 2003); Lori B. Girshick, "I Leave in the Dark of Morning," *Prison Journal* 73 (1994): 93–97; Petersilia, "Prisoner Reentry."

55. Sharp and Marcus-Mendoza, "It's a Family Affair."

56. Clear, "Backfire: When Incarceration Increases Crime."

57. Barbara Bloom, "Why Punish the Children? A Reappraisal of the Children of Incarcerated Mothers in America," *IARCA Journal* 6 (1993): 14–17; Joan Moore, "Bearing the Burden: How Incarceration Weakens Inner-City Communities," *Journal of the Oklahoma Criminal Justice Research Consortium* 3 (1996); Petersilia, "Prisoner Reentry."

58. Hugh Adam Bedau, *The Case against the Death Penalty* (Washington, DC: American Civil Liberties Union, 1997).

CHAPTER 2   DEALING WITH THE HORROR

1. Lewis et al., "Neuropsychatric, Psychoeducational, and Family Characteristics," 584–589; Michael L. Radelet, Margaret Vandiver, and Felix M. Berardo, "Families, Prisons, and Men with Death Sentences: The Human Impact of Structured Uncertainty," *Journal of Family Issues* 4 (1982): 593–612; Vandiver, "Coping with Death"; Margaret Vandiver, "Beyond All Justice: The Death

Penalty and Families of the Condemned," *Odyssey* (1992): 56–63; Vandiver, "Impact of the Death Penalty"; Vandiver and Berardo, "'It's Like Dying Every Day'"; King and Norgard, "What about Our Families?"

2. Bedau, *Case against the Death Penalty*. For a more in-depth discussion of this, see Phillip J. Cook and Donna B. Slawson with Lori Gries, *The Cost of Processing Murder Cases in North Carolina* (Raleigh, NC: Administrative Office of the Courts, 1993); Margot Garey, "The Cost of Taking a Life: Dollars and Sense of the Death Penalty," *University of California–Davis Law Review* 18 (1985): 1221–1273; Robert L. Spangenberg and Elizabeth Walsh, "Capital Punishment or Life Imprisonment? Some Cost Considerations," *Loyola–Los Angeles Law Review* 23 (1989): 45–58.

3. Mumia Abu-Jamal, *Live from Death Row* (Reading, MA: Addison-Wesley, 1995); Kenneth Bolton, "Book Review: Live from Death Row," in *The International Sourcebook on Capital Punishment*, ed. W. A Schabas, 102–106 (Boston: Northeastern University Press, 1997).

4. Amnesty International, *State Cruelty against Families*, AMR 51/132/2001.

5. Vandiver and Berardo, "'It's Like Dying Every Day,'" 3349.

6. Elizabeth Beck et al., "Seeking Sanctuary: Interviews with Family Members of Capital Defendants," *Cornell Law Review* 88 (2003): 343–381; Boss, *Ambiguous Loss;* King and Norgard, "What about Our Families?"; Vandiver, "Impact of the Death Penalty"; Vandiver and Berardo, "'It's Like Dying Every Day.'"

7. Vandiver and Berardo, "'It's Like Dying Every Day.'"

8. Ibid.

9. Snell, *Capital Punishment, 2001;* James Liebman et al., *A Broken System, Part II: Why There Is So Much Error in Capital Cases, and What Can Be Done about It,* Columbia Law School, 2002, http://www2.law.columbia.edu/brokensystem 2/index2.html (accessed October 14, 2003).

10. Citizens United for the Reform of Errants (CURE) is a group that advocates for prisoners and their families.

11. An open-ended schedule of questions was utilized. The questions covered how the subjects found out their relative had been arrested and might be charged with a capital offense, how they had initially reacted, and the subsequent effects on their lives. Subjects were asked at the end of each interview what they wanted known about the effects of the death penalty on the families of offenders. The initial face-to-face interviews took approximately two hours each, although one lasted over four hours. Several subjects were reinterviewed at subsequent points in time.

12. There is a large body of literature dealing with the use of interview schedules and with instruments for in-depth interviews. See, for example, John S. Lofland and Lyn Lofland, *Analyzing Social Settings: A Guide to Qualitative Observation and Analysis* (Belmont, CA: Sage, 1995).

13. Earl Babbie, *The Practice of Social Research* (Belmont, CA: Wadsworth, 1992); Bruce L. Berg, *Qualitative Research Methods for the Social Sciences* (Boston, MA: Allyn & Bacon, 2001); W. Lawrence Neuman, *Social Research Methods: Qualitative and Quantitative Approaches,* 2nd ed. (Boston: Allyn & Bacon, 1994); Donald Polkinghorne, *Methodology for the Human Sciences: Systems of Inquiry* (Albany, NY: SUNY Press, 1983); Leonard Schatzman and Anselm Strauss, *Field Research: Strategies for a Natural Sociology* (Englewood Cliffs, NJ: Prentice-Hall, 1973); Dorothy Smith, "A Sociology for Women," in *The Prism of Sex,* ed. J. Shermon and E. T. Beck, 135–187 (Madison: University of Wisconsin Press, 1979).

14. Lofland and Lofland, *Analyzing Social Settings,* 19.
15. Jeff Ferrell and Mark S. Hamm, "True Confessions," in *Ethnography at the Edge,* ed. J. Ferrell and M. S. Hamm, 2–10 (Boston: Northeastern University Press, 1998); Barry Glaser and Anselm Strauss, *The Discovery of Grounded Theory: Strategies for Qualitative Research* (Chicago: Aldine, 1967).
16. Mark Fleisher, "Ethnographers, Pimps, and the Company Store," in *Ethnography at the Edge,* ed. J. Ferrell and M. S. Hamm, 44–64 (Boston: Northeastern University Press, 1998). Fleisher argues that the neutral approach of criminology results in crime statistics, transforming those who commit crime into "faceless agents of crime" and victims into "faceless statistics" (p. 9). The families of those facing the death penalty are not "faceless," and I have chosen to "put a face on death" by letting their own words and experiences tell the story of family members of the accused.
17. Graham Kalton, *An Introduction to Survey Sampling* (Newbury Park, CA: Sage, 1983).

CHAPTER 3   TRYING TO COPE

1. John Bowlby, *Attachment and Loss: Loss, Sadness, and Depression* (New York: Basic Books, 1980); Sanders, *Grief: The Mourning After.*
2. R. J. Kastenbaum, *Death, Society and Human Experience,* 6th ed. (Boston: Allyn & Bacon, 1998); Sanders, *Grief: The Mourning After.*
3. James Liebman, Jeff Fagan, and Valerie West, "Technical Errors Can Kill," *National Law Journal,* special ed., September 2000.
4. Mark Fuhrman, *Death and Justice: An Expose of Oklahoma's Death Row Machine* (New York: William Morrow, 2003). Mark Fuhrman gained national fame, or more appropriately notoriety, for his role in the O. J. Simpson murder trial. Since his retirement, he has written several "true crime books" prior to his book on Oklahoma's system of capital punishment. His book about capital punishment in Oklahoma arose out of his Spokane talk show, where an Oklahoma defense attorney raised the issue of incompetence and unethical testimony by a police chemist who had testified in numerous capital cases.
5. Paula's quotes are from an unpublished manuscript written by the subject.
6. Barry Scheck and Peter Neufeld established the Innocence Project in the early 1990s to deal with the flood of requests from prisoners around the country wanting to establish their innocence through DNA testing. For more detail, see Barry Scheck, Peter Neufeld, and Jim Dwyer, *Actual Innocence: When Justice Goes Wrong and How to Make It Right* (New York: Penguin Putnam, 2001).

CHAPTER 4   THE GRIEF PROCESS

1. Elisabeth Kübler-Ross, *On Death and Dying* (New York: Scribner Classics, 1997 [1969]).
2. Boss, *Ambiguous Loss;* Stephen Freeman, "Identity Maintenance and Adaptation: A Multilevel Analysis of Response to Loss," *Research in Organizational Behavior* 21 (1998): 247–294; Kastenbaum, *Death, Society and Human Experience;* G. L. Villereal, "A Comparison of Vietnam Era Veterans and Their Combat Exposure with the Symptomatology of Dying," *Omega: Journal of Death and Dying* 36 (1998): 305–330.

3. David Adams, "The Consequences of Sudden Traumatic Death: The Vulnerability of Bereaved Children and Adolescents and Ways Professionals Can Help," in *Complicated Grieving and Bereavement,* ed. G. R. Cox, R. A. Bendiksen, and R. G. Stevenson, 23–20 (Amityville, NY: Baywood, 2002); Thomas Attig, "Relearning the World: Always Complicated, Sometimes More Than Others," in *Complicated Grieving and Bereavement,* ed. G. R. Cox, R. A. Bendiksen, and R. G. Stevenson, 7 (Amityville, NY: Baywood, 2002); Kastenbaum, *Death, Society and Human Experience;* Sheila Payne, Sandra Horn, and Marilyn Relf, *Loss and Bereavement* (Buckingham, England: Open University Press, 1999); Frank, *At the Will of the Body* (Boston: Houghton Mifflin, 1991).

4. Margaret S. Stroebe and Henk Schut, "The Dual Process Model of Coping with Bereavement: Rationale and Description," *Death Studies* 23 (1999): 197–224; William Worden, *Grief Counselling and Grief Therapy* (London: Routledge, 1991).

5. Bowlby, *Attachment and Loss;* Sigmund Freud, "Mourning and Melancholia," in *The Pelican Freud Library,* vol. 11, *On Metapsychology: The Theory of Psychoanalysis,* 245–268 (London: Penguin, 1984 [1917]); Harry Stack Sullivan, *Clinical Studies in Psychiatry* (New York: W. W. Norton, 1956).

6. Dennis Klass, Phyllis R. Silverman, and Steven L. Nickman, *Continuing Bonds: New Understandings of Grief* (Philadelphia: Taylor & Francis, 1996); M. Osterweis, Frederic Solomon, and Morris Green, eds., *Bereavement Reactions, Consequences and Care* (Washington, DC: National Academy Press, 1984); Payne, Horn, and Relf, *Loss and Bereavement;* Camille Wortman and Roxanne Silver, "The Myth of Coping with Loss," *Journal of Consulting and Clinical Psychology* 57 (1989): 349–357.

7. Attig, "Relearning the World"; Gerry R. Cox, Robert A. Bendiksen, and Robert G. Stevenson, *Complicated Grieving and Bereavement: Understanding and Treating People Experiencing Loss* (Amityville, NY: Baywood, 2002); Larry Darrah, "Camouflaged Grief: Survivor Grief in Families of Soldiers Still Listed as MIA," in *Handbook of Bereavement Research: Consequences, Coping and Care,* ed. M. S. Stroebe et al., 85–97 (Washington, DC: American Psychological Association, 2002); Robert A. Neimeyer, Holly G. Prigerson, and Betty Davies, "Mourning and Meaning," *American Behavioral Scientist* 46 (2002): 235–251.

8. Darrah, "Camouflaged Grief."

9. Darrah, "Camouflaged Grief."

10. Boss, *Ambiguous Loss.*

11. Susan Folkman, "Revised Coping Theory and the Process of Bereavement," in *Handbook of Bereavement Research: Consequences, Coping and Care,* ed. M. S. Stroebe et al., 563–584 (Washington, DC: American Psychological Association, 2001).

12. J. Dominion, "Commentary on 'Normal Grief: Good or Bad? Health or Disease?'" *Philosophy, Psychiatry and Psychology* 1, no. 4 (1994): 221–222.

13. Ginnie Graham, "There's Always Those Left Behind," *Tulsa World,* September 24, 2000.

14. Furhman, *Death and Justice;* Barry Scheck, Peter Neufeld, and James Dwyer, *Actual Innocence: When Justice Goes Wrong and How to Make It Right* (New York: Penguin Putnam, 2001).

15. Boss, *Ambiguous Loss.*

16. Letter from Father Gregory Gier, Rector, Holy Family Cathedral, Tulsa, Oklahoma, undated.

17. Electronic message, January 4, 2001.
18. Cynthia Hubert, "Role in Capture Haunts Kaczynski's Brother," *Sacramento Bee,* January 19, 1997, http://www.unabombertrial.com/archive/1997/ 011997–2.html (accessed January 26, 2004).
19. David Kaczynski, "The Death Penalty Up Close and Personal," New Yorkers Against the Death Penalty, http://www.nyadp.org/main/david.html (accessed January 26, 2004).
20. Kaczynski, "The Death Penalty Up Close and Personal."
21. Ibid.
22. Ibid.

CHAPTER 5   FACING THE END

1. James R. Acker and Charles S. Lanier, "Beyond Human Ability? The Rise and Fall of Death Penalty Legislation," in *America's Experiment with Capital Punishment,* 2nd ed., ed. J. R. Acker, R. M. Bohm, and C. S. Lanier, 85–119 (Durham, NC: Carolina Academic Press, 2003). Some have argued that the last public execution was in Missouri in 1937. In the execution of Roscoe "Red" Jackson in Galena, Missouri (May 26, 1937), invitations were issued to more than four hundred people. Children were not allowed. It was not truly public. Instead, it was held within a ten-foot stockade (Perry T. Ryan, "The Last Public Execution," *The Last Public Execution in the United States,* http://www.geocities.com/lastpublichang/LastPublicExecution.htm [accessed on May 9, 2004]).
2. Sarat, *When the State Kills.* For a more detailed discussion of the viewing of capital punishment, see Michel Foucault, *Discipline and Punish: The Birth of the Prison* (New York: Vintage Books, 1977). Foucault traces the history of punishment from punishment of the corporal body to punishment of the mind through imprisonment. He goes into the history of capital punishment and the transfer of responsibility for revenge from the individual victim to the state.
3. Wendy Lesser, *Pictures at an Execution: An Inquiry into the Subject of Murder* (Cambridge, MA: Harvard University Press, 1993); Sarat, *When the State Kills.*
4. Maj. Daniel Hudson, *Managing Death-Sentenced Inmates: A Survey of Practices,* 2nd ed. (Lanham, MD: American Correctional Association, 2000).
5. Sarat, *When the State Kills.*
6. ALIVE, "In Memoriam: Gerald Bivins," http://www.todesstrafe-usa.de/death_penalty/memoriam_e_bivins.htm (accessed January 16, 2003).
7. Ann B. Sherer, "A United Methodist Pastor's Vigil on Death Row," *Hoosier United Methodist News,* 2001, http://www.inareaumc.org/april101/comment.htm (accessed January 16, 2003).
8. *The Free Dictionary,* 2004, http://www.thefreedictionary.com/executive %20clemency.
9. *Herrera v. Collins,* 506 U.S. 390 (1993).
10. Acker and Lanier, "Beyond Human Ability?"
11. Death Penalty Information Center, 2004. See also Michael L. Radelet and Barbara A. Zsembik, "Executive Clemency in Post-*Furman* Capital Cases," *University of Richmond Law Review* 27 (1993): 289–314.
12. Bohm, *DeathQuest II.*
13. National Public Radio, "Witness to an Execution," *All Things Considered,*

October 20, 2000, http://www.soundportraits.org/on-air/witness_to_an _execution/ (accessed January 16, 2004).

14. For an in-depth description of the methods of execution, see chapter 4 in Bohm, *DeathQuest II.*

15. Michael L. Radelet, "Botched Executions," Death Penalty Information Center, http://deathpenaltyinfo.org/article.php?scid=8&did=478 (accessed January 16, 2003).

16. Phil Magers, "Analysis: Is Lethal Injection Humane?" *Washington Times,* http://washingtontimes.com (accessed January 12, 2003).

CHAPTER 6 AFTERMATH

1. Cox , Bendiksen, and Stevenson, *Complicated Grieving and Bereavement.*

2. Hudson, *Managing Death-Sentenced Inmates.* See appendix A of this book for a listing of state policies on contact visits.

3. Wortman and Silver, "The Myth of Coping with Loss," 349–357.

4. See Camille Wortman and Roxanne Silver, "The Myth of Coping with Loss Revisited," in *Handbook of Bereavement Research: Consequences, Coping and Care,* ed. M. S. Stroebe et al., 405–429 (Washington, DC: American Psychological Association, 2001).

5. Neimeyer, Prigerson, and Davies, "Mourning and Meaning," 235–251.

6. These words were printed in the bulletin for Mark Fowler's memorial service.

7. Fuhrman, Death and Justice.

CHAPTER 7 "BUT HE'S INNOCENT"

1. William M. Holmes, "Who Are the Wrongfully Convicted on Death Row?" in *Wrongly Convicted: Perspectives of Failed Justice,* ed. S. A. Westervelt and J. A. Humphrey, 99–113 (New Brunswick, NJ: Rutgers University Press, 2002). Holmes examined Bureau of Justice statistics data from 1970 through 1992, finding 688 overturned convictions. Of these, 58 either had charges dropped or were found not guilty at retrial. Some cases had not reached final disposition, making the estimate low. This analysis only includes those cases in which a higher court found serious flaws in the trial. It is thus a very conservative estimate. It is entirely possible that there are innocent men and women condemned to death in cases that have not been overturned. For further information, see Michael L. Radelet and Hugh Adam Bedau, "Erroneous Convictions and the Death Penalty," in *Wrongly Convicted: Perspectives on Failed Justice,* ed. S. D. Westervelt and J. A. Humphrey, 269–280, (New Brunswick, NJ: Rutgers University Press, 2002); Michael L. Radelet and Hugh Adam Bedau, "The Execution of the Innocent," in *America's Experiment with Capital Punishment: Reflections on the Past, Present, and Future of the Ultimate Penal Sanction,* 2nd ed., ed. J. R. Acker, R. M. Bohm, and C. S. Lanier, 325–344 (Durham, NC: Carolina Academic Press, 2003); Michael L. Radelet, Hugh Adam Bedau, and Constance Putnam, *In Spite of Innocence: The Ordeal of 400 Americans Wrongly Convicted of Crimes Punishable by Death* (Boston: Northeastern University Press, 1992); Michael L. Radelet, William S. Lofquist, and Hugh Adam Bedau, "Prisoners Released from Death Rows Since 1970 Because of Doubts about Their Guilt," *Thomas M. Cooley Law Review* 13 (1996): 907–666; Radelet and Bedau, "Erroneous Convictions"; Radelet and Bedau, "Execution of the Innocent."

2. Death Penalty Information Center.
3. Stanley Cohen, *The Wrong Men: America's Epidemic of Wrongful Death Row Convictions* (New York: Carroll & Graf, 2003).
4. Ken Armstrong and Steve Mills, "Until I Can Be Sure": How the Threat of Executing the Innocent Has Transformed the Death Penalty Debate," in *Beyond Repair? America's Death Penalty,* ed. S. P. Garvey, 94–120 (Durham, NC: Duke University Press, 2003).
5. George Castelle and Elizabeth Loftus, "Misinformation and Wrongful Convictions," in *Wrongly Convicted: Perspectives on Failed Justice,* ed. S. D. Westervelt and J. A. Humphrey, 17–35 (New Brunswick, NJ: Rutgers University Press, 2002); Elizabeth Loftus, *Eyewitness Testimony* (Cambridge, MA: Harvard University Press, 1996); Scheck, Neufeld, and Dwyer, *Actual Innocence.* One problem with eyewitness testimony is transference, wherein the eyewitness finds a face familiar and assumes, because of the familiarity of the individual's appearance, that this is the person they saw commit the crime. However, the individual may look familiar to the eyewitness because he or she has had contact with the "identified perpetrator" in some other situation or has seen pictures of that person.
6. Radelet and Bedau, in "Execution of the Innocent," make the argument that the greatest cause of wrongful convictions is the use of prosecution witnesses who are hoping for some type of leniency in their own cases. Many of these "snitches" turn out to have some involvement in the crime about which they are testifying, and in some cases the actual offender has testified that another person committed the crime (See Scheck, Neufeld, and Dwyer, *Actual Innocence.*)
7. Radelet and Bedau, "Erroneous Convictions"; Scheck, Neufeld, and Dwyer, *Actual Innocence.* Visual hair analysis is a major problem in criminal cases yet consistently used to convict accused murderers. Human hairs do not have characteristics that allow for absolute visual identification. Additionally, forensic testimony has been provided in cases where no analysis had occurred. Medical examiner Ralph Erdmann filed autopsy reports on cases where no autopsy had been done.
8. See Scheck, Neufeld, and Dwyer, *Actual Innocence;* Barry Scheck and Peter Neufeld, "DNA and Innocence Scholarship," in *Wrongly Convicted: Perspectives on Failed Justice,* ed. S. D. Westervelt and J. A. Humphrey, 241–252 (New Brunswick, NJ: Rutgers University Press, 2002). See also Radelet and Bedau, "Execution of the Innocent."
9. Proponents of capital punishment point to this as a technicality rather than evidence of innocence. However, in Sandra's brother's case, the new trial resulted in an acquittal. The state's only evidence was testimony by a dentist with little experience that the bite mark matched her brother's bite impression. In the second trial, a number of highly skilled forensic odontologists provided evidence that there was no way the bite could have come from her brother.
10. Scheck, Neufeld, and Dwyer, *Actual Innocence;* Fuhrman, *Death and Justice.*
11. After this chapter was written, I received information that other evidence has been found that strongly points to the innocence of Misty's father. I spoke with his attorney, who has indicated that they are proceeding in efforts to get his conviction overturned.
12. The previous quote is from the Truth in Justice Web site. To preserve the anonymity of this family, no further information is given.

CHAPTER 8   DOUBLE LOSERS

1. This percentage was calculated using the Federal Bureau of Investigation Uniform Crime Report statistics. Of the 14,054 murders tracked by the FBI, 133 victims of were husbands, 601 were wives, 113 were mothers, 110 were fathers, 239 were sons, 210 were daughters, 87 were brothers, 20 were sisters, and 271 were other family members. An additional 3,217 involved acquaintances, 154 involved boyfriends, 444 were murders of girlfriends, 110 were murders of neighbors, 5 were of employees, and 10 were of employers. The victim-offender relationship information for 42.8 percent of the cases was not provided (6,015), suggesting that it is quite likely that the estimates for murder of family members are far too low. For further information, see the Federal Bureau of Investigation, *Crime in the United States: Uniform Crime Reports, 2001* (Washington, DC: Federal Bureau of Investigation, 2002).
2. Rynearson, "Psychotherapy of Bereavement"; Sanders, *Grief: The Mourning After.*
3. Borg, "Vicarious Homicide Victimization."
4. For a discussion of this in regard to the family of prisoners, see Sharp and Marcus-Mendoza, "It's a Family Affair."
5. Murder Victims' Families for Reconciliation, *Not in Our Name: Murder Victims' Families Speak Out against the Death Penalty* (Cambridge, MA: MVFR, 2003).
6. Murder Victims' Families for Reconciliation.
7. Although the Fowlers had resolved their relationship with Mark in the years prior to his death, the relationship at the time of his offense was conflicted due to his drug use and other criminal behavior. Mark worked for his father in Jim's remodeling business part of the time, but his behavior made it difficult to depend on him. After his conviction, the Fowlers did not visit him for over a year.
8. Payne, Horn, and Relf, *Loss and Bereavement.* The authors describe these factors in addition to age, gender, personality, health problems, initial grief reactions, and social support as factors that should be taken into account in assessing grief reactions. In the Fowlers's case, not only did they have the two murders to cope with, but a few years later Jim's other son was killed in a motorcycle accident.
9. Murder Victims' Families for Reconciliation, *Not in Our Name,* includes the story of Kerry Max Cook, who spent more than two decades on death row in Texas. While he was on death row, his only sibling was killed, leading Cook to evaluate his own position on capital punishment.
10. Bella English, "Kerry Max Cook Spent 20 years on Death Row. His Message is Clear: 'Being Innocent Is Not Enough to Save You,'" *Boston Globe,* January 25, 2003.

CHAPTER 9   FAMILY AFTER THE FACT

1. Frederick Paine, "Looking for a Pen Pal on Death Row?" *New Abolitionist* 15 (May 2000), http://www.nodeathpenalty.org/newab015/fredrickPaine.html (accessed February 13, 2004).
2. Valerie Wallace, "Join the Pen Pal Program," *New Abolitionist* 3, no. 3 (1999). http://www.nodeathpenalty.org/newab012/valerieWallace.html (accessed February 10, 2004).
3. Jan Arriens, "My Pen Pals Await Execution," *BBC News World Edition,* May 8,

2003, http://news.bbc.co.uk/2/hi/uk_news/3008439.stm (accessed February 13, 2004).

4. Canadian Coalition to Abolish the Death Penalty, "Prisoners' Pen Pals Speak on Writing to Prisoners," http://ccadp.org/ccadp-experience.html (accessed February 10, 2004).

5. Canadian Coalition to Abolish the Death Penalty.

6. Correspondence from the warden's assistant to the Oklahoma coordinator for LifeLines.

7. Alan Elsner, "European Women Marry U.S. Death Row Inmates," Prisonerlife .com, 2002, http://www.prisonerlife.com/deathrow/deathrow16.cfm (accessed January 24, 2004).

8. *The Execution of Wanda Jean,* 2002, directed by Liz Garbus, HBO Productions. The film chronicles the last three months of the life of Wanda Jean Allen, who was the first African American woman executed in the United States in the post-*Furman* era of capital punishment.

9. Wanda Jean Allen, executed on January 11, 2001, had a history of brain damage and borderline mental retardation. At her clemency hearing, the attorney general's office argued that she was not retarded because she had attended college. Wanda Jean Allen never attended college and did not even complete high school. She had said that she did, thinking it would get her more lenient treatment.

10. Johnnie Carter, "Forgiving the Unforgivable," *Family Circle,* August 6, 2002.

11. Carter, "Forgiving the Unforgivable."

CHAPTER 10   THE DEATH PENALTY AND FAMILIES, REVISITED

1. Boss, *Ambiguous Loss.*

2. Costanzo, *Just Revenge;* Miller, Cohen, and Wiersema, *Victim Costs and Consequences.*

3. Sister Helen Prejean, *Dead Man Walking* (New York: Random House/Vintage Books, 1994). Sister Helen provides the statistic that the marriages of 70 percent of couples who have lost a child end in divorce.

4. Prejean, *Dead Man Walking,* 238. In chapter 11, Sister Helen talks about her involvement with victim's family members and the groups supporting them. She provides the reader with excellent insight into the suffering of these families. She describes attending the two different support groups, Parents of Murdered Children and Survive. The demographic composition of the two groups is very different, and the experiences of the members reflect this. Parents of Murdered Children, at the meeting described in her book, was composed of primarily white middle-class family members. In most cases, the perpetrators of their children's murders had been tried and sentenced. In contrast, the members of Survive were primarily poor black women. In the overwhelming majority of the cases, the women did not expect to see the offender brought to trial. The attendees reported being ignored by the criminal justice system and treated more like criminals themselves than like crime victims.

5. Federal Bureau of Investigation, *Crime in the United States: Uniform Crime Reports, 2002* (Washington, DC: Federal Bureau of Investigation, 2003). Table 2.4 provides the following information: Of the 14,054 murders reported in 2002, 6,730 (47.8 percent) were black and 377 (2.6 percent) were designated "other race."

6. King and Norgard, "What about Our Families?"; Vandiver and Berardo, " 'It's Like Dying Every Day.' "
7. Vandiver, "Coping with Death."
8. Costanzo, *Just Revenge.*
9. Cohen, Miller, and Rossman. "Costs and Consequences of Violent Behavior in the United States."
10. Mark S. Umbreit, "Restorative Justice through Victim-Offender Mediation"; Umbreit and Vos, "Homicide Survivors Meet the Offender Prior to Execution."
11. Girshick, "I Leave in the Dark of Morning"; Petersilia, "Prisoner Reentry."
12. For a detailed description of state policies concerning contact visits on death row, see appendix A.

Chapter 11   Conclusion

1. Michael L Radelet, "Humanizing the Death Penalty," *Social Problems* 48, no. 10 (2001): 83.
2. Amnesty International, *State Cruelty against Families.*
3. The order is not published. I received a copy from Sharon. In order to protect her confidentiality, I am not providing identifying information.

Appendix C   Demographics of Interview Subjects

1. Criminal Justice Project of the NAACP Legal Defense and Educational Fund, *Death Row U.S.A, Summer 2003.* Approximately 60 percent of the executions in Oklahoma have been of white offenders. Current death row population is 38 percent African American.
2. I have not included race and age information for these subjects because I do not have it for all of them. I also had brief messages from other family members that are not listed here, although examples from their correspondence appear in the book.

Bibliography

Abramson, Stacy, and David Isay. "The Stopping Point: Interview with a Tie Down Officer." In *Machinery of Death: The Reality of America's Death Penalty Regime,* edited by D. R. Dow and M. Dow, 169–173. New York: Routledge Press, 2002.

Abu-Jamal, Mumia. *Live from Death Row.* Reading, MA: Addison-Wesley, 1995.

Acker, James R., and Charles S. Lanier. "May God—or the Governor—Have Mercy: Executive Clemency and Execution in Modern Death Penalty Systems." *Criminal Law Bulletin* 36 (2000): 200–237.

———. "Beyond Human Ability? The Rise and Fall of Death Penalty Legislation." In *America's Experiment with Capital Punishment,* 2nd ed., edited by J. R. Acker, R. M. Bohm, and C. S. Lanier, 85–119. Durham, NC: Carolina Academic Press, 2003.

Acker, James R., Thomas Brewer, Ramon Cunningham, Allison Fitzgerald, Jamie Flexon, Julie Lombard, Barbara Ryn, and Bivette Stodghill. "No Appeal from the Grave: Innocence, Capital Punishment, and the Lessons of History." In *Wrongly Convicted: Perspectives of Failed Justice,* edited by S. D. Westervelt and J. A. Humphrey, 154–173. New Brunswick, NJ: Rutgers University Press, 2002.

Adams, David. "The Consequences of Sudden Traumatic Death: The Vulnerability of Bereaved Children and Adolescents and Ways Professionals Can Help." In *Complicated Grieving and Bereavement,* edited by G. R. Cox, R. A. Bendiksen, and R. G. Stevenson, 23–20. Amityville, NY: Baywood, 2002.

ALIVE—Coalition to Abolish the Death Penalty. "In Memoriam: Gerald Bivins." ALIVE, http://www.todesstrafe-usa.de/death_penalty/memoriam_e_bivins.htm.

Altheide, David L. *Creating Fear: News and the Construction of Crisis.* New York: Aldine de Gruyter, 2002.

Amnesty International. *State Cruelty against Families.* AMR 51/132/2001.

Armstrong, Ken, and Steve Mills. "Until I Can Be Sure": How the Threat of Executing the Innocent Has Transformed the Death Penalty Debate." In *Beyond Repair? America's Death Penalty,* edited by S. P. Garvey, 94–120. Durham, NC: Duke University Press, 2003.

Arriens, Jan. "My Pen Pals Await Execution." *BBC News World Edition,* May 8, 2003, http://news.bbc.co.uk/2/hi/uk_news/3008439.stm.

Arrigo, Bruce A., and Christopher R. Williams. "Victims Vices, Victim Voices, and Impact Statements: On the Place of Emotion and the Role of Restorative Justice in Capital Sentencing." *Crime and Delinquency* 49 (2003): 603–626.

Attig, Thomas. "Relearning the World: Always Complicated, Sometimes More Than Others." In *Complicated Grieving and Bereavement,* edited by G. R. Cox, R. A. Bendiksen, and R. G. Stevenson, 7–19. Amityville, NY: Baywood, 2002.

Babbie, Earl. *The Practice of Social Research*. Belmont, CA: Wadsworth, 1992.

Beck, Elizabeth, Brenda Sims Blackwell, Pamela Blume Leonard, and Michael Mears. "Seeking Sanctuary: Interviews with Family Members of Capital Defendants." *Cornell Law Review* 88 (2003): 343–381.

Bedau, Hugh Adam. *The Death Penalty in America*. New York: Oxford University Press, 1982.

———. *The Case against the Death Penalty*. Washington, DC: American Civil Liberties Union, 1997.

Beeghley, Leonard. *Homicide: A Sociological Explanation*. Lanham, MD: Rowman & Littlefield, 2003.

Berg, Bruce L. *Qualitative Research Methods for the Social Sciences*. Boston: Allyn & Bacon, 2001.

Bernstein, Nell. "Relocation Blues." In *Prison Nation,* edited by T. Herivel and P. Wright, 106–111. New York: Routledge Press, 2003.

Blackman, P. H., V. L. Leggett, B. L. Olson, and J. P. Jarvis, eds. *The Varieties of Homicide and Its Research: Proceedings of the 1999 Meeting of the Homicide Working Group*. Washington, DC: Federal Bureau of Investigation, 2000.

Bloom, Barbara. "Why Punish the Children? A Reappraisal of the Children of Incarcerated Mothers in America." *IARCA Journal* 6 (1993): 14–17.

Bohm, Robert M. "Retribution and Capital Punishment: Toward a Better Understanding of Death Penalty Opinion." *Journal of Criminal Justice* 20 (1992): 227–236.

———. *DeathQuest II*. Cincinnati: Anderson, 2003.

Bolton, Kenneth, Jr. "Book Review: Live from Death Row." In *The International Sourcebook on Capital Punishment,* edited by W. A. Schabas, 102–106. Boston: Northeastern University Press, 1997.

Bonczar, Thomas, and Tracy L. Snell. *Capital Punishment, 2002*. Washington, DC: U.S. Department of Justice, Bureau of Justice Statistics, 2003.

Borg, Marian J. "Vicarious Homicide Victimization and Support for Capital Punishment: A Test of Black's Theory of Law." *Criminology* 36, no. 3 (1998): 537–567.

Boss, Pauline. *Ambiguous Loss: Learning to Live with Unresolved Grief*. Cambridge, MA: Harvard University Press, 1999.

Bowlby, John. *Attachment and Loss: Loss, Sadness, and Depression*. New York: Basic Books, 1980.

Bright, Stephen B. "Legalized Lynching: Race, the Death Penalty and the United States Courts." In *The International Sourcebook on Capital Punishment,* edited by W. A. Schabas, 5–29. Boston: Northeastern University Press, 1997.

Burgess, A. W. "Family Reaction to Homicide." *Journal of Orthopsychiatry* 45 (1975): 391–398.

Butterfield, Fox. "Killings Increase in Many Big Cities," *New York Times,* December 21, 2001. http://www.nytimes.com/2001/12/21/national/21CRIM.html.

Canadian Coalition to Abolish the Death Penalty, "Prisoners' Pen Pals Speak on Writing to Prisoners," Canadian Coalition to Abolish the Death Penalty, http://ccadp.org/ccadp-experience.html.

Carter, Johnnie. "Forgiving the Unforgivable." *Family Circle,* August 6, 2002.

Castelle, George, and Elizabeth Loftus. "Misinformation and Wrongful Convictions." In *Wrongly Convicted: Perspectives on Failed Justice,* edited by S. D. Westervelt and J. A. Humphrey, 17–35. New Brunswick, NJ: Rutgers University Press, 2002.

Cavanaugh, Kerry. "Children's Experiences of Death: Three Case Studies." In *Complicated Grieving and Bereavement,* edited by G. R. Cox, R. A. Bendiksen, and R. G. Stevenson, 69–82. Amityville, NY: Baywood, 2002.

Clear, Todd. *Harm in American Penology: Offenders, Victims and Their Communities.* Albany, NY: SUNY Press, 1994.

———. "Backfire: When Incarceration Increases Crime." *Journal of the Oklahoma Criminal Justice Research Consortium* 3 (1996): 7–17.

Cohen, M. A., T. R. Miller, and S. B. Rossman. "The Costs and Consequences of Violent Behavior in the United States." In *Understanding and Preventing Violence.* Vol. 4, edited by J. Roth and A. Reiss, 67–116. Washington, DC: National Academy Press, 1994.

Cohen, Stanley. *The Wrong Men: America's Epidemic of Wrongful Death Row Convictions.* New York: Carroll & Graf, 2003.

Cook, Phillip J., and Donna B. Slawson with Lori Gries. *The Cost of Processing Murder Cases in North Carolina.* Raleigh, NC: Administrative Office of the Courts, 1993.

Correia, Isabel, Jorge Vala, and Patricia Aguiar. "The Effects of Belief in a Just World and Victim's Innocence on Secondary Victimization, Judgments of Justice and Deservingness." *Social Justice Research* 14, no. 3 (2001): 327–342.

Costanzo, Mark. *Just Revenge: Costs and Consequences of the Death Penalty.* New York: St. Martin's Press, 1997.

Cox, Gerry R., Robert A. Bendiksen, and Robert G. Stevenson. *Complicated Grieving and Bereavement: Understanding and Treating People Experiencing Loss.* Amityville, NY: Baywood, 2002.

Criminal Justice Project of the NAACP Legal Defense and Educational Fund. *Death Row U.S.A., Summer 2003,* NAACP, http://www.deathpenaltyinfo.org/DEATHROWUSArecent.pdf.

Cushing, Robert Renny, and Susannah Sheffer. *Dignity Denied: The Experience of Murder Victims' Family Members Who Oppose the Death Penalty.* Cambridge, MA: Murder Victims' Families for Reconciliation, 2002.

Daniel, S. W., and C. J. Barrett. "The Needs of Prisoners' Wives: A Challenge for the Mental Health Professionals." *Community Mental Health Journal* 17 (1981): 310–322.

Darrah, Larry. "Camouflaged Grief: Survivor Grief in Families of Soldiers Still Listed as MIA." In *Handbook of Bereavement Research: Consequences, Coping and Care,* edited by M. S. Stroebe, R. O. Hansson, W. Stroebe, and H. Schut, 85–97. Washington, DC: American Psychological Association, 2002.

Death Penalty Information Center, 2004, http://www.deathpenaltyinfo.org.

Dominion, J. "Commentary on 'Normal Grief: Good or Bad? Health or Disease?'" *Philosophy, Psychiatry and Psychology* 1, no. 4 (1994): 221–222.

Dow, David R. "Introduction: The Problem of 'Innocence.'" In *Machinery of Death: The Reality of America's Death Penalty Regime,* edited by D. R. Dow and M. Dow, 1–8. New York: Routledge Press, 2002.

———. "How the Death Penalty Really Works." In *Machinery of Death: The Reality of America's Death Penalty Regime,* edited by D. R. Dow and M. Dow, 11–35. New York: Routledge Press, 2002.

Dow, David R., and Mark Dow. *Machinery of Death: The Reality of America's Death Penalty Regime.* New York: Routledge Press, 2002.

Dow, Mark. "'The Line between Us and Them': Interview with Warden Donald Cabana." In *Machinery of Death: The Reality of America's Death Penalty Regime,* edited by D. R. Dow and M. Dow, 175–191. New York: Routledge Press, 2002.

Elsner, Alan. "European Women Marry U.S. Death Row Inmates," Prisonerlife .com, 2002, *http://www.prisonerlife.com/deathrow/deathrow16.cfm.*

English, Bella. "Kerry Max Cook Spent 20 Years on Death Row. His Message Is Clear: 'Being Innocent Is Not Enough to Save You,'" *Boston Globe,* January 25, 2003.

Erez, Edna, and L. Roeger. "The Effect Victim Impact Statements Have on Sentencing Patterns and Outcomes: The Australian Experience." *Journal of Criminal Justice* 23 (1995): 363–375.

Espy, M. Watt, and John Smykla. *Executions in the United States, 1608–1987: The Espy File.* Machine-readable data file. Ann Arbor, MI: ICPSR, 1987.

Feagin, Joe R., Anthony M. Orum, and Gideon Sjoberg. *A Case for the Case Study.* Chapel Hill: University of North Carolina Academic Press, 1991.

Federal Bureau of Investigation. *Crime in the United States: Uniform Crime Reports, 2000.* Washington, DC: Federal Bureau of Investigation, 2001.

———. *Crime in the United States: Uniform Crime Reports, 2001.* Washington, DC: Federal Bureau of Investigation, 2002.

———. *Crime in the United States: Uniform Crime Reports, 2002.* Washington, DC: Federal Bureau of Investigation, 2003.

Ferrell, Jeff, and Mark S. Hamm. "True Confessions." In *Ethnography at the Edge,* edited by J. Ferrell and M. S. Hamm, 2–10. Boston: Northeastern University Press, 1998.

Field, Nigel P., George A. Bonanno, Patricia Williams, and Mardi J. Horowitz. "Appraisal of Blame in Adjustment in Conjugal Bereavement." *Cognitive Therapy and Research* 24, no. 5 (2000): 551–569.

Fishman, L. T. "The World of Prisoners' Wives." In *Long-Term Imprisonment: Policy, Science and Correctional Practice,* edited by T. J. Flanagan. Thousand Oaks, CA: Sage, 1995.

Flatt, Bill. "Some Stages of Grief." *Journal of Religion and Health* 26 (1987): 143–148.

Flavin, Jeanne. "Feminism for the Mainstream Criminologist: An Invitation." *Journal of Criminal Justice* 29 (2001): 271–285.

Fleisher, Mark. "Ethnographers, Pimps, and the Company Store." In *Ethnography at the Edge,* edited by J. Ferrell and M. S. Hamm, 44–64. Boston: Northeastern University Press, 1998.

Folkman, Susan. "Revised Coping Theory and the Process of Bereavement." In *Handbook of Bereavement Research: Consequences, Coping and Care,* edited by M. S. Stroebe, R. O. Hansson, W. Stroebe, and H. Schut, 563–584. Washington, DC: American Psychological Association, 2001.

Foucault, Michel. *Discipline and Punish: The Birth of the Prison.* New York: Vintage Books, 1977.

Frank, Arthur W. *At the Will of the Body.* Boston: Houghton Mifflin, 1991.

Free Dictionary. http://www.thefreedictionary.com/executive%20clemency.

Freeman, Stephen. "Group Facilitation of the Grieving Process with those Bereaved by Suicide." *Journal of Counseling and Development* 69, no. 4 (1991): 328–331.

———. "Identity Maintenance and Adaptation: A Multilevel Analysis of Response to Loss." *Research in Organizational Behavior* 21 (1999): 247–294.

Freud, Sigmund. "Mourning and Melancholia." In *The Pelican Freud Library.* Vol. 11, *On Metapsychology: The Theory of Psychoanalysis,* 245–268. London: Penguin, 1984 [1917].

Fuhrman, Mark. *Death and Justice: An Expose of Oklahoma's Death Row Machine.* New York: William Morrow, 2003.

Gabel, Katherine, and Denise Johnston. *Children of Incarcerated Parents.* New York: Lexington Books, 1995.

Galliher, John F., Larry W. Koch, David Patrick Keys, and Teresa J. Guess. *America without the Death Penalty: States Leading the Way.* Boston: Northeastern University Press, 2002.

Garey, Margot. "The Cost of Taking a Life: Dollars and Sense of the Death Penalty." *University of California–Davis Law Review* 18 (1985): 1221–1273.

Girshick, Lori B. "I Leave in the Dark of Morning." *Prison Journal* 73 (1994): 93–97.

Glaser, Barry, and Anselm Strauss. *The Discovery of Grounded Theory: Strategies for Qualitative Research.* Chicago: Aldine, 1967.

Graham, Ginnie. "There's Always Those Left Behind," *Tulsa World,* September 24, 2000.

Grisham, John. *The Chamber.* New York: Doubleday, 1994.

Gross, Samuel R., and Phoebe C. Ellsworth. "Second Thoughts: Americans' Views on the Death Penalty at the Turn of the Century." In *Beyond Repair? America's Death Penalty,* edited by S. P. Garvey, 7–57. Durham, NC: Duke University Press, 2003.

Hagan, John. "The Next Generation: Children of Prisoners." *Journal of the Oklahoma Criminal Justice Research Consortium* 3 (1996): 19–28.

Hairston, Creasie Finney. "Family Ties during Imprisonment: Important to Whom and for What?" *Journal of Sociology and Social Welfare* 18 (1991): 87–104.

———. "The Forgotten Parent: Understanding the Forces that Influence Incarcerated Fathers' Relationships with Their Children." *Child Welfare* 77 (1998): 617–630.

Haney, Craig. "The Social Context of Capital Murder: Social Histories and the Logic of Mitigation." *Santa Clara Law Review* 547 (1995): 548–559.

———. "Mitigation and the Study of Lives: On the Roots of Violent Criminality and the Nature of Capital Justice." In *America's Experiment with Capital Punishment,* edited by J. R. Acker, R. M. Bohm, and C. S. Lanier, 351–384. Durham, NC: Carolina Academic Press, 1998.

Holmes, William M. "Who Are the Wrongfully Convicted on Death Row?" In *Wrongly Convicted: Perspectives of Failed Justice,* edited by S. A. Westervelt and J. A. Humphrey, 99–113. New Brunswick, NJ: Rutgers University Press, 2002.

Hubert, Cynthia. "Role in Capture Haunts Kaczynski's Brother," *Sacramento Bee,* January 19, 1997. *http://www.unabombertrial.com/archive/1997/011997-2.html.*

Hudson, Maj. Daniel. *Managing Death-Sentenced Inmates: A Survey of Practices,* 2nd ed. Lanham, MD: American Correctional Association, 2000.

Humphrey, John A., and Saundra D. Westervelt. Introduction to *Wrongly Convicted: Perspectives of Failed Justice,* edited by S. A. Westervelt and J. A. Humphrey, 1–16. New Brunswick, NJ: Rutgers University Press, 2002.

Hutch, Richard A. "Mortal Losses, Vital Gains: The Role of Spirituality." *Journal of Religion and Health* 39, no. 4 (2000): 329–338.

Jackson, Rev. Jesse L., Sr., Rep. Jesse L. Jackson Jr., and Bruce Shapiro. *Legal Lynching: The Death Penalty and America's Future.* New York: New Press, 2001.

Johnston, Denise. "Effects of Parental Incarceration." In *Children of Incarcerated Parents,* edited by K. Gabel and D. Johnston. New York: Lexington Books, 1995.

Kaczynski, David. "The Death Penalty Up Close and Personal." New Yorkers Against the Death Penalty, *http://www.nyadp.org/main/david.html.*

Kalton, Graham. *An Introduction to Survey Sampling.* Newbury Park, CA: Sage, 1983.

Kampfer, C. "Post-Traumatic Stress Reactions in Children of Incarcerated Mothers." In *Children of Incarcerated Parents,* edited by K. Gabel and D. Johnston. New York: Lexington Books, 1995.

Kastenbaum, R. J. *Death, Society and Human Experience,* 6th ed. Boston: Allyn & Bacon, 1998.

King, Rachel. *Don't Kill in Our Names: Families of Murder Victims Speak Out against the Death Penalty.* New Brunswick, NJ: Rutgers University Press, 2003.

King, Rachel, and Katherine Norgard. "What about Our Families? Using the Impact on Death Row Defendants' Family Members as a Mitigating Factor in Death Penalty Sentencing Hearings." *Florida State Law Review* 26 (1999): 1119–1173.

Klass, Dennis, Phyllis R. Silverman, and Steven L. Nickman. *Continuing Bonds: New Understandings of Grief.* Philadelphia: Taylor & Francis, 1996.

Kübler-Ross, Elisabeth. *On Death and Dying.* New York: Scribner Classics, 1997 [1969].

Lazarus, Richard S., and Susan Folkman. *Stress, Appraisal and Coping.* New York: Springer, 1984.

Leo, Richard A. "False Confessions: Causes, Consequences, and Solutions." In *Wrongly Convicted: Perspectives on Failed Justice,* edited by S. A. Westervelt and J. A. Humphrey, 36–54. New Brunswick, NJ: Rutgers University Press, 2002.

Lesser, Wendy. 1993. *Pictures at an Execution: An Inquiry into the Subject of Murder.* Cambridge, MA: Harvard University Press, 1993.

Lewis, D. O., J. H. Pincus, B. Bard, E. Richardson, L. Prichep, M. Feldman, and C. Yeager. "Neuropsychatric, Psychoeducational, and Family Characteristics of 14 Juveniles Condemned to Death in the United States." *American Journal of Psychiatry* 14, no. 5 (1988): 584–589.

Liebman, James, Jeff Fagan, and Valerie West. "Technical Errors Can Kill." *National Law Journal,* special ed., September 2000.

Liebman, James, Jeff Fagan, Andrew Gelman, Valerie West, Garth Davies, and Alexander Kiss. *A Broken System, Part II: Why There Is So Much Error in Capital Cases, and What Can Be Done About It.* Columbia Law School, 2002. *http://www2.law.columbia.edu/brokensystem2/index2.html.*

Lofland, John S., and Lyn Lofland. *Analyzing Social Settings: A Guide to Qualitative Observation and Analysis.* Belmont, CA: Sage, 1995.

Lofquist, William A. "Whodunit? An Examination of the Production of Wrongful Convictions." In *Wrongly Convicted: Perspectives on Failed Justice,* edited by S. D. Westervelt and J. A. Humphrey, 174–196. New Brunswick, NJ: Rutgers University Press, 2002.

Loftus, Elizabeth F. *Eyewitness Testimony.* Cambridge, MA: Harvard University Press, 1996.

Magers, Phil. "Analysis: Is Lethal Injection Humane?" *Washington Times, http://washingtontimes.com.*

Mawby, R. I., and S. Walklate. *Critical Victimology.* Thousand Oaks, CA: Sage, 1995.

Miller, T. R., M. A. Cohen, and B. Wiersema. *Victim Costs and Consequences: A New Look.* Washington, DC: National Institute of Justice, 1996.

Moore, Joan. "Bearing the Burden: How Incarceration Weakens Inner-City Communities." *Journal of the Oklahoma Criminal Justice Research Consortium* 3 (1996).

Mumola, Christopher J. *Bureau of Justice Special Report: Incarcerated Parents and Their Children* (BJS Publication No. NCJ 1832335). Washington, DC: Department of Justice: Bureau of Justice Statistics, 2000.

Murder Victims' Families for Reconciliation. *Not in Our Name: Murder Victims' Families Speak Out against the Death Penalty.* Cambridge, MA: MVFR, 2003.

Nathanson, Stephen. "Does It Matter If the Death Penalty Is Arbitrarily Administered?" In *Punishment and the Death Penalty: The Current Debate,* edited by R. M. Baird and S. E. Rosenbaum, 161–174. Amherst, NY: Prometheus Books, 1985.

National Public Radio. "Witness to an Execution." *All Things Considered,* October 20, 2000, http://www.soundportraits.org/on-air/witness_to_an_execution.

Neimeyer, Robert A., Holly G. Prigerson, and Betty Davies. "Mourning and Meaning." *American Behavioral Scientist* 46 (2002): 235–251.

Neuman, W. Lawrence. *Social Research Methods: Qualitative and Quantitative Approaches,* 2nd ed. Boston: Allyn & Bacon, 1994.

Nolen-Hoeksema, Susan, and Judith Larson. *Coping with Loss.* Mahwah, NJ: Erlbaum, 1999.

Orth, Uli. "Secondary Victimization of Crime Victims by Criminal Proceedings." *Social Justice Research* 15 (2002): 313–325.

Osterweis, M., Frederic Solomon, and Morris Green, eds. *Bereavement Reactions, Consequences and Care.* Washington, DC: National Academy Press, 1984.

Paine, Frederick. "Looking for a Pen Pal on Death Row?" *New Abolitionist* 15 (May 2000), http://www.nodeathpenalty.org/newab015/fredrickPaine.html.

Parker, Karen F., Mari A. Dewees, and Michael L. Radelet. "Racial Bias and the Conviction of the Innocent." In *Wrongly Convicted: Perspectives on Failed Justice,* edited by S. D. Westervelt and J. A. Humphrey, 114–131. New Brunswick, NJ: Rutgers University Press, 2002.

Paternoster, Raymond. *Capital Punishment in America.* New York: Lexington Books, 1991.

Payne, Sheila, Sandra Horn, and Marilyn Relf. *Loss and Bereavement.* Buckingham, England: Open University Press, 1999.

Petersilia, Joan. "Prisoner Reentry: Public Safety and Reintegration Challenges." *Prison Journal* 81 (2001): 360–375.

Polkinghorne, Donald. *Methodology for the Human Sciences: Systems of Inquiry.* Albany, NY: SUNY Press, 1983.

Prejean, Sister Helen. *Dead Man Walking.* New York: Vintage Books, 1993.

Prokosch, Eric. "Death Penalty Developments." In *The International Sourcebook on Capital Punishment,* edited by W. A. Schabas, 66–80. Boston: Northeastern University Press, 1997.

Radelet, Michael L. "Botched Executions." Death Penalty Information Center, *http://deathpenaltyinfo.org/article.php?scid=8&did=478.*

———. "Book Review: Deadly Innocence?" In *The International Sourcebook on Capital Punishment,* edited by W. A. Schabas, 93–96. Boston: Northeastern University Press, 1997.

———. "Humanizing the Death Penalty." *Social Problems* 48, no. 10 (2001): 83–87.

Radelet, Michael L., and Hugh Adam Bedau. "Erroneous Convictions and the Death Penalty." In *Wrongly Convicted: Perspectives on Failed Justice,* edited by S. D. Westervelt and J. A. Humphrey, 269–280. New Brunswick, NJ: Rutgers University Press, 2002.

———. "The Execution of the Innocent." In *America's Experiment with Capital Punishment: Reflections on the Past, Present, and Future of the Ultimate Penal Sanction,* 2nd ed., edited by J. R. Acker, R. M. Bohm, and C. S. Lanier, 325–344. Durham, NC: Carolina Academic Press, 2003.

Radelet, Michael, Hugh Bedau, and Constance Putnam. *In Spite of Innocence: The Ordeal of 400 Americans Wrongly Convicted of Crimes Punishable by Death.* Boston: Northeastern University Press, 1992.

Radelet, Michael L., William S. Lofquist, and Hugh Adam Bedau. "Prisoners Released from Death Rows Since 1970 Because of Doubts about Their Guilt." *Thomas M. Cooley Law Review* 13 (1996): 907–666.

Radelet, Michael L., Margaret Vandiver, and Felix M. Berardo. "Families, Prisons, and Men with Death Sentences: The Human Impact of Structured Uncertainty." *Journal of Family Issues* 4 (1982): 593–612.

Radelet, Michael L., and Barbara A. Zsembik. "Executive Clemency in Post-*Furman* Capital Cases," *University of Richmond Law Review* 27 (1993): 289–314.

Rafter, Nicole. *Shots in the Mirror: Crime Films and Society.* New York: Oxford University Press, 2000.

Reed, Mark D., and Brenda Sims Blackwell. "Families of Homicide Victims: A Review and Recommendations for Current Research and Practice." Paper presented at the American Society of Criminology meetings, Chicago, November 2002.

Reidy, Thomas J., Mark D. Cunningham, and Jon R. Sorensen. "From Death to Life: Prison Behavior of Former Death Row Inmates in Indiana." *Criminal Justice and Behavior* 28 (2001): 62–82.

Reinharz, Shulamit. *Feminist Methods in Social Research.* New York: Oxford University Press, 1992.

Rimer, Sarah. "A Father Feels the Weight of His Son's Sins." *New York Times,* April 29, 2001. *http://www.nytimes.com/2001/04/29/national/MCVE.html.*

Ryan, Perry T. "The Last Public Execution," Last Public Execution, *http://www.geocities.com/lastpublichang/LastPublicExecution.htm.*

Rynearson, E. K. "Psychotherapy of Bereavement after Homicide: Be Offensive." *Psychotherapy in Practice* 2 (1996): 421–428.

SacBee. "David Kaczynski: Defendant's Brother," *Sacramento Bee* [online]. *http:// www.unabombertrial.com/players/david.html.*

Sanders, Catherine M. *Grief: The Mourning After.* New York: John Wiley & Sons, 1999.

Sarat, Austin, ed. *The Killing State: Capital Punishment in Law, Politics and Culture.* New York: Oxford University Press, 1999.

―――. *When the State Kills: Capital Punishment and the American Condition.* Princeton, NJ: Princeton University Press, 2001.

Schabas, William A., ed. *The International Sourcebook on Capital Punishment.* Boston: Northeastern University Press, 1997.

―――. "African Perspectives on Abolition of the Death Penalty." In *The International Sourcebook on Capital Punishment,* edited by W. A. Schabas, 30–65. Boston: Northeastern University Press, 1997.

―――. "International Law and the Abolition of the Death Penalty." In *Beyond Repair? America's Death Penalty,* edited by S. P. Garvey, 178–211. Durham, NC: Duke University Press, 2003.

Schatzman, Leonard, and Anselm Strauss. *Field Research: Strategies for a Natural Sociology.* Englewood Cliffs, NJ: Prentice-Hall, 1973.

Scheck, Barry, and Peter Neufeld. "DNA and Innocence Scholarship." In *Wrongly Convicted: Perspectives on Failed Justice,* edited by S. D. Westervelt and J. A. Humphrey, 241–252. New Brunswick, NJ: Rutgers University Press, 2002.

Scheck, Barry, Peter Neufeld, and Jim Dwyer. *Actual Innocence: When Justice Goes Wrong and How to Make It Right.* New York: Penguin Putnam, 2001.

Sharp, Susan F. "Mothers in Prison: Issues in Parent-Child Contact." In *The Incarcerated Woman: Rehabilitative Programming in Women's Prisons,* edited by S. F. Sharp, 151–165. Upper Saddle River, NJ: Prentice-Hall, 2003.

Sharp, Susan F., and Susan Marcus-Mendoza. "It's a Family Affair: Incarcerated Mothers and Their Families." *Women and Criminal Justice* 12 (2001): 21–49.

Sharp, Susan F., Susan T. Marcus-Mendoza, Robert Bentley, Debra Simpson, and Sharon Love. "Gender Differences in the Impact of Incarceration on the Children and Families of Drug Offenders." In *Interrogating Social Justice,* edited by M. Corsianos and K. A. Train, 218–246. Toronto: Canadian Scholars' Press, 1999.

Sherer, Ann B. "A United Methodist Pastor's Vigil on Death Row." *Hoosier United Methodist News,* 2001. *http://www.inareaumc.org/april01/comment.htm.*

Simon, Jonathan, and Christina Spaulding. "Tokens of Our Esteem: Aggravating Factors in the Era of Deregulated Death Penalties." In *The Killing State: Capital Punishment in Law, Politics, and Culture,* edited by A. Sarat, 81–113. New York: Oxford University Press, 1999.

Smith, Dorothy. "A Sociology for Women." In *The Prism of Sex,* edited by J. Shermon and E. T. Beck, 135–187. Madison: University of Wisconsin Press, 1979.

Smykla, J. O. "The Human Impact of Capital Punishment: Interviews with Families of Persons on Death Row." *Journal of Criminal Justice* 15 (1987): 331–347.

Snell, Tracy. *Capital Punishment, 2001.* Washington, DC: U.S. Department of Justice, Bureau of Justice Statistics, 2002.

Spangenberg, Robert L., and Elizabeth Walsh. "Capital Punishment or Life Imprisonment? Some Cost Considerations." *Loyola–Los Angeles Law Review* 23 (1989): 45–58.

Sprang, M. Virginia, John S. McNeil, and Roosevelt Wright. "Psychological Changes after the Murder of a Significant Other." *Social Casework* 70, no. 3 (1989): 159–164.

Spungen, Deborah. *Homicide: The Hidden Victims: A Guide for Professionals.* Belmont, CA: Sage, 1997.

Steiker, Carol, and Jordan M. Steiker. "Judicial Developments in Capital Punishment Law." In *America's Experiment with Capital Punishment: Reflections on the Past, Present and Future of the Ultimate Penal Sanction,* 2nd ed., edited by J. R. Acker, R. M. Bohm, and C. S. Lanier, 55–83. Durham, NC: Carolina Academic Press, 2003.

Street, Paul. "Color Blind." In *Prison Nation,* edited by T. Herivel and P. Wright, 30–40. New York: Routledge Press, 2003.

Stroebe, Margaret S., and Henk Schut. "The Dual Process Model of Coping with Bereavement: Rationale and Description." *Death Studies* 23 (1999): 197–224.

———. "Models of Coping with Bereavement: A Review." In *Handbook of Bereavement Research: Consequences, Coping and Care,* edited by M. S. Stroebe, R. O. Hansson, W. Stroebe, and H. Schut, 375–403. Washington, DC: American Psychological Association, 2001.

Stroebe, Margaret S., Robert O. Hansson, Wolfgang Stroebe, and Henk Schut, eds. *Handbook of Bereavement Research: Consequences, Coping and Care.* Washington, DC: American Psychological Association, 2001.

Stroebe, Wolfgang, Margaret Stroebe, Georgios Abakoumkin, and Henk Schut. "The Role of Loneliness and Social Support in Adjustment to Loss: A Test of Attachment versus Stress Theory." *Journal of Personality and Social Psychology* 70 (1996): 1241–1249.

Sullivan, Harry Stack. *Clinical Studies in Psychiatry.* New York: W. W. Norton, 1956.

Surette, Ray. *Media, Crime and Criminal Justice: Images and Realities.* Belmont, CA: West/Wadsworth, 1998.

Travis, Jeremy, and Joan Petersilia. "Reentry Reconsidered: A New Look at an Old Question." *Crime and Delinquency* 47 (2001): 291–313.

Turow, Scott. *Ultimate Punishment: A Lawyer's Reflections on Dealing with the Death Penalty.* New York: Farrar, Straus & Giroux, 2003.

Umbreit, Mark S. "Restorative Justice through Victim Offender Mediation: A Multi-Site Assessment." *Western Criminology Review* 1 (1998). *http://wc.sonomo.edu/v1n1/umbreit.html.*

Umbreit, Mark S., and Betty Vos. "Homicide Survivors Meet the Offender Prior to Execution: Restorative Justice through Dialogue." *Homicide Studies* 4 (2000): 63–87.

Vandiver, Margaret. "Coping with Death: Families of the Terminally Ill, Homicide Victims, and Condemned Prisoners." In *Facing the Death Penalty: Essays on a Cruel and Unusual Punishment,* edited by M. Radelet, 123–138. Philadelphia: Temple University Press, 1989.

———. "Beyond All Justice: The Death Penalty and Families of the Condemned." *Odyssey* (1992): 56–63.

———. "The Impact of the Death Penalty on the Families of Homicide Victims and of Condemned Prisoners." In *America's Experiment with Capital Punishment,* 2nd ed., edited by J. R. Acker, R. M. Bohm, and C. S. Lanier, 613–645. Durham, NC: Carolina Academic Press, 2003.

Vandiver, Margaret, and Felix M. Berardo. "'It's Like Dying Every Day': The Families of Condemned Prisoners." *Families, Crime and Criminal Justice* 2 (2000): 339–358.

Villereal, G. L. "A Comparison of Vietnam Era Veterans and Their Combat Exposure with the Symptomatology of Dying." *Omega: Journal of Death and Dying* 36 (1998): 305–330.

Wallace, Valerie. "Join the Pen Pal Program." *New Abolitionist* 3, no. 3 (1999). http://www.nodeathpenalty.org/newab012/valerieWallace.html.

Weisheit, R. A., and J. M. Klofas. "The Impact of Jail: Collateral Cost and Affective Response." *Journal of Offender Counseling, Services and Rehabilitation* 14 (1989): 51–65.

Weissman, Marsha, and Candace M. LaRue. "Earning Trust from Youths with None to Spare." *Child Welfare* 77 (1998): 579–590.

Worden, William. *Grief Counselling and Grief Therapy.* London: Routledge Press, 1991.

Wortman, Camille, and Roxanne Silver. "The Myth of Coping with Loss." *Journal of Consulting and Clinical Psychology* 57 (1989): 349–357.

———. "The Myth of Coping with Loss Revisited." In *Handbook of Bereavement Research: Consequences, Coping and Care,* edited by M. S. Stroebe, R. O. Hansson, W. Stroebe, and H. Schut, 405–429. Washington, DC: American Psychological Association, 2001.

Wright, Paul. "'Victims' Rights' as a Stalking-Horse for State Repression." In *Prison Nation,* edited by T. Herivel and P. Wright, 60–65. New York: Routledge Press, 2003.

Yant, Martin. *Presumed Guilty: When Innocent People Are Wrongly Convicted.* Buffalo, NY: Prometheus Books, 1991.

Zimmerman, Clifford S. "From the Jailhouse to the Courthouse: The Role of Informants in Wrongful Convictions." In *Wrongly Convicted: Perspectives on Failed Justice,* edited by S. D. Westervelt and J. A. Humphrey, 55–76. New Brunswick, NJ: Rutgers University Press, 2002.

Zimring, Franklin E. *The Contradictions of American Capital Punishment.* New York: Oxford University Press, 2003.

———. "Postscript: The Peculiar Present of American Capital Punishment." In *Beyond Repair? America's Death Penalty,* edited by S. P. Garvey, 212–229. Durham, NC: Duke University Press, 2003.

Zisook, Sidney, and Stephen R. Shuchter. "Grief and Bereavement." In *Comprehensive Review of Geriatric Psychiatry,* Vol. 2, edited by J. Sadavoy and L. W. Lazarus, 529–562. Washington, DC: American Psychiatric Association, 1996.

INDEX

About the Author

Susan F. Sharp is an associate professor in the department of sociology at the University of Oklahoma. Her research interests have recently explored the impact of criminal justice policies on the families of offenders. Her first book, the edited volume *The Incarcerated Woman: Rehabilitative Programming in Women's Prisons* (Prentice-Hall, 2003) focused on the problems of women prisoners and the correctional system response to those problems. She contributed a chapter about mothers in prison for that book, in addition to several articles about the impact of incarceration on children and other family members. In addition to her current interest in the effects of capital punishment, her research has focused on the study of gender, crime, and deviance. She is the 2003–2005 Chair of the Division on Women and Crime of the American Society of Criminology.